Butterfly Life in a Caterpillar World

Discover the Unbounded Joy of the Butterfly Life

Betty Moni

"Therefore if any man be in Christ, he is a new creature: old things are passed away; behold, all things are become new." 2 Corinthians 5:17

Butterfly Life In A Caterpillar World

Printed in India

Dedication

In the words of Andrae Crouch in his song, *My Tribute*, "How can I say thanks for the things You have done for me?" Those are my exact feelings! I owe **everything** to God! When I think of all that He has done for me, His Word (the Bible) that He has given me, and the people that He has sent to influence my life and ministry, I know that through all these He has given me a clearer knowledge of Himself. Yet, the more I know about God, the more I know there is still more to know! Perhaps the best way to say thanks is to give everything back to Him—all the time. Still, I am learning:

"Brethren, I count not myself to have apprehended: but this one thing I do, forgetting those things which are behind, and reaching forth unto those things which are before, I press toward the mark for the prize of the high calling of God in Christ Jesus." (Philippians 3:13-14)

The best I know how, I commit this book into the hands of Almighty God and dedicate it completely to Him for His use and for His glory.

Acknowledgements

Thanks be to God for my faithful and loving husband and family as well as our many friends who have encouraged and prayed for me during the writing, rewriting, and completion of this book. It has taken years! Many times during the process I have heard the question, "How long have you been working on the book?" Thankfully, along the way some have reassured me with this comment, "God's timing is always right, and He will finish the book in His way and in His time." Some have suggested that a portion of the contents were probably not quite there—things I had yet to experience in order to be included in their proper place—come to think of it, they were right!

Thanks be to God for my longtime friend in the faith, Colleen Sexton, through whom many years ago (though unknown to both of us at that time) God planted in me the seed for the butterfly life message and ministry.

Thanks be to God for our loving and gifted friends, Cathi & David Winkler, who skillfully edited the manuscript. They have been a special blessing—an answer to prayer.

And, thanks be to God for His Unspeakable Gift (2 Corinthians 9:15), without which there would be no hope—no "butterfly life!"

"The wages of sin is death; but the gift of God is eternal life through Jesus Christ our Lord." (Romans 6:23)

✳

Contents

Introduction

We don't live in a butterfly world. Evil and ugliness abound. Life is really hard and very painful at times. We don't live in a Utopia. We do live in a caterpillar world! Is it possible, in this kind of environment, to live a butterfly kind of life—to fly above, and in spite of, all the troubles and terrors of this life? We have it on the best authority, the Word of God, that we can! The real question is a personal and individual one—not, can you, but, "Will you live that butterfly kind of life?"

This book is written, not by an expert, but rather by an "experiencer." One might think that for all my "butterfly" lessons over the years, I should have reached perfection by now, but I'm not there yet. I'm not yet all I ought to be, or even all I'm going to be, but thanks be to God, I'm not what I used to be. I remember where God brought me from, and I know He is still at work in my life; however, this does not allow license to live any old way, but rather, gives liberty to keep on learning and growing as God leads, and to hold on to and enjoy His encouragement in the process: *"For it is God which worketh in you both to will and to do of His good pleasure." (Philippians 2:13) "Being confident of this very thing, that He which hath begun a good work in you will perform it until the day of Jesus Christ." (Philippians 1:6)*

Within the pages to follow, many personal experiences will be related—some funny, and others downright painful. I'm convinced that these events are simply answers to a prayer of many years ago. When I first entered the music ministry, I asked God to never let me sing or say anything I did not know for certain was absolutely true, and then I asked God to speak to me in everything, even the little things, in a way that I could clearly understand. Though I have been surprised and sometimes initially disappointed in the some of the ways He has answered, His methods have always proven to be the right ones! My hope and prayer is that, somehow, within these pages, God will speak to you. May He express His great love to you personally, and may He both whisper and shout the sheer necessity and the unbounded joy of the "butterfly life," and may He gently yet firmly instruct you in the perfect way to "wing it."

Betty Moni

Part I

The Butterfly Life—How To Find It

Chapter 1
Butterfly Life—
A New Kind of Creature

Everybody knows that butterflies begin as caterpillars. Almost everyone would agree that butterflies are beautiful, and caterpillars are, well, disgusting! In fact, comparisons of the two yield very marked contrasts.

What words come to mind when considering the butterfly? Beauty, peace, joy, love, gentleness, gracefulness, freedom, and other good things. What words come to mind when considering the caterpillar? Ugly, creepy, nasty, bondage, earthbound—the caterpillar is just a low-down critter destined for the dirt! A glimpse of the butterfly brings lovely exclamations, such as, "ooh...ahhh!" While some caterpillars are interesting in appearance, one look usually provokes quite the opposite response: "ughh...yuck!"

Over many years of "Butterfly Life in a Caterpillar World" conferences and retreats, the question has often been asked: "If you had the choice of being either a caterpillar or a butterfly and you had to choose one or the other, which would you rather be?" How many said they would rather be a caterpillar? Zero! Every single one preferred to be a butterfly. And, why? Because basically, every human being wants love, acceptance, joy, freedom (all those things mentioned above)—and these are the qualities of life suggested in the butterfly life.

Obviously, the caterpillar will never fly if it remains in its "caterpillar state." The only way this little worm will ever fly is to somehow gain wings! Some time ago, I heard a story about a conversation between two caterpillars. They were discussing ordinary caterpillar things when, suddenly, they observed a bright and beautiful butterfly, obviously having a marvelous time airborne—dancing, diving, and circling about. One caterpillar remarked to the other, "You'll never get me up in one of those things!"

We can never achieve God's great design for us in the state we are in—sin

Sometimes we are like that—we look only at what we can do, never realizing the wonderful plan God has for us, and what He can do. He has already made provision—He, Himself, can and will empower us for fabulous flight!

There are many different kinds of butterflies, but really, they all started out the same way, as caterpillars. They change from caterpillars to butterflies because that's what God designed them to do. By natural instinct these little creatures obey His purpose, plan (pattern), and process.

Human beings have to be changed also—we can never achieve God's great design for us in the state we are in—sin. Sin has separated us from God, and death is our destiny:

"As it is written, ' There is none righteous, no, not one.' " *(Romans 3:10)*

"For all have sinned, and come short of the glory of God." (Romans 3:23)

"The soul that sinneth, it shall die." (Ezekiel 18:20)

Death is clearly our destiny, but there is hope. God has made a way to reverse that awful sentence. Jesus, Himself, took the death penalty, He *"washed us from our sins in His own blood,"* (Revelation 1:5), and now offers us reconciliation with Himself—eternal life and freedom:

"For the wages of sin is death; but the gift of God is eternal life through Jesus Christ our Lord." (Romans 6:23)

"For God so loved the world, that He gave His only begotten Son, that whosoever believeth in Him should not perish, but have everlasting life." (John 3:16)

Even though the caterpillar and the human being both have natural instincts, there's one thing the caterpillar will never have that every human being is created with—Choice! That is the big difference between us and the caterpillar (as well as every other kind of life on this planet). God not only created man (and woman) a living soul, but He gave man (and woman) free will. Even if we make the wrong choice, He still allows us the freedom to make that decision.

For many years, Texas Baptist Evangelists have held an annual evangelism conference, usually in January, and it has been my privilege to attend many of those meetings. Because of my husband's occupation, however, it has not always been possible for him to attend with me. The 1982 conference was one of those times.

Since God knows and cares about every detail of our lives, it just makes sense to pray about everything. On the first evening of the 1982 conference, as I prayed for God's protection and

His direction for a safe place to park the van, I was really surprised when the only spot available (even though only about a block away from the convention center) was squarely in front of an all-night, adult X-rated type movie house.

I said, "Lord, you can't be serious—this is no place for a Christian lady to park!" And though I heard no audible sound, He clearly spoke to my heart, simply confirming that this was the right place and that He would take care of me. So, that is where I parked, and sure enough, I didn't have a single problem.

The second evening of the conference, again I prayed for protection and direction in where to park, and—you guessed it, the only place to park was the exact same spot as the day before. "Wait a minute, Lord," I protested, "I don't like this place— surely you don't want me to park here again!" And, again, though not audible, His answer was swift and clear. He assured me that just as He took care of me before, He would do it again. This was obviously where God wanted me to be, and once again He spoke: "You can trust me. Just do what I say. I have my reasons." So I parked there again.

As I walked a few steps from the van, I was approached by a woman I had seen go into the movie house just moments before. She was tall and thin, so sad-looking, and she smelled awful. Her jeans and shoes were very shabby, and she wore old, black gloves. Her speech was coarse, "What's a lady like you doin' out here on the street at night?" she questioned. "Well, I'm on my way to an evangelism conference." I replied. "But, this is no place for a lady like you—you shouldn't be out here—it's dangerous on the street," she warned, "I know, I'm a street person—I'll bet you never met a street person before."

My heart was breaking for that woman! Suddenly I was filled with a love for her that I could not explain. "It's all right," I said,

"I'm not going far—just over there to the Convention Center to hear about Jesus—would you like to go with me?" The invitation had just sort of fallen out of my mouth before I knew it.

To my surprise, the woman said, "Yes, I've been wantin' to go, but didn't want to go by myself." She introduced herself— "My name's Kathy—actually, my real name's Betty, but I hate that name, so they call me Kathy. What's your name?"

"My name is Betty," I replied.

We must have made an odd-looking pair—our appearances were so very opposite. I took her by the hand, and we walked together to the conference. She kept saying, "You're different— I see God in you—you really care about me, don't you?" I did care about her, for in His own mysterious way Jesus was filling my heart with His wonderful love for her. Surely the Lord had purposely directed me to park in that particular place at that particular time so I could meet Kathy. It was a divine appointment designed by Almighty God. If Kathy could just meet Jesus, He would change her heart and transform her into a brand new creature.

Kathy related part of her life to me—mostly tragic. She was dying of cancer, and her husband was an alcoholic. By the smell of her breath, she too, while not completely intoxicated right then, was, no doubt, fairly fond of the bottle. Incidentally, she said she used to be a Baptist—I had the feeling that she must have been Baptist in name only because some of the things she said made it pretty clear that she had never accepted Christ as her Savior.

We took our seats, and the conference began, but before long, Kathy became very uncomfortable, and began to talk rather loudly. Some of her words shouldn't be said anywhere, much less at an evangelism conference. People began to turn and look. I wondered what they were thinking—were they seeing her need, or were they just annoyed? One couple in front of us did get up and leave. Silently, from my heart, I cried out, "Oh God, here we are in the midst of an evangelism conference, and there is one right here in the midst of us in such deep need—oh, touch her life—help her, please!"

Kathy only got louder—she insisted she was leaving. "I don't belong here, she said, "I'm gettin' out of here."

"I'll go with you then," I said. "I want to tell you about Jesus."

"No! You belong here—I don't! You stay!" she argued.

"If you go, I'm going with you," I answered, "Please, let me talk with you about Jesus."

She answered with an emphatic "No! I mean it! You're not goin'—I am! You're a good lady, and I know you care about me, but you're not goin' with me!"

With that, Kathy left, and I just sat there and wept. "Oh God," I cried, "I was so sure you wanted me to bring her here— did I make a mistake?"

In a moment, a man leaned over from behind me, and whispered. "What was her name? I'd like to pray for her." Then another man from down the row quietly slipped over to me and said, "We were praying for you both the whole time— who is she? We want to pray for her." Then another from across the aisle stepped over and said, "Tell me her name—we will take her name back to our church and pray for her." Praise God, these precious friends had all seen Kathy's desperate need, and were filled with compassion for her.

Then a dear evangelist friend, Dr. Rudy Hernandez, knelt

beside my seat and whispered that he had watched the whole time, and when Kathy left, he had followed her outside and talked with her, and before she left him, he prayed for her.

After that conference session ended, a tall lady in red came over and just wrapped me up completely in her arms. "I saw how you loved her," she said. "Tell me her name—our church will be praying for her."

Then I knew that God had indeed scheduled that meeting for Kathy and me, knowing she would go with me to the conference, knowing she would not stay, knowing that many would be drawn to pray for her, and even knowing how she would respond. The parking place, our meeting, the events that followed—God knew it all in advance, and I believe He orchestrated it all so that Kathy would hear how she could become a new creation in Christ, and so that many believers would pray for her. She was so close that night, yet so far away! Only God knows whether she ever believed and accepted Jesus Christ.

Whether a street person or a king, every individual has to make his or her own choice to receive or reject Jesus. Remember the account of King Agrippa? The Apostle Paul testified before him to the truth of Jesus Christ. In considerable detail and with great passion he explained to the king how this Jesus had changed his own life completely. The Scripture records the king's response: *"Then Agrippa said unto Paul, Almost thou persuadest me to be a Christian." (Acts 26:28)* There is no recorded dialog between Paul and King Agrippa after that, and no evidence in the Scriptures that this king ever became a Christian—a new creature in Christ. He was so close, yet so far away. King Agrippa had a choice, and his answer was "almost," a choice that was clearly "no." Almost...not yet...maybe...later...these are all dangerous words—all procrastination answers. Whatever word is used, to postpone a "yes" to Jesus is actually to say, "No!"

I don't know what has become of Kathy. I have not seen or heard from her since that night at the conference. That may have been her last chance to become a new creation in Christ. Every time a person says "no" to Jesus, it is like a drop of cement around the heart of that one. And it is possible for a heart to become so hardened by continual rejection of Jesus that one day that heart can no longer hear and respond. *"While it is said, Today, if ye will hear His voice, harden not your hearts..." (Hebrews 3:15)* Kathy had a choice. How I hope she said "yes" before it was too late.

God has a purpose, a plan, and a process for every individual, but these things will never be realized automatically or by natural instinct. All human beings are, indeed, created equal (albeit different), but until and unless we are transformed into a new creature (born again by believing in Jesus Christ and receiving Him as our personal Savior and Lord), we will remain forever in that caterpillar state—dead in our sins. But there is good news—God's Word—to all who say "yes" to Jesus:

Every time a person says "no" to Jesus, it is like a drop of cement around the heart of that one

"And you, being dead in your sins...hath He quickened together with Him, having forgiven you all trespasses; Blotting out the handwriting of ordinances that was against us, which was contrary to us, and took it out of the way, nailing it to His cross." (Colossians 2:13-14)

To become a new creation, there is one way only—His name is Jesus. He said: *"I am the way, the truth, and the life; no man cometh unto the Father but by Me." (John 14:6)*

"He came unto His own, and His own received Him not, But as many as received Him, to them gave He power to become the sons of God, even to them that believe on His Name." (John 1:11-12)

"Therefore if any man be in Christ, he is a new creature: old things are passed away; behold, all things are become new." (2 Corinthians 5:17)

Chapter 2
Butterfly Life—Who Can Qualify?

There are billions of people on this Earth! Which ones qualify to become new creatures? Everyone! The wonderful news is that the transformation is made by God through His grace—not by anything we have to offer, not by anything we can win, pay, earn, or do!

"For by grace are ye saved through faith; and that not of yourselves; it is the gift of God: Not of works, lest any man should boast. For we are His workmanship, created in Christ Jesus unto good works, which God hath before ordained that we should walk in them." *(Ephesians 2:8-10)* Now that is GRACE!

G - God's

R - Riches

A - At

C - Christ's

E - Expense

"…Christ Jesus, Who, being in the form of God, thought it not robbery to be equal with God: But made Himself of no reputation,

and took upon Him the form of a servant, and was made in the likeness of men: And being found in fashion as a man, He humbled Himself, and became obedient unto death, even the death of the cross." (Philippians 2:5-8)

"But He was wounded for our transgressions, He was bruised for our iniquities: The chastisement of our peace was upon Him; and with His stripes, we are healed. All we like sheep have gone astray; we have turned every one to his own way; and the Lord hath laid on Him the iniquity of us all. (Isaiah 53:5-6)

No wonder *Amazing Grace* is one of the most favorite hymns in all of history!

The world (this world system) has a whole different type of acrostic--I call it the World's WEB, and I'm not referring to the World Wide Web internet system. If the world could (and it can't, but if it could) give anyone a new, successful kind of life, this would likely be its appropriate acrostic:

W - Wealth

E - Education

B - Beauty

The world says you need all three of these things, but if you can't have them all, you surely must at least have one.

W—WEALTH

To begin with, if God had said that I would have to have wealth and riches in order to know Him, I'd be in big trouble. I was born into a poor preacher's family, and for a long time my daddy preached in little bitty churches way back in the "sticks" of Arkansas. Most of the time he got paid in beans and chickens—more beans than chickens—but I loved beans and cornbread, and if we had fried potatoes to go with it, I thought that was near about Heaven! Sometimes all we had to eat was dried bread crusts—they call them "croutons" these days—but back then, sometimes that was just all we had to eat.

We didn't have money for store-bought clothes, so my mother used to make clothing for my two sisters and me. Mother didn't have a sewing machine and couldn't afford to buy fabric, but sometimes people gave her their old clothing, and she carefully ripped those garments apart, saving the snaps, hooks and eyes, buttons, and whatever else was still good—even the thread. She made up her own patterns out of whatever paper she could find. Tissue paper was the best, but that wasn't always available, so many times she used old newspapers. She then pressed out the old garment pieces on the ironing board, and pinned the homemade patterns on the best parts of those old garments, and then carefully cut out each piece. By hand, with tiny and precise stitches, using that "second-hand" thread, she sewed our "new" clothes.

Mother never told us we were poor—her motto was, "Well, we'll just make the best of it!" And she always did. She sometimes made clothes for our dolls. I remember the beautiful coats she made for them, using scraps of casket material. One Christmas when Daddy was away in the Army, she even made cradles for our dolls—she used old orange crates! When we were asleep, she stayed up late sanding and painting. On Christmas morning we were completely delighted and surprised with those beautiful hand made cradles!

Once my dad completed his military service he felt strongly that, even though he already had college degrees, he should continue his education at the Seminary in Fort Worth, Texas. So, when I was twelve years old, we packed up, "lock, stock, and barrel," and moved to Fort Worth. It was an exciting move, but I have to admit, it was also a little disappointing—I really thought there would be cowboys in the dusty streets, and horses tied up to hitching rails. That's the way it was in the movies, but that's not the way it was when we moved to Fort Worth—progress had come. I just had to get over the wild-west idea.

My dad labored diligently, not only in his studies at the Seminary, but also worked very hard organizing little churches. Perhaps it was all too much, because at the age of 50 he suffered a massive stroke, so severe that he lost the use of the entire right side of his body. He also lost his memory and all ability to read and speak or even make a sound. Still his dream, his goal, was to preach again. Throughout his illness, he continued to affirm, "Well, it could be worse!"

My dad struggled valiantly to recover, and did make marked progress, even regaining the ability to speak fairly well, but he never came close to a complete recovery. He was sick for 26 years before he went home to Heaven. I should hasten to say that I don't know the "whys," but I do know that God is still good, and none of this happened without His knowledge or consent. One day we will understand, but in the meantime, we can rest in the fact that God is absolutely sovereign, and that His love for us will never cease or even lessen. And, someday, we will know "the rest of the story."

My dad loved me, and if he could have given me this world's wealth and riches, he surely would have—he just never had it to give.

I married young, but I married an enlisted man in the Air Force. His salary back then was a whopping $120 per month, and although that was more then than it is now, it was still very challenging to make it from one paycheck to the next. It had not occurred to us that we should discuss finances in much detail before we married. I think because we were so in love, we just figured that everything would work out. Having been raised in a Christian home, my automatic assumption was that we would tithe—I thought all Christians did that. My husband (Don), however, was not raised the same way I was. Most of his life he had been a church-goer, but actually became a Christian only a year before we married.

So, when we began our life together, we had some very interesting discussions about finances. I thought we should tithe—give ten percent of our income to the church where we were members. Don agreed that he would like to, and wished we could, but said we just didn't have enough money. He would even get a pencil and paper and show me how it would not work. And I would say, "I know, I know, but I think it's what they call faith—you just give the money, and trust God to get you through." Don wasn't convinced. He did finally agree to a compromise. He said, "OK, when we get paid, we'll take the $12 out and hold it aside, and if we still have it by the time we get the next paycheck, we'll give it." That did not work at all— the $12 was long gone by the time the next paycheck came, and in fact, we even had added expenses!

At last, Don agreed to "try" tithing. Either I had bugged him about it so long that he finally gave in just to get me "off his back," or we were simply both under conviction at the same time, but we did agree that we would give the tithe to our church when we the next paycheck came. We still couldn't make it work on paper—this would be a big leap of faith. More than once Don worried out loud, "I don't see a way in the world we can make it. If we get through this month, God will have to do it."

When that next paycheck came, we put the tithe in the offering plate that first Sunday, and I confess I was a little worried—in fact, I never prayed so hard in all my life! Though I don't remember my exact words, I know my prayer was that God would provide the money we needed, because if He didn't come through then Don would say, "I told you it wouldn't work," and that would be the end of it. I thought we were really putting God on the spot! Can you believe it? Wondering if the God Who put all the gold in the hills would be able to come up with $12! (Oh me, oh we, of little faith!)

> Can you believe it? Wondering if the God Who put all the gold in the hills would be able to come up with $12!

The next day we received a check in the mail—an insurance dividend that we didn't know we were going to get, and it was for more than $12. But, that wasn't all—three days later, Don was out in front of our apartment working on the car (which he had to do a lot), when a man drove up in a pick-up truck, leaned out the window and said, "Say, would you like a part-time job?" Don had been looking for part-time work and hadn't been able to find anything. The man in the truck owned a service station— the kind that used to provide real service, not only pumping the gas, but also checking tire pressure, engine oil level, radiator water level, and even cleaning the windshield.

Anyway, the man with the service station needed someone to work for him on Friday nights and Saturdays. You have to appreciate the fact that we lived in a low-rent housing area that wasn't on the way anywhere—you had to be going there on purpose, and you had to know how to get there. But God knew our need, He knew where we lived, and how to get there, and He sent that man to offer my husband that job. Don took the job, and kept it until we moved to another city.

When we took that first trembling step of faith in tithing, God poured out His blessings, just as He said He would do:

"Bring ye all the tithes into the storehouse, that there may be meat in mine house, and prove me now herewith, saith the Lord of hosts, if I will not open you the windows of heaven, and pour you out a blessing, that there shall not be room enough to receive it." *(Malachi 3:10)*

Some of the blessings have been financial, and some of other kinds, but from the day we began to put God first in our finances, He has always made a way for us. We have had some rough times (and there may be more), but God has never failed to bring us through.

From time to time, my husband made rank in the Air Force, but we just kept having more kids, so it seemed we were always trying to catch up. We even had the funny idea that as the children got older they'd be less expensive—almost everybody knows it turns out quite the opposite! Still, God continued to meet all our needs.

After retiring from the Air Force, Don attended school and at the same time worked at a Christian bookstore part time. His job soon became full time, and before long he became manager of the store. After about 8 years, he left managing that store and got his own store, and about a year later, a second store. Unfortunately, shortly after taking on that second store, the economy in our city took a drastic turn downward, and subsequently, so did we! It became obvious that by the end of the year, we were going to lose the second store, and we did. By the end of the following year, we knew we were going to lose the first store as well.

We did find some buyers for that store, well, "sort-of" buyers—they would not give us any money for the store, but they would agree to take the half of the debts and we would keep half, and maybe everybody could make it, and the store could remain open. So, we signed the contract, and it looked like things would work out OK, and they did…for about 6 months. Suddenly the store was closed, the merchandise repossessed, and the new owners seemed to have disappeared from the face of the Earth. Not only did we still have our part of the debt, but, since the "new owners" could not be found, we had the additional financial burden of obligations the new owners had left behind.

Talk about difficult days! Don was already in his 50's and was looking for employment, and not being very successful— seems he was either over- or under-qualified. Talk about discouragement! I will admit that I had some "pity-parties" during those times. A pity party, of course, is when one feels extremely sorry for oneself; "No one has ever been hurt like me; no one has ever suffered as much as I have; no one has ever had such a hard life as me; oh poor me!"

If you've ever had any of those pity parties, you know they are really no fun—you're the only one invited, and the longer they last, the worse you feel! I know this for a fact because of a particular pity party during the demise of the bookstores and the problems that followed. It didn't help that Don would make remarks like, "Honey, I've got it all figured out. If we both work as hard as we can till we are 123, we'll be out of debt." I got to thinking about how bad our circumstances really were!

Incidentally, that is the classic way that a pity party begins—when we get our eyes off of God and onto ourselves, our problems, and our circumstances. The problems and circumstances that day loomed larger than they had ever been. I felt completely overwhelmed. I cried out, "God, sometimes I think I can't last much longer!" Immediately the thought occurred to me, "But, I always do!" And God gave me a song, right on the spot, and lifted me completely out of my despair:

The Pity Party Song
(He Will Bring Us Through)[1]

Sometimes I think I can't last much longer,

But I always do!

I just keep trusting my Blessed Savior,

And, God just keeps bringing me through!

So, there's no need for a pity-party—

Everybody's got a valley!

That's just part of life for me and you.

But, there is one who knows all about it,

And He is able, don't you doubt it—

Jesus Christ, our Lord, will bring us through!

God did provide a job for Don, still in the Christian bookstore field, not in retail sales, but on the wholesale side as a sales representative, and he worked in that capacity for about twelve years.

Still, life wasn't easy, since most of those 12 years Don worked on a "straight commission" basis, meaning no salary, no allowances, and no expense accounts—all expenses had to come out of his commission, which was sometimes nonexistent! I've heard that commission sales can be fantastic. I've also heard they can be really good, and sometimes only fair. We found out for a fact that commissions can be pretty good part of the time, fair to moderate most of the time, lousy at times, and sometimes not even there! But God always made a way, although a number of those ways have been quite unique and even funny.

God does have a sense of humor! One particular weekend while in ministry in another state, I called home on a Sunday night to check on Don (he had been sick and had to stay home). I asked how things were going, and he said he was feeling better, but that a funny thing had happened—we had been "papered!" This was a popular prank by either "friends" or "enemies" of teenagers. This playful little trick involved throwing rolls of toilet paper over tree branches at the home of the teenage "target," so that the end result would be yards and yards of toilet paper hanging from the trees. (At the time of this incident, one of our daughters and her teenaged sons were living with us, and apparently one of her boys was the designated target.)

Back to the telephone conversation, however. Don continued, "But, a funny thing," he said, "I think our dog scared the kids off, because they left 24 rolls of unopened toilet paper!" You know, we didn't have to buy toilet tissue for a long time! God truly does supply **all** our needs, albeit in unusual ways on occasion.

While we know God will always provide, we are still sometimes surprised at the way God uses ordinary events in extraordinary ways. Several years ago we were planning a baby shower—another little granddaughter would be arriving soon, and we wanted a special celebration.

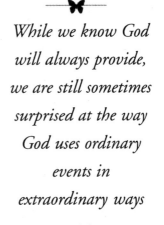

While we know God will always provide, we are still sometimes surprised at the way God uses ordinary events in extraordinary ways

The shower was scheduled for 2:00 p.m. on a Saturday in March, at our home. I had ordered a cake from a local grocery store, and it was to be ready for pick-up anytime on the day of the shower. I began preparing early on the day of the shower, trying to make sure everything was just right. Suddenly, about 10 A.M., even though preparations were not quite complete, I felt the strong sense to stop everything, go immediately to the grocery store and get the cake. When I told Don that I wanted to go right then, he suggested it would be just as good to wait until after lunch since it was less than a mile to the store, but, whatever… It wasn't a big deal—I could have waited, but still somehow felt compelled to go right then.

When I arrived at the store, I half expected the cake would be broken or messed up somehow, but thankfully, it was fine—beautiful! I carefully placed the cake in the shopping cart and proceeded to select a few other things, such as Sprite for the punch, which I actually put back on the shelf and got 7-Up instead, since it was less expensive that day.

As I stood looking at paper plates, napkins, etc., sort of lost in thought, a man walked up to me and said, "I see you have 7-

Up in your basket." I didn't know what business that was of his, but I was nice anyway, and replied, "Well, yes, as a matter of fact, I do." He responded with, "Well then, you have just won $77 worth of groceries…and, a gift certificate from a sporting goods store, and four tickets to a San Antonio Spurs basketball game!" The man went on to explain that they were doing a promotion that day at that particular store, and the very first person he spotted with 7-Up in their basket would be the winner of the prizes. And that was me! I had not heard a thing about that special promotion, but God knew all about it. I am totally convinced that strong "go now" suggestion at ten o'clock in the morning was His way of sending me at just the right time to receive the wonderful provision He had waiting for me.

Incidentally, when I got home with the groceries and gifts and examined the game tickets, the effective date stamped on them was March 31—our son's birthday! What is more, the tickets were for really good seats, not the kind way up in the "nosebleed" section. Our son and three of our grandsons went to that game, and did they ever have a blast! What a game! The Spurs won big-time! They couldn't do anything wrong that night! They didn't do much of anything the rest of that season, but on that particular March 31st, they were absolutely terrific! Isn't that just like our great and loving Heavenly Father, not only to supply all our needs, but also to throw in a special surprise birthday present just for fun!

Many other times and in many other ways our great God has faithfully supplied our needs, and even many of our "wants." It would take several more chapters, maybe even another whole book, to recount them all! The point is—if God said I had to have this world's wealth and riches in order to know Him, there's not a time in my life, from my birth up to and including this very moment, that I could qualify. That would be the first strike against me. On the basis of this world's wealth and riches, I could not know God—I could not hope to qualify to become a new creation.

The second letter in the World's Web is E—for Education.

E—EDUCATION

Could I qualify on the basis of education? Once again, I'd be in big trouble, even though I graduated from high school with very high honors. I graduated on Tuesday night, but I married on Saturday night of that very same week, and I never did get those college and university degrees. So, if God had said I had to have that higher education in order to know Him, that would be the second strike against me. On the basis of education, I could not know God—I could not hope to qualify to become a new creation.

The last letter in the World's Web is B—for Beauty (or "looks" if you're a guy).

B—BEAUTY

My last chance! I always thought I wanted to be the "step-out-of-the-shower-dripping-wet-gorgeous" type. Not only has that not happened in the past, it is becoming patently obvious that it will never happen in the future. I am getting older, and a lot of things change with age. Gravity takes over, and things move around—they don't stay in the same places they used to be. Luci Swindoll says that everything either falls down or falls off!

That's just the way it is—our bodies do change with age! Our hair turns gray or turns loose, or both; our eyes get weak—first it's single vision glasses, then bifocals, then trifocals, then coke bottle focals, maybe even implants; and they say the time even comes that whatever doesn't hurt doesn't work anymore. It is a fact that the physical body is perishing, but we can take great comfort in the promise of God that for all who have become new creatures in Christ, there is a bright and beautiful future beyond this earthly existence, which includes a wonderful, glorified body!

Back to the "beauty" thing—I do think it is all right for women to use cosmetics—within reason, of course. I once heard a pastor say that "any old barn looks better with a coat of paint!" I have been told that the word "cosmetic" comes from the root word, cosmos, meaning, "to bring order out of chaos!" Enough said!

There was a time when I thought I had a chance at this thing called beauty. It was the first time I ever saw my husband-to-be. I was sixteen. I had been invited to a Fourth of July picnic/party, and the plan was for the guys and girls to meet together at our sponsor's home the night before the party. The guys would then go to the lake and camp out by the gate so they could be first in on the morning of the 4th—that way, we would get one of the best picnic spots. The girls were to spend the night at the sponsor's house and then drive out and meet the guys in the morning at the lake.

It sounded like a perfect plan. On that particular July 3rd, as we gathered at the sponsor's home, I was seated on the floor not far from the front door when in walked a couple of guys I had never met. One of them was, without a doubt, the most handsome, gorgeous hunk of man I had ever seen. Suddenly, I was in love! I don't think he even noticed me, since he stepped right over me as though I wasn't even there, but I surely did notice him! I know, some people say you don't fall in love instantly, but I did! We met at the picnic the next day, and it wasn't long before we began dating. Almost a year later, we married.

Some months after we married, in an especially tender moment, I was thinking about the time I first saw my husband, remembering how I had instantly fallen "head-over-heels" in love with him. I wondered if he had felt the same way—he had never mentioned it. I asked him, "Honey, what did you think of me the first time you ever saw me?" And he answered, "Why?" I thought he was teasing me, so I pressed on, "Oh, I just wondered—I'd just like to know." "Are you sure?" he questioned. "Yeah, yeah, tell me," I begged. "Well then," he said, "if you really want to know, I thought you were the littlest, whitest thing I had ever seen!" I was totally surprised, and crushed. "You mean...you didn't fall in love with me at first sight?" I asked. I will never forget his answer, "Naw, honey, you just sort of grew on me." I'm glad I didn't have to "grow" on God. He loved me long before I ever knew Him. But, if God had said I had to have this world's beauty and glamour to know Him, that would be strike three. I would be "out!" On the basis of this world's concept of beauty and glamour, I could not know God—I could not hope to qualify to become a new creation.

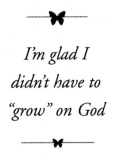

I'm glad I didn't have to "grow" on God

But God has a better plan. He says there is only one kind of person that can qualify to know God. This kind is described in one word in many places in the Bible, but I'm thinking about this particular Scripture: *"For whosoever shall call upon the name of the Lord shall be saved." (Romans 10:13)* Well, I am a "whosoever," and so is everybody who has ever been born or ever will be, from the beginning of time until the end of the age.

No matter who you are or who you are not;

No matter what you have or what you have not;

No matter where you have been or where you have not been;

No matter what you have done or what you have not done;

No matter whether you are beautiful/handsome or not;

No matter whether you are rich or poor;

No matter whether you have many degrees of education,

or no degrees;

None these or any other things can qualify or disqualify you to know God.

Whosoever? Absolutely! God loves every person, everywhere, and it is His will that everyone would come to know Him. The Lord *"...is not willing that any should perish, but that all should come to repentance." (2 Peter 3:9)*

"For God so loved the world, that He gave His only begotten Son, that whosoever believeth in Him should not perish, but have everlasting life." (John 3:16)

God so loved! Can we even begin to comprehend such love? That God values each of us so very much? Although I have been unable to find the source of the following illustration, it is just too good not to be shared:

A well-known speaker started off his seminar by holding up a $20 bill. In the room of 200 he asked, "Who would like this $20 bill?" Hands started going up.

He said, "I am going to give this $20 to one of you, but first, let me do this." He proceeded to crumple the bill up. He then asked, "Who still wants it?" Still the hands were up in the air.

"Well," he replied, "What if I do this?" And he dropped it on the ground and started to grind it into the floor with his shoe. He picked it up, now crumpled and dirty. "Now who still wants it?" Still the hands went into the air.

"My friends, you have all learned a very valuable lesson. No matter what I did to the money, you still wanted it because it did not decrease in value. It was still worth $20."

"Many times in our lives, we are dropped, crumpled and ground into the dirt by the decisions we make and the circumstances that come our way. We feel as though we are worthless. But no matter what has happened or what will happen, you will never lose your value: dirty or clean, crumpled or finely creased, you are still priceless to the One who died on the cross for you. The worth of our lives comes not in what we do or who we know, but by THE GOD WHO LOVES US. You are special—don't ever forget it. Count your blessings, not your problems. You have a Savior who wants to spend eternity with you."

God **already** loves you! It is only by His grace and mercy that anyone can ever come to know Him. No one can buy, win, earn, or otherwise qualify for God's favor. There is **nothing** in us that will ever commend us to God. It is quite the other way around—when we could not reach God, He came to us:

"But God commended His love toward us, in that, while we were yet sinners, Christ died for us." (Romans 5:8)

You must come to God with nothing in your hands, no credits, no suggestions, no deals—you must come just as you are—as a "whosoever."

The insignificant little caterpillar just does what God designed him for, and God makes him brand new. How much more should we do what God designed us for—come to Him just as we are—let Him make us new and give us "wings"!

Chapter 3
Butterfly Life—But, HOW?

Butterfly Life in a Caterpillar World [2]

Butterfly life in a caterpillar world—
How does it happen to be?
How can a wooly little caterpillar critter
Be changed so beautifully?

Once a little caterpillar critter,
Now flies with grace so free;
There must be a lesson in the little caterpillar
Just for you and me.

Well, the little caterpillar simply does
The thing it's s'posed to do;
Obeys what God designed him for,
And God makes him brand new!

We're the reason Jesus came,
He conquered death's cold grave,
Paid sin's debt to set us free,
And now we know the way.

Butterfly life can now be yours,
You'll never be the same!
Butterfly life can now be yours
By trusting Jesus' name.

Butterfly life in a caterpillar world,
That's how it happens to be!
That's how a wooly little caterpillar critter
Can change so beautifully.

Once a little caterpillar critter,
Now flies with grace so free—
Yes, there's a lesson in the little caterpillar
Just for you and me.

Butterfly life in a caterpillar world,
Now it can happen to you!
You can leave that caterpillar living
And find a life brand new.

In HIM you must be born again,
His Word you must obey,

Butterfly life can now be yours
By trusting Jesus' name.

Butterfly life can now be yours,
You'll never be the same!
Butterfly life can now be yours
By trusting in His name!

"Therefore if any man be in Christ, he is a new creature: old things are passed away; behold, all things are become new." (2 Corinthians 5:17)

Some years ago I traveled with a mission team to Africa. My major assignment was ministry in song. For a portion of the time, I was with the medical team at Dandora Baptist Church in Kenya. The medical clinic was held in one of the rooms of the church building, but the area was not large enough to accommodate all the people who came for medical care, so they waited outside the building for their turn. And while they waited, I sang to them about Jesus. After the clinic closed, we had an evangelistic service in the church "auditorium" (which was a very small and simple room, with rough, backless, wooden benches for seating).

It was interesting to note that the church building itself had modern-looking light fixtures, wall switches, and electrical outlets, but none of them worked! They weren't connected to anything—they were just there! The building had all the outward appearances of electricity, but no power!

That is a pretty good illustration of the big difference

between a religious person and a Christian. Those who have religion alone may look good and have the outward appearance of light, but there will be no light because religion alone is powerless, not being connected to the power source, the Lord Jesus Christ.

In contrast, true Christians are filled with light, because they are **united** with the power source—the Lord Jesus Christ. That vital connection is made the moment we are born into God's family by receiving Jesus Christ as Savior. In that instant we are transformed by God from death to life, into a new creature!

The electrical system in a building is not disconnected and reconnected every time the light is needed—it is only necessary to flip the switch on the wall. It is also true with Christians— we don't have to continue to be born again time after time. Then how is it that some Christians **seem** to be "in the dark?" Even a Christian can have an *outward* appearance of light and a life of victory, yet miss the real power to live it, because even though he or she is still connected, united with Christ (having been born again), the "switch on the wall" is in the off position (control has not been given to God—more about this in Chapter 8).

What does the caterpillar **do** to become a butterfly? He simply obeys what God designed him for—follows the instincts God has placed within him. There is within every human being a "God-shaped" vacuum (a sense far greater than natural instinct) that HE alone can fill. Once again, we are reminded that the caterpillar has no choice but to become what God designed him to be. Human beings were not only created with the choice to say "yes" to God, but also the freedom to make the wrong choice—we can say "no" to God—no new birth, no new creature—and God will not override that choice, even though it means eternal separation from Him.

How can you or I become a new creature? What must we do? In our world today, if you have enough money, you can buy almost anything. During that same mission trip to Kenya, I learned that African children often have combination Christian and African names. I was told that when a child is old enough, for 300 shillings the child can be baptized, and at that time can choose a Christian name. The child's first communion costs 200 shillings. Since many in Africa believe that both baptism and first communion are required to go to Heaven, it follows that eternal life can only be obtained if you comply with those two requirements and pay 500 shillings. **Eternal life for 500 shillings???** God's plan is so much better—a "whosoever" doesn't have to have 500 shillings or anything else!

In the concluding session of the "Butterfly Life in a Caterpillar World" conferences and retreats, I usually demonstrate how to make butterflies out of magazine pictures. It is obvious that the pictures are not alive—they are powerless to change themselves—they can become butterflies only if some higher power transforms them. For those particular magazine picture butterflies, that "higher power" is me.

In 2 Corinthians 5:17, we read, *"if any man be in Christ, he is a new creature."* So, **how** do we get **"in Christ?"** Until we are **in** Him, we are as lifeless as those magazine pictures—dead in our sins and powerless to do anything about it. Dead people can do nothing! The only way we will ever be changed into a new creature is to submit ourselves to a "higher power" that can make the transformation, and there is only one power Who can do that—He is Almighty God, through Jesus Christ our Lord.

God will never wave a magic wand over a group of people

and then declare them all righteous and forgiven—new creatures. To become a new creature in Christ, each and every one of us must personally, by the individual act of our own will, humbly come to God in prayer. There are three critical steps involved in this specific "ACT" of prayer:

A – Acknowledge

C – Confess/Believe

T – Trust/Receive

A – Acknowledge to God that you are a sinner.

He already knows that, but each one of us must be willing to recognize—concede and agree with Him—that we are sinners. Until God transforms us, we are all dead in our sins, and remember, dead people can't do anything.

As mentioned before, the Bible says that **all** are sinners: *"For all have sinned, and come short of the glory of God." (Romans 3:23)* "All" means, well, **ALL**! That includes you, me, everybody—no one is left out of this equation. The result of sin is the same for everyone: *"The wages of sin is death,"* and the way out is the same for everyone—*"but the gift of God is eternal life through Jesus Christ our Lord." (Romans 6:23)*

In Revelation 1:5, we are told clearly that Jesus *"loved us, and washed us from our sins in His own blood."* Why did Jesus have to give His own blood for us? Sin has always required a blood sacrifice. When we go all the way back to the beginning, we will see that God Himself shed the blood of animals to provide skins to cover Adam and Eve after they sinned. *"Unto Adam also and to his wife did the Lord God make coats of skins, and clothed them." (Genesis 3:21)* Fast-forward to the New

Testament, and we read: *"...without shedding of blood is no remission." (Hebrews 9:22)*

Back again to the Old Testament—we read in the book of Leviticus: *"For the life of the flesh is in the blood: and I have given it to you upon the altar to make an atonement for your souls; for it is the blood that maketh an atonement for the soul." (Leviticus 17:11)* In Old Testament times animal sacrifices were required. Each year, on the day of Atonement the priest would offer the blood of a lamb as a sacrifice for the sins of the people. This sacrificial offering (atonement) could never take away their sins, but only cover them for that year. Each year those sins were rolled forward (not taken away or eradicated, but only covered), until the day **all** those sins rolled to the foot of the cross, where the spotless, sinless Son of God, Jesus Christ, paid for those sins with His own pure and perfect blood: *"Forasmuch as ye know that ye were not redeemed with corruptible things, as silver and gold...But with the **precious blood of Christ, as of a lamb without blemish and without spot."** (1 Peter 1:18-19)*

"For He hath made Him (Jesus) *to be sin for us, Who knew no sin, that we might be made the righteousness of God in Him." (2 Corinthians 5:21)*

*"But Christ being come an high priest of good things to come, by a greater and more perfect tabernacle, not made with hands, that is to say, not of this building: Neither by the blood of goats and calves, but **by His own blood** He entered in **once** into the holy place, **having obtained eternal redemption for us."** (Hebrews 9:11-12) "In Whom we have **redemption through His blood,** even the forgiveness of sins." (Colossians 1:14)*

Salvation is free, but not cheap. It cost Jesus the greatest sacrifice ever made. The cross did not *happen* to Jesus. He came on purpose to die—to pay a debt He did not owe—a debt we could not pay—the awful debt of sin.

The Cross Did Not *Happen* to Jesus

The cross did not *happen* to Jesus,
His death was no cruel trick of fate,
The grave was no final vanquish,
It was only a three-day wait.

The cross did not *happen* to Jesus,
There He willingly took all our sins,
Paid our debt with His own blood completely
So that we could be perfectly clean.

Jesus rose from the dead in victory—
It is finished, the battle's been won,
His triumph complete and eternal,
Son of man, and yet God the Son.

The cross did not *happen* to Jesus,
It was His plan from the start,
Because He lives, we can live also,
When we trust Him with all of our heart.

At the cross Jesus paid with His own blood for the sins of all the people of the Old Testament who looked forward to the coming of the Lamb of God (Jesus) who would take away their sins. And at the cross Jesus paid with His own blood for the sins of all the people of the New Testament times who would trust in Him. For **all** people of **all** time who believe on and receive Jesus Christ as Savior and Lord, **JESUS PAID IT ALL!**

C - Confess/Believe

I have met people all over the world who know "about" Jesus—they can tell me that He is the Son of God, that He died on the cross, was buried, and rose from the grave. Some have had this knowledge *about* Jesus for most of their lives. But, living in a Christian home or even going to church for years and years does not make a person a Christian any more than living in a barn makes a person a cow!

A person can practice flying a jet plane by way of a flight simulator, and may even log hundreds of hours in that simulator, but if that person never gets into a **real** jet airplane and takes off, no matter how much he knows or how long he has practiced on the simulator, he has never had the **genuine** experience of an **authentic** jet flight! If he is a real jet pilot he must personally fly a real jet airplane. Until and unless you, personally, believe with your heart on the Lord Jesus Christ, open the door of your life, ask Him to come in, and receive Him, you cannot really experience that new life—the best you can do will only be a "simulation." One can only be a new creature by being "in Christ." So, how does one get "in Christ?"

"... The word is nigh thee, even in thy mouth, and in thy heart; that is, the word of faith, which we preach; That if thou shalt confess with thy mouth the Lord Jesus and shalt believe in thine heart that God hath raised him from the dead, thou shalt be saved. For with

*the heart man believeth unto righteousness; and with the mouth confession is made unto salvation. For the Scripture saith, Whosoever believeth on Him shall not be ashamed…For whosoever shall call upon the name of the Lord shall be **saved**." (Romans 10:8-11,13)*

Saved! Changed! Transformed into a new creation! That is just what God does in the life of any "whosoever" who will make that conscious choice to believe on the Lord Jesus Christ.

T – Trust/Receive

There is one thing we can and must **do** to become a new creation, and that is to **trust (receive)** Jesus Christ.

Repentance is a part of trusting (receiving) Jesus. To "repent" is more than to be sorry—it also means to turn around and go the opposite direction. Instead of walking away from God, one must make a U-turn, or a "you" turn, and walk toward God.

> *Instead of walking away from God, one must make a U-turn, or a "you" turn, and walk toward God*

MAKE A "YOU" TURN

No one can do this for you—you must make that decisive turn from self and this world system to Jesus Christ, confess Him as Lord and Savior, **receive** and **trust** Him.

"He came unto His own, and His own received Him not. But as many as received Him, to them gave He power to become the sons of God, even to them that believe on His name." (John 1:11-12)

When and Where

When, and where does one need to be to trust in/receive Jesus Christ? In a church? In a prayer room? At Sunday School? At a Bible Study meeting? **Wherever** you are **When** you hear God calling to you!

Saul was on his way to Damascas that he might persecute Christians, when he was not only **blinded** by the light of God, but **shaken** by the voice of God. Saul (who came to be known later as Paul the Apostle) was led by the hand of his companions to the city of Damascus. For three days he was without food and drink, and without sight. Then God sent a man named Ananias to witness to Saul. And when Saul received that witness and responded to Jesus Christ, he was transformed. Not only did he receive his sight physically, but also spiritually. Now his eyes were truly open! The Jesus he had once hated he now loved with all his heart, and he began to tell the world boldly about this Jesus Christ, Son of God, Savior. He definitely and dramatically made that "you" turn, and became a fantastic new creation. You can read all about it in Acts 9:1-31.

On a log at a mobile home park! Some years ago during a Western ministry tour, I was visiting in a mobile home park in Yuma, Arizona. During a morning walk, I met a woman who was deeply burdened. We began to talk, and then sat down together on a log, as I shared with her about Jesus Christ, and how she could find new life in Him, and know the hope, joy, and peace that comes with that new life. In a few moments, sitting right there on the log, that precious lady simply prayed and asked Jesus to forgive her, and come into her life. She believed and received Him, and she was born again—that's how one gets "in Christ"—by the miracle of being born again—into God's family. This kind of "birth" day can occur anywhere, any time of the night or day.

On a plane—Captive Audience! "But God…it would be so much better if I could change my flight." Sometimes God says no to my reasonable request to change the plan, and I don't understand why. Such was the case when I was returning home from another concert tour. I wanted to get an earlier, more direct, flight from San Francisco to San Antonio, and eliminate the long way around—via Phoenix. It certainly made more sense to me—it would save time and be a lot less tiring. I had been out in ministry, away from home, long enough! Why couldn't I get an earlier flight?

As I boarded the plane in San Francisco bound for Phoenix, I noticed an available seat by the window in the second row, and felt irresistibly drawn to that seat. The girl in the center seat of that row indicated that the seat was available. I attempted to politely move past the lady in the aisle seat, hoping she would move a bit so I could get to my seat, but nothing happened— she just sat there. After a couple more "excuse me's," the girl in the center seat said, "She's blind, and can't speak any English— you'll just have to sort of step over her."

Struggling past the two ladies, I began to wonder if I had made the wrong decision—but it was too late by then: the plane was filling fast, and anyway, the only seats left were probably in the tail section. I would just have to make the best of it, and hope I wouldn't have to get in and out too much, if at all.

My thoughts were interrupted as Pat, the girl in the center seat, explained that at first she had been farther back in the plane, but had watched this little Spanish lady, who was accompanied by her family long enough to see that she was safely seated, and then they had kissed her goodbye and left the plane. The little Spanish lady was very lonely and scared—with no one to talk to and no one to help. Pat had felt so sorry for her that she left her "safe" spot over the aircraft wings, to come and sit and talk with this helpless little woman. (Unknown to us all, God was using all these things to fit into a very special plan.)

As the plane began to taxi onto the runway, both Pat and the Spanish lady were trembling, and tears were beginning to well up in their eyes. Pat turned and began to tell me of her terrible fear of flying. I could not help but smile as I told her, "You know what—you don't ever have to be afraid if you know Jesus." Then I told her how God had put me into the music ministry 20 years prior, and had given me His promise—*"And I will preserve your going out and your coming in from this time forward, and even forevermore." (Psalm 121:8)* I could say with certainty that God had kept that promise all those years. And, well, since God was going to keep me safe, and Pat was on the same plane with me, she would be safe too.

When I asked Pat if she knew Jesus, she said she knew He had always been near. As she began to recount some of her experiences, it became increasingly clear that while God had been "near," Pat had only known **about** Him, and had never really come to **know Him personally**. There is a big difference!

Pat related how that some years back, her 7-year-old son had been killed—hit by a truck while riding his bicycle. As the details began to unfold, I commented that it must have been hard for her after his death, and she replied that it had been very hard at times—she had even tried twice to commit suicide. I asked, "What did you do—how, I mean, well, what did you do?" She told me that she would be driving her car and see a curb, and say to herself, "Just hit that curb and end it all!" But, both times, instantly, she had heard a voice, saying, "If you do, you will never see your son again."

God had, indeed, been near—near enough to warn Pat. If she had ended her life either of those times, she could not have joined her son in Heaven. When I explained how she could know God personally through His Son, the Lord Jesus Christ, Pat prayed to receive Jesus Christ right there on the plane, right out loud. I couldn't hear the angels in Heaven rejoicing, but I'm sure they were, and Pat's son, too!

Pat got off the plane in Phoenix to catch another flight to El Paso where she lives. Funny, I had tried so hard to get an earlier return flight to San Antonio, but it simply was not available—thank God! And, I'm thankful I didn't change seats when it looked so difficult to get to the "chosen" one. Oh, I know God could have used somebody else, some other time, but I am so thankful that He rearranged my life and let me be a part of His plan to reach Pat.

In Prison—Even more captive audience! God has given many opportunities of ministry in prisons all across the United States and even in Australia. While we will never know, this side of Heaven, how many of those inmates made that "you-turn" and received Jesus Christ as Savior, becoming new creations in Christ Jesus, there have been times that we have seen people changed. In personal conversation with some, we have heard comments such as this from a prisoner in Jean, Nevada: "You have ministered to my hurting heart."

I will never forget a particular young man who was incarcerated at a maximum security penitentiary. As I began to sing and speak, I noticed a man seated at the back of the room—perhaps he caught my attention because he was wearing sunglasses, and seemed to have an "I dare you" look about him. I half expected he might leave, but instead, as I continued to sing and speak, he moved to the middle of the room, and then all the way to the front. It was obvious that he was really listening.

After the service we were given just a few minutes to talk with inmates, and the man with the sunglasses came to me immediately. He said his name was Mark, and that this was the first time in his entire life that he had been in any kind of church service—he had **never** heard about Jesus!

I had explained during that afternoon service how to receive Jesus Christ, and Mark had heard but had not made that "you-turn," and he was anxious to know more. Suddenly, however, the time was gone. I wanted to give Mark one of my little "Where To Go When It Hurts" books, for it would explain more about how to know Jesus, but the officials would not allow me to give him anything.

Later I was told that Mark had been "in the hole" for five years. One can only imagine what kind of place that is! I was told that out of every 24 hours of every day the prisoner has **one** hour of light. The rest of the time is spent in solitary confinement—in darkness. The day God sent me to that prison was Mark's first day out of "the hole"—that was the reason for the sunglasses. As far as I know, the little book that I wanted to give to Mark was later delivered to him by a prison chaplain.

This much I know—God sent me to that prison that day to share the Truth with Mark and others like him, and they heard enough to know how to get to Him through Jesus Christ. My prayer is that whether through the little book or someone else or something else, Mark and others who came to that service will come to know Jesus Christ as Savior.

Anywhere! A number of years ago I was invited to speak for our first Coffee Cup Ministries meeting. This was a new women's outreach from our church, patterned after the teas that had been a part of recent evangelistic meetings in Australia. The idea was to meet in private homes and invite neighbors and friends who did not know Jesus Christ. In Australia, the ladies would invite their friends to come and meet their American friends, to which many responded (although I have to admit some had already met other Americans, and really weren't that interested).

On the day of the Coffee Cup outreach, we had a very full room, including several guests. As I recall, we began by asking each lady to give her name and tell something about herself, a sort of get-acquainted time. Then I was to sing and give my testimony about our time in Australia. Unknown to me, one of the guests, Tonya, came only because she heard that the speaker was going to talk about Australia, and she thought it might be interesting since that is where she and her husband had spent their honeymoon. Besides, she had run out of excuses to give her friend who was always inviting her to some sort of church thing—she figured this home meeting would be fairly safe.

At this point, I should back up enough to say that God had already impressed me that I should give a copy of my little book, "Where To Go When It Hurts," to every guest at the Coffee Cup meeting. I prepared to do just that—in fact, I was **very** willing—God had already dealt with me on the issue of giving while on my way to Melbourne, Australia.

We first landed in Sydney, where we had to deplane for an hour and then get back on the same plane to continue our flight to Melbourne. While in the Sydney airport, I noticed three young ladies that were obviously Australian, and obviously not Christians, so I gave each one of them a little tract. On the front of the tract were the words, "You Are Loved"—and on the inside, the words of John 3:16, personalized. On the back of the tract, the way to receive Jesus Christ was explained. As a group, we had been told that we should be careful in sharing the Gospel—not to be too overwhelmingly bold.. So, I figured that I had done the right thing in just giving the girls a tract—surely that wasn't too bold.

When we got on the plane, I noticed where the girls were sitting, and I continued on further back in the plane to my assigned seat. As I started to sit down, God spoke to my heart—"Give each of those girls one of your books (Where To Go When It Hurts)." I argued silently with God, "But, they cost money, and besides I don't even know if I have three books in my bag." I continued to protest, but God wouldn't let me alone until I looked into my bag—there were exactly three books! So, I went back up the aisle to where the girls were sitting, and though I felt a little foolish, I smiled and offered each of them a book, and each one accepted.

Feeling that God must surely be satisfied now, I proceeded back to my seat, but just as I started to sit down, God spoke to my heart again—"Now, go and sign each book." This time I didn't argue—I went back to ask the girls if I could sign the books I had given them. God opened the door for me to share the Gospel with the first girl (the other two were somewhere else on the plane).

I explained the little tract, and shared with her how we are all sinners (Romans 3:10, 23) and separated from God—"*The wages of sin is death, but the gift of God is eternal life through Jesus Christ our Lord.*" *(Romans 6:23)* Suddenly, I knew how to explain "the gift"—it was like the book I had given her. **It was a gift!** I had already paid for it—I did not ask her for money. I had just offered the book to her, and she had accepted it. She didn't have to—she could have refused, but she did accept the gift, and now the book was hers to keep. It was such a joy to tell her that God loved her so much that He sent His only Son, Jesus Christ, to die on the cross to pay for her sin, and that if she would turn from herself and her sin to Jesus, and receive/accept Him, the gift of God (eternal life through Jesus Christ) would be hers. God would give her that new birth––new life in Him. I told the girl that she could pray anywhere, even there on the plane, and God would hear her, and she could be born into His family right then. But, she said she wasn't ready—she would think about it. I told her not to think about it too long—this plane could fall out of the sky, and it could be eternally too late for her.

As the first girl left her seat, one of the other girls came and sat down, and I shared with her about the gift of God in the same way. Then she left, and the third girl came and sat down, and once again I shared the truth of the gift of God. Each of the girls were offered the gift of the book, and each accepted it. Each girl was offered the gift of eternal life through Jesus Christ our Lord, but none accepted. Each girl was warned not to wait too long. I have never heard from those girls again—perhaps some time after our encounter they did accept Jesus Christ— I hope so.

Back to the first Coffee Cup Ministry—as part of my Australia testimony that day, I shared the story of the three girls and the three books, and I gave each of the guests a copy of that same book. After our meeting, one of the guests who came to talk with me was Tonya—she thanked me for the book, and promised she would read it—that she wouldn't put it down until she finished it. One week later, she called and said that she missed me at the Coffee Cup Meeting that week, and she wanted to come by to see me right then. I had just had a tooth extracted, and was feeling lousy (looked that way too), but she wanted so much to come by that I agreed that she could come if she didn't mind the way I looked.

She soon arrived—carrying smiles, flowers and balloons (with the words "Thank You, Thank You, Thank You" all over them). But the most wonderful thing of all was her story. True to her promise, she had gone home, put the children to bed early, and read the book all the way to the end—then she went into her closet and got down on her knees, and asked Jesus to forgive her and come into her life. Tonya was already a beautiful woman physically, but that moment she became a gorgeous new creation in Christ Jesus! She purchased some of my recordings for friends, and then she asked, "Could I please pay for the books you gave those Australian girls on the plane?" Through that request came the soft reminder that I must never hesitate when God directs me to give anything. We can never out-give God. *"He that spared not His own Son, but delivered Him up for us all, how shall He not with Him also freely give us all things?" (Romans 8:32)*

✖

*This gift is free
—not cheap—
but free to all
who will
receive
Jesus Christ*

✖

The story doesn't end there—this precious new friend began a weekly Bible study in her own home, along with an excellent, experienced Bible teacher who agreed to conduct the studies. This Bible study grew tremendously—sometimes there were 90-100 ladies in attendance. There are many things I could tell you about Tonya, but probably one of the most outstanding things is that she goes about doing good, and everywhere she goes she tells people about Jesus. She is still walking and talking with Jesus, and looks more like Him every day. She and many others have traded their old caterpillar state of being for the gift of God—Eternal life through Jesus Christ our Lord.

"For the wages of sin is death; but the gift of God is eternal life through Jesus Christ our Lord." (Romans 6:23) This gift is free—not cheap—but free to all who will receive Jesus Christ. *"Now then we are ambassadors for Christ, as though God did beseech you by us: we pray you in Christ's stead, be ye reconciled to God. For He hath made Him* (Jesus Christ) *to be sin for us,* (He) *Who knew no sin; that we might be made the righteousness of God in Him." (2 Corinthians 5:20-21)*

The Gift

Fortunes are spent to find beauty,
Seeking the fountain of youth,
But one honest look in the mirror
Will surely reveal the truth!

The tent of this flesh that I live in
Is perishing every day—
Perhaps I could prolong the process,
But it's clear that I **will** pass away!

What is the cost of eternal life?
Money? Materials? Fame?
How far would you go to obtain it?
Possessions and deeds would be vain!

Eternal life is **so** costly,

The price we never could pay,

But God loved us all so deeply

That He sent His Son, Jesus—the Way!

His Word says that we are all sinners,

Eternal death and hell our end.

But Jesus paid with His own blood

To take away our sin.

Eternal life cannot be bought,

Cannot be won or earned.

The gift of life is only found

In Jesus Christ, God's Son.

The only begotten Son of God—

On Him you must believe.

The Gift, Eternal Life, is yours

When Jesus you receive.

The Bible tells us (speaking of Jesus): *"He was in the world, and the world was made by Him, and the world knew Him not. He came unto his own, and his own received Him not. But as many as received Him, to them gave He power to become the sons of God, even to them that believe on His Name."* *(John 1:10-12)*

A true gift can only be received! Receive! That's the key! If you pay or work, or in any way try to earn or achieve it, then it is not a gift. Unlike the butterfly, which becomes a new creature, not by choice but rather automatically as it goes through the stages of its life, you and I **have choice.** Even though Jesus paid for every sin of every person who has ever been born into this world, from the beginning of time to the end of the age, and God is not willing that any should perish, it is still our choice—have you received God's gift? If not, will you?

For the multitude of times the wonderful good news of the Lord Jesus Christ has been shared, both in this ministry, and personally, there have been, basically, three kinds of responses: An enthusiastic "yes"; an emphatic "no"; and a pathetic "not now" (which is also "no").

Now that you know **how** to become that new creation, would you be willing to **A C T** on that knowledge? Wherever you are, if you can sense God calling to you, reach out to Him in prayer. It's your move...

Chapter 4
Butterfly Life—
Isn't There Some Other Way?

A caterpillar can become a butterfly in just **one** way—by specifically following its God-designed process of transformation. There are, of course, damaging and destructive forces that can prevent completion of that process and keep the caterpillar from ever becoming a butterfly. Even well-meaning outside forces can have devastating effects, like in the story that follows.

Whether this is a true account, I cannot say, but I heard about a man who found a cocoon, and out of curiosity, set the cocoon in a safe place, and watched it carefully day by day. One day he noticed slight movement, and realized it must be time for the butterfly to emerge. A small opening appeared at one end of the cocoon, and the man watched for several hours as the butterfly struggled to force itself through that small hole.

Then the movement stopped, and from all outward signs, it appeared that without help, the small creature would never make it out of the cocoon. Out of compassion, the man took a sharp blade and very carefully slit the cocoon down the side.

> *A person can become a new creation by one and only one process—God's forgiveness and redemption through Jesus Christ His Son*

Sure enough, the little creature emerged easily—but, the poor little thing had a swollen body and shriveled wings, and in just a short time the misshapen little butterfly died. The man had wanted only to help, but his best intentions only resulted in crippling the little creature and hastening its death.

God has a specific process that will transform a little caterpillar critter into a beautiful free-flying butterfly, but it can only happen one way—God's way. In our "Butterfly Life" conferences and retreats, this principle is demonstrated through our paper butterflies. A magazine picture can only become a paper butterfly if the directions are explicitly followed—otherwise the result could be a mosquito-looking thing!

Someone has wisely said, "If you lose the process, then you lose the product." A person can become a new creation by one and only one process—God's forgiveness and redemption through Jesus Christ His Son.

Forgiven Forever

Do you know what it means to be forgiven?
Do you know what it means to taste God's grace?
Have you ever felt His touch of love and mercy?
Have you ever known the joy of His embrace?

If your answer is "no" to all those questions,

But in your heart you're longing to say, "yes"!

Come to Jesus and receive Him as your Savior.

He will set you free and give you rest!

You will know what it means to be forgiven!

You will know what it means to taste His grace!

You will know His tender touch of love and mercy!

Every sin and stain He will erase!

You can sing: I'm in Him a new creation!

Forgiven! Oh, what great amazing grace!

Forgiven! All my sins are gone forever!

Forgiven—and **forever** in His marvelous embrace!

Over the years, there have been many occasions to minister in countries far from our home in Texas. Some of those times have been in countries where English was not the primary language. While English is my most fluent language, God has also given me the ability to do fairly well with Portuguese. During the time my husband was in the United States Air Force, three of those years were spent in Brazil, where Portuguese is the national language. Twice since leaving the military, God has given opportunity for ministry in Brazil, and what a blessing it has been to be able to communicate in the language of the people there. In case you're wondering, this **is** all leading somewhere, specifically to the spring of 1999.

I was participating with Sammy Tippit Ministries in an evangelistic effort in the city of Rio de Janeiro, and was assigned to Primeira Igreja Batista na Penha to sing for evangelistic services each night of the week. Every day our team went out to share the good news of Jesus Christ with Brazilians in their homes. Most of their houses were very humble dwellings, often with dirt floors and just very basic furnishings. What a joy it was to share the gospel and see many precious ones come to know Jesus Christ. I especially remember one particular 101-year-old woman. Although she could not get out of bed, her mind was clear and sharp—and when she heard about Jesus, she believed and received Him. By now she has probably left that earthly bed for her new home in Heaven—I think she must have been just existing—just waiting for someone to come to her and tell her about Jesus.

Each evening before the crusade service began, our team met in the church office to pray with the pastor. During the Thursday evening pre-service meeting, the pastor surprised me with a change in plans. He told me that I would not be singing the following night because he wanted me to go and see a particular family that had requested a visit; however, the only time they had available was at the very same time as our evangelistic service. It was decided that on Friday evening, immediately after the pre-service meeting, our small team would go directly to visit the family. I was fine with that.

The next morning, I prepared for the day, knowing that once we left our hotel that morning, there would be no time to return until late that night, after the evening crusade service. I dressed more casually than I would have if I were singing that evening—I chose black slacks and a dark green knit, golf-type shirt—the kind with a collar and two-button neck opening.

Our day was going well until we stopped for lunch at a little café. The meal was delightful. I noticed that the café signs advertised the very same brand of ice cream we used to enjoy when we lived in Brazil many years ago. Remembering how delicious that ice cream was in the past was more than I could stand—I ordered a big vanilla bar completely covered with a thick layer of chocolate! And, it was every bit as good as I expected—in fact, I enjoyed it **so** much, that without even realizing it, I dripped chocolate all down the front of my shirt! When I noticed what had happened, I tried to use dampened paper napkins to get the chocolate off, but the paper only balled up in little bits and did nothing to eradicate the stains.

Well, I thought to myself, at least I'm not singing before all those people tonight, and maybe when we get to the church I can get the stains out. However, when we got to the pre-service meeting, the pastor gave me plan "B." He wanted me to sing at the **beginning** of the service and then, right after that I should leave for the scheduled family visit. "Oh boy!" I thought, "What am I going to do about the stains?" Silently, I began to pray—surely God would give me a way to get the shirt clean.

I hurried to the ladies restroom, and did my best to wash out the chocolate stain (while still wearing the shirt). I used lots of cold water and soap, and by the time I was finished, my whole shirt front was wet. It hadn't occurred to me that it might not dry before our services were to begin. Just then, one of the church members saw my plight, and graciously offered to take my shirt and iron it. She explained that they had an iron in the basement, and I could wear her jacket while she ironed my shirt. That would work! However, when the lady returned with my shirt, although it was definitely dry, it was also obvious that the stains were still there—she had only ironed them in. Of course, that wasn't her fault, because that particular fabric, when wet, is so dark that it would have been next to impossible to tell if the stains were there or not.

What to do? Well, what if I turn my shirt around and wear it backwards? I tried that, and it looked really odd. The front wasn't too bad—it had a kind of high turtle-neck effect, but the back was, well, just weird-looking. I asked the opinion of a friend—she just shook her head.

I kept on praying, and the thought occurred to me that the evangelist usually carried an extra shirt in his briefcase—if he had brought an extra shirt that evening, perhaps he would loan it to me. I knew his shirt would be too big for me, but "clean" would be better than "too big." As soon as the evangelist arrived, I asked him about the spare shirt, and he responded, "Yes, I did bring an extra, but I've been sweating all day, and I'm wearing the clean one!"

"Now what?" I thought, still praying. It appeared that there was only one option—to wear my own stained shirt backwards. But, how would I get from the back of the church to the front, and up to the platform? There was a long aisle that I would have to walk down, and people would notice that my shirt was on backwards, and would probably question my sanity. Then another thought occurred to me—I could walk through the basement (which ran the entire length of the auditorium), go up the stairs at the back, then enter through a door that led right onto the platform. I would be facing the congregation— they wouldn't see my back, so maybe it would escape their notice that things weren't quite right. I still had a problem though; I had not yet figured out how to leave when I finished singing. Obviously, to reverse my entry and walk backwards off the platform would look peculiar. Well, at least I knew how to get started—surely God would give me a graceful exit.

As I proceeded through the basement area toward the back stairs, about halfway there a man stopped me and tapped me on the shoulder. He asked me if I knew my shirt was on backwards. I smiled and said yes, thanked him, and continued on my way. "If that man noticed the 'backward' shirt," I thought, "everyone would have noticed if I had gone down the aisle upstairs, and I would be the laughingstock of the whole church!" In all honesty, though that would be embarrassing, my big concern was that people would be so distracted by the stain or the backward shirt that they would miss the message of the music.

I wondered what possible good could come of this whole experience—after all, God's Word says, *"And we know that all things work together for good to them that love God, to them who are the called according to His purpose." (Romans 8:28)* So far, I had not found anything good about this situation.

As I climbed the stairs and entered the platform area and sat down in the chair reserved for me, I continued to puzzle over that question—"what possible good?" At the very moment I stood to sing, God spoke to my heart. Though there was no audible sound, I could not mistake His voice. By the way, God does speak to His children: *"My sheep hear my voice, and I know them, and they follow me." (John 10:27)* He simply

We can scrub with all our might, but no matter how hard we try we can never wash away our own sins!

instructed me to just tell the people the truth about my chocolate-stained shirt—tell them that's exactly the way it is with sin. So, after I sang the first song, I related the whole lunch experience—

how I had really enjoyed the chocolate-covered ice cream bar, and the way the chocolate had dripped ever-so-silently, leaving dark stains on my shirt. I explained that, like that shirt, we are all deeply stained with sin *("all have sinned,"* Romans 3:23). I related how desperately I had tried to wash the chocolate stains out of my shirt, but the shirt would not come clean. We can scrub with all our might, but no matter how hard we try we can never wash away our own sins!

I went on to say that I tried wearing my shirt backwards, and even turned around to show the people. The stains were still there. We can try to turn our lives around, and we may even look good from certain angles, but no matter what human effort or clever plan we come up with, the sin stains remain! Oh, they may not be visible from the front, but they are far from gone!

Then I related my idea of borrowing a shirt from the evangelist—great idea, but this didn't work either. We cannot borrow someone else's cleansing.

Nothing could help my shirt except a thorough cleansing—one that would take the stain **completely away.** No matter what method we try, we can**not** get the awful sin stain out of our lives. **What can wash away my sin? Nothing but the blood of Jesus!** That's the way it is with every individual—we can never be cleansed from our sins until we ask Jesus Christ to forgive us and come into our lives and make us clean. Sin has left a crimson stain, but He **can** and **will** wash away our sins—He **can** and **will** make us as white as snow:

"Come now, and let us reason together, saith the Lord; though your sins be as scarlet, they shall be as white as snow; though they be red like crimson, they shall be as wool." (Isaiah 1:18)

I closed my testimony that night by singing, *Jesus Paid It*

All. Then I bravely walked the length of the aisle to the back of the church to go with my friends to make the scheduled home visit. (God had, indeed, given me a graceful exit.) When sharing my testimony in the home we visited, and explaining to those dear people about their need to receive Jesus Christ, once again God led me to tell about the "stained shirt." Two people in that home accepted Christ as their Savior and Lord. Did God bring good out of the "chocolate-stain" disaster? No question about it!

Just a few years prior to this Brazilian crusade, Don and I were in Puerto Rico for ministry. We had been there only a few days when a call came from the company my husband worked for. There had been a change in their sales conference schedule, and it would be necessary for Don to leave immediately for Florida. But, ministry was not finished there in Puerto Rico!

It seemed quite unfair that his company would change their meeting at the last minute, especially since we had checked with them before confirming the Puerto Rico ministry, in order to be **certain** there would be no conflict. There was nothing to do but make adjustments to accommodate the company schedule. I was to stay in Puerto Rico and complete the ministry there, and Don would leave immediately for the Florida conference.

When I left Puerto Rico, though still a little puzzled about why Don had to leave early and feeling a little lonely that he couldn't be with me for our return home, I still felt encouraged that the time in Puerto Rico had been wonderful. God had ministered in many special ways, and accomplished much good through the ministry.

God is never surprised, and He had no problem with those "unexpected" changes. They were only unexpected to us, and were all part of His plan to begin with, a part which He began to unveil as he introduced Mary Lou into my life. Apparently she was really supposed to occupy the seat that we thought should have been Don's.

Once we were airborne, Mary Lou asked what I was doing in Puerto Rico, so I explained about this ministry—that through music I share with people how to know Jesus Christ. When I asked Mary Lou if she knew Jesus as her Savior, she told me she didn't need Jesus, that she didn't need anything because she already had everything she needed and wanted. What she could not see was that there was **one** thing she lacked, **one** thing she desperately needed—a personal relationship with God through Jesus Christ His Son…but she wasn't interested.

We kept in touch by mail once in a while over a period of time. For about five years I prayed for an opportunity of ministry somewhere close to Mary Lou, hoping that if I was ever near her area she would come to a concert and maybe this time she would hear and respond to Jesus.

God did open a door of ministry only a few miles from her home, and Mary Lou even invited us to stay in her home. She came to the church and politely listened to me as I shared in music, Scripture and testimony, but as far as we know, her heart was unchanged. My heart still longs to know that Mary Lou has received Jesus Christ as her Savior, but there has been no news that she has said "yes" to Him. These are the words of my last personal plea to her:

"Dear Mary Lou,

I have hesitated sending this poem though I've had it in my daytimer for quite awhile—guess I just kept waiting for a better time. This is it—can't wait any longer—life on this earth is too short. So, because I love you, I'm sending this. It may make you mad—that's OK—God has really put you on my heart.

So, even though I may never hear from you again, here is the poem God gave me for you. Please read it, and know that I love you—it was no accident that you got my husband's seat on that plane.   God has been calling to you for a long time—if you haven't said "yes" to Him yet, please don't wait any longer.

You are in my heart, in my prayers…"   Love, Betty

Mary Lou

The Bible says that all have sinned,
None righteous—no, not one;
But God so loved the world (that's us),
He sent His only Son.

Oh, Mary Lou, He came for you,
Your debt of sin He paid—
For you Jesus endured the cross,
On Him your guilt was laid.

You've had all this world could offer
Which never truly satisfies,
There's an emptiness within your heart,
And yet, you have your pride.

But your righteousness will never do—
As filthy rags it is.
The righteousness that God approves
Is Jesus'—only His!

He took your punishment and mine,
He didn't have to die—
He could have called ten thousand angels,
But He chose to pay the price.

He rose in victory from the grave,
He reigns in power above.
There's an open door to Heaven now
Because of Jesus' love.

When your human heart stops beating,
It will then be much too late,
For what you do with Christ on earth
Forever seals your fate!

If He never was your Savior,
He now your judge will be.
And He'll say, "I never knew you—
Go—depart from me!"

You will suffer in the pit of Hell,
Eternal torment, pain and fear,
With the words, "I never knew you"
Forever ringing in your ears.

Oh, Mary Lou, He's calling you—
His arms are open wide,

Jesus offers you salvation—
And you must now decide.

He may never call your name again—
Please answer while you may.
Ask Jesus to forgive you,
And accept Him now—today!
Receive God's greatest gift—His Son—
Please, Mary Lou, today.

There was a popular song some years ago called, *I Did it My Way.* That only works in the imagination. Whether Mary Lou stayed with "her way" I do not know, but my prayer is that before it is eternally too late she will come to Jesus— God's Way.

There is only one way: *Jesus said, "I am the way, the truth, and the life; no man cometh unto the Father but by me." (John 14:6)*

There is no other way! *"Neither is there salvation in any other; for there is none other name under heaven given among men, whereby we must be saved." (Acts 4:12)*

Tomorrow there may be no way: Ready or not, eternity is only a heartbeat away. *"…To day if ye will hear His voice, harden not your hearts." (Hebrews 4:7)*

Chapter 5
Butterfly Life—Flight Design

The butterfly is fashioned for flight! This is a major part of its ultimate design. If the butterfly should stay a caterpillar, flying would forever remain impossible. Because the caterpillar simply obeys what God designed it for, it is changed into a butterfly—and with that transformation, God furnishes that new creature with wonderful wings.

When a human being follows God's design, HE transforms that person into a new creature, and in a real sense, provides "wings" (in the Person of His Holy Spirit), evidenced by the fruit of the Spirit, which He alone can produce in us. *"But the fruit of the Spirit is love, joy, peace, long-suffering, gentleness, goodness, faith, meekness, temperance…" (Galatians 5:22-23)* The life of the butterfly seems to exhibit some of these qualities— love, joy, beauty, freedom and peace.

What does the butterfly do to get these things? Nothing! These qualities are inherent in the butterfly design! Throughout history, mankind has spent all kinds of time, money and effort to procure these very things. For some, this has been a lifelong pursuit, only to find at the end of earthly existence that whatever success they thought they had was only temporary, with no real value after all. Apart from God's design, there is **no real** love, joy, beauty, freedom, or peace, but only **imitations** of the "real thing." At the end (beyond the grave) for all who have refused to follow God's plan, there lies an eternity of hatred, anguish, ugliness, bondage, terror and torment. But each and every person who, during his or her earthly existence, has followed God's plan (become a new creature in Christ by accepting Jesus Christ as Savior) will, at the end of this earthly life, step into an eternity of incredible beauty, love, joy, freedom, peace, and more—all the things we've always wanted.

Love, joy, beauty, freedom, and peace—all these are **already** ours in Christ! The big problem is that we sometimes don't know how to access what we already have! It is sort of like the telephone system we purchased for our home, which has lots of good features, including speakerphone and intercom capability. I am embarrassed to say we had the system two years before we actually used the intercom feature—one day I accidentally stumbled onto it, and it worked! What a surprise! I had not taken the time to read the owner's manual thoroughly to begin with, so I did not even know all the features that came with the phone, much less how to use them.

A few months after learning about the intercom on our phone system, we discovered another feature. One day I accidentally hit the "SP-Phone" button on one of the handsets, and, there was another surprise! I discovered the speakerphone feature worked on the handset! What a wonderful convenience, especially when subjected to the endless automated menus often encountered this day and age! We thought the speakerphone feature was only available from the base set—we didn't know it could be used with any portable handset in the house! All we had to do was push the "SP-Phone" button! It was there all the time!

The phones would have been adequate even if we had never found out about the intercom and speakerphone—obviously the system is much more than just adequate with these special assets. Because we did not know what we had, access to these great features was delayed two years! If we had just read the instructions thoroughly to start with, we could have enjoyed these wonderful blessings right from the beginning!

Perhaps that is why we do not always enjoy the peace, beauty, joy, freedom, and all the other things that became ours the moment we were transformed by Christ. We don't know what we have! The moment we are born into God's family, we become new creatures in Christ, transformed by God, the Holy Spirit. With that transformation, the Holy Spirit comes to dwell within every believer. And He, the Holy Spirit, not only resides within us, but it is He who produces the fruits of the Spirit. It is He who empowers us to live according to God's design. Why do we not know what we have and who we are in Christ?

You may have heard the story of a missionary and his wife who were returning to America from a long stay overseas. They had scrimped and saved a long time so they could purchase fare on a cruise ship to return home. Once aboard the ship, they settled in nicely, having prepared as best they could. It had taken all the money they had for tickets, so they had brought along their own food, consisting of peanut butter, jelly, bread, crackers, canned tuna fish and the like. The couple often walked past the beautiful dining room, and every time they looked in, the people seemed to be having such a wonderful time, and the tantalizing aroma of wonderfully fine food seemed to invite, yet forbid this good man and woman. How they would have enjoyed such fare; however, they consoled themselves by reminding each other that at least they had the privilege of being on the ship.

At the end of the cruise, as the couple waited for their turn to leave the ship, another passenger turned to them and remarked, "Wasn't the food wonderful? Don't you think it was some of the most delicious you've ever tasted?" Though a little embarrassed, the couple had to answer truthfully, "Well, quite frankly, we didn't have the money to go to the dining room—we brought our own food." "Oh, but, didn't you know?" questioned the lady, "The meals were included in the price of the tickets!" Every provision for the finest of food had already been made for these dear ones—it was theirs for the taking, but they didn't get a single taste! They never got to enjoy what was already theirs because they didn't know about all the benefits that automatically came with their tickets!

All who are born again, transformed by the power of God, are from the moment of that transformation endowed with His design, automatically loaded with benefits and blessings!

There is no lack (no want) in any area:

*"The Lord is my Shepherd; **I shall not want**." (Psalm 23:1)*

*"O taste and see that the Lord is good; blessed is the man that trusteth in Him. O fear the Lord, ye His saints; for there is **no want** to them that fear Him." (Psalm 34:8-9)*

*"Blessed be the God and Father of our Lord Jesus Christ, who **hath** blessed us with **all** spiritual blessings in heavenly places in Christ." (Ephesians 1:3)*

We who have been born again **already have all** spiritual blessings, including those things we see and envy in the butterfly—beauty, joy, freedom, and peace. The problem is how to gain access to what we already have.

One of the most sought after blessings is peace! If peace is a part of the "package," how can we gain access to it? To begin with, we must remember that there are two kinds of peace—the peace **of** God, and peace **with** God. The peace **of** God is impossible unless we first have peace **with** God. Until a person is "saved" (has been born again by receiving Jesus Christ as Savior), he is an enemy of God, and no enemy of God has peace

If peace is a part of the "package," how can we gain access to it?

with Him. The very moment a person is saved—forgiven and born into the family of God, that person is placed into Christ by God, and from that moment forward, and forever, has peace **with** God.

The peace **of** God is literally **"Himself!"** *"For **He is** our peace..."* (Philippians 2:14) *"Christ in you, the hope of glory."* *(Colossians 1:27)* This is why we can go through anything and still be at peace as we experience what is already ours—the peace **of** God—perfect peace! Perfect, in Webster's Dictionary, is defined as "Having no defect or fault; flawless, accurate, absolute." That is the kind of peace God gives when we "stay" (maintain the position of) our minds on Him. *"Thou wilt keep him in perfect peace, whose mind is stayed on Thee: because he trusteth in Thee. Trust ye in the Lord for ever: for in the Lord Jehovah is everlasting strength."* (Isaiah 26:3-4)

That is the kind of peace God gave Horatio Spafford, a prominent lawyer in Chicago. He and his family were good friends with D. L. Moody and Ira Sankey. It is said that Ira Sankey's music had a great influence in leading the Spafford children to Christ. Horatio and his wife, Anna, had one son and four daughters. Not long before the great Chicago fire in 1871, the Spaffords' son died, and the family felt utterly devastated. But another blow came when the ravaging Chicago fire destroyed a great deal of real estate in the downtown area, where Mr. Spafford had heavy investments. This brought about his financial ruin. Even though they had suffered much, however, the Spaffords felt great compassion for the homeless and desperately needy people of the city, and so began focusing their efforts to help them.

After two years of their ministry of mercy to the people of Chicago, Mr. Spafford felt the need of a vacation for his family. When he learned that D. L. Moody and Ira Sankey were holding meetings in England, and that thousands were coming to Christ, Mr. Spafford decided that he and his family should go to England for their vacation, and at the same time help his friends in the evangelistic campaign there.

Reservations were made for the Spafford family to sail to England on the *S.S. Ville de Havre*; however, last minute business prevented Mr. Spafford from traveling with his wife and daughters, so arrangements were made for him to follow a few weeks later. Tragically, enroute to England the *S.S. Ville de Havre* collided with another ship, the English *Lochearn*. In only 12 minutes, the *S.S. Ville de Havre* sank, and the 226 lives that were lost included the four Spafford daughters. Ten days after Mrs. Spafford's rescue from a floating piece of debris, she finally arrived in Wales, and cabled just two words to her husband— "Saved alone."

Mr. Spafford boarded the next ship to England. He stood at the railing as the ship crossed the area where his precious daughters died, and it was there that God gave him great peace.

Mr. Spafford left the railing and went to his cabin where he penned the words to one of history's greatest, most comforting hymns of all time:

It Is Well with My Soul

When peace, like a river, attendeth my way,
When sorrows like sea billows roll;
Whatever my lot, Thou has taught me to say,
It is well, it is well, with my soul.

Chorus
It is well with my soul,
It is well, it is well, with my soul!

Though Satan should buffet, though trials should come,
Let this blest assurance control,
That Christ has regarded my helpless estate,
And hath shed His own blood for my soul.

Chorus
My sin, oh, the bliss of this glorious thought!
My sin, not in part, but the whole
Is nailed to the cross, and I bear it no more,
Praise the Lord, praise the Lord, O my soul!

Chorus

For me, be it Christ, be it Christ hence to live:

If Jordan above me shall roll,

No pang shall be mine, for in death as in life

Thou wilt whisper Thy peace to my soul.

Chorus

But, Lord, 'tis for Thee, for Thy coming we wait,

The sky, not the grave, is our goal;

Oh the trump of the angel! Oh the voice of the Lord!

Blessed hope, blessed rest of my soul!

Chorus

And, Lord, haste the day when my faith shall be sight,

The clouds be rolled back as a scroll;

The trump shall resound, and the Lord shall descend,

"Even so," it is well with my soul.

It is well with my soul,

It is well, it is well, with my soul!

Mr. Spafford surely must have known the scriptural account of the Shunammite woman (2 Kings 4:8-37), for he knew the very same kind of peace she had. Peace is defined as: "completeness, soundness, a state of wholeness, welfare, harmony, peace, ease, quietness, calmness, and rest." In fact, another word for "It is well" in Hebrew is *shalom*, which also means "peace."

Perhaps the woman from Shunem was really the first to write the song, *It Is Well*. If anyone ever had a right to be filled with anger and despair, it would be this woman! She and her husband were good people who revered and worshipped God. The Shunammite woman was so filled with the love of God that she wanted to make a room in their own home where Elisha, the prophet of God, could come aside from his travels and rest comfortably. The Shunammite and her husband, with no other motive than to help the prophet of God, provided that special room. And, oh, how God rewarded them! Until that time the woman had been childless, and the scriptures tell us *"her husband was old"*—the prospect of children for this couple was absolutely nil! But God did the impossible—and He gave them a son!

If we stopped right there, we might expect the rest of her story would be "and they lived happily ever after," and for a while it did seem to be that way. But, suddenly, *"When the child was grown, it fell on a day, that he went out to his father to the reapers. And he said unto his father, my head, my head: And he said to a lad, Carry him to his mother. And when he had taken him, and brought him to his mother, he sat on her knees till noon, and then died."* (2 Kings 4:18-20)

What would you or I do? Would we shake our fist at God and cry out at the injustice, the unfairness of it all? The Shunammite woman did not react in anger or fear—she responded in faith: *"And she went up, and laid him on the bed of the man of God, and shut the door upon him, and went out. And she called unto her husband and said, Send me, I pray thee, one of the young men, and one of the asses, that I may run to the man of God, and come again. And he said, Wherefore wilt thou go to him today? It is neither new moon, or Sabbath. And she said, **It shall be well.**"* (2 Kings 4:21-23) She had no positive word that it would be well, and she did not know what God was going to do—but she **did** know and trust **Him** above all else. That is the peace **of** God!

This kind of peace is not necessarily a state of inactivity. The Shunammite woman did what she knew to do: she went to find the prophet Elisha. As he saw her riding toward him in the distance, he instructed his servant to go out to meet her and ask, *"Is it well with thee? Is it well with thy husband? Is it well with the child? And she answered, It is well."* (2 Kings 4:26) From the looks of things, it was not well, and she had not read the end of the chapter for it was yet unwritten, but she trusted God and refused to allow her circumstances to dictate her perspective or her peace.

From what we have already seen of this woman, I believe she was absolutely certain that the God who had already done the impossible in giving her a son could and would do the impossible again, and bring him back to life. Though not yet seeing the outcome, by faith she could say, **"It is well!" Peace!** The rest of the story? God **did** restore life to the son of the Shunammite.

Incidentally, the Bible calls the woman from Shunem a "great" woman, but never once gives us her name! Why not? Perhaps it is to demonstrate that **anyone** who knows and loves God and trusts Him completely can experience His mighty power and perfect peace in the midst of life's most devastating circumstances.

Oh, and just in case you are interested in the "rest of the story" of the Spafford family—ten years later, they (Horatio, Anna, and two daughters born after the shipwreck disaster) moved to Jerusalem, Israel, and started a group called "The American Colony," organized to serve the poor.

The *It Is Well...* song may be a dramatic testimony in your own life. I know it has been in mine—several times! Probably the first time was when I went to Poland in ministry with the Tom Popelka evangelistic team. Since I don't speak or sing in the Polish language, the idea was that prior to singing, I would give testimony and explain the songs, which an interpreter would translate. Then I would sing the songs in English. Some of the songs I chose were older, more well-known tunes, so that the people listening might already be somewhat familiar with them and could understand even though not hearing them in their own language. For this reason, one of the songs I selected was, *It Is Well with My Soul.* Though I had heard that song all of my life, this would be my first time ever to use it as a solo.

It is well! That was my testimony to the people who came to the crusade service in Bialystok, Poland, on the night of September 29, 1987. I boldly stated, "No matter what happens in my life, even if I never make it back to America, it is well! It is well because Jesus makes it so! It doesn't depend upon my circumstances. Jesus is in my heart, and HE makes it well—it is well with my soul." This testimony was translated into the Polish language, and then I sang, *It Is Well with My Soul.*

Shortly after the service that evening, I proceeded down some steps to another part of the church building. I thought I was all the way down the steps, but the area was dimly lit, and unfortunately there was one more step that I did not see! I came crashing down, mostly on my left foot. Instantly, there was intense pain and swelling, I knew something was desperately wrong with that foot.

Friends carried me to my room and helped me onto my bed. After they left, questions began to flood my mind, "Why? Why now? Why this? Is my foot broken? If it is, will I need surgery? Will I be able to stay? If so, how will I get around?" "God," I said, "I don't understand..." My time with Him that morning had been wonderful—I really had yielded everything to Him, and had felt such perfect assurance as I asked Him to order my steps and direct my paths...and now, this!

As I lay there, so far from home, feeling alone, starting to cry, and wondering why—I heard this silent question, "Is it still well?" My own testimony of that evening returned to mind, "No matter what happens in my life..." Did I really believe that? "Yes," I began to smile as I said it right out loud, "Yes! It **is** well! Lord, I worship and praise You! I still don't understand, but I do thank you, and believe You to work all this for my good and for your glory." And God gave me peace, and rest.

> *"Is it still well?" My own testimony of that evening returned to mind, "No matter what happens in my life..." Did I really believe that?*

The next day, X-rays confirmed a broken bone in my left foot. The doctors were very kind, and said I could probably safely stay there in Poland for the rest of the crusade. But still, there were doubts—I needed a second opinion, a confirmation—I prayed for a word from God. Miraculously, by phone, we reached Dr. Pat Wilson, an orthopedic surgeon and good friend back home in San Antonio. He not only gave further instructions and warning signs to watch for, but also the assurance that, though it would probably be uncomfortable and inconvenient, if I wanted to stay for the remaining eight days of ministry, it should be OK. That was a direct word from God—His confirmation that I had asked for.

He didn't say it would be easy, and in fact, it was not only hard for me, but also for my friends on the evangelistic team. They got a literal taste of "bearing one another's burdens" because they often carried me where crutches could not go.

That evening, with a strap-on plastic cast from just below my knee all the way to the tip of my toes, and with the help of borrowed crutches, I once again stood before the people in the same church as the night before. "Last night, I said that no matter what happens in my life, it is well." Then I told them what had happened in my life right after the service of the night before, and reaffirmed, "Tonight, I stand here to tell you, it **is** well! It doesn't depend on my circumstances—it is well because Jesus is in my heart, and HE makes it well." Once again I sang, *It Is Well with My Soul.* Though still uncertain why God allowed the accident, I did have His certain peace. Could it be that God wanted a visible as well as spoken testimony? After sharing further testimony of our wonderful Lord Jesus, I sang, *Rise Again* (in the Polish language—the ability to do that is another whole story). That night there were eight precious souls saved—born again—into the family of God.

The story of the Shunammite woman has become an integral part of the "Butterfly Life in a Caterpillar World" ministry, and there have been many more "it is well" experiences to go with it. In fact, it seems that every time I give the "it is well" testimony, almost invariably something else happens—something which I am sure the adversary hopes will damage that testimony, but instead it just demonstrates Romans 8:28. God always works **all things** (good and bad) *"together for good to them that love God, to them who are the called according to His purpose." (Romans 8:28)* Through it all, He continues to prove His peace and strengthen our faith.

In a 1995, while in Japan for a "Butterfly Life" retreat, I was just getting ready to give my "it is well" testimony, when a long-distance phone call came for me. Our daughter, Cathy, was calling from home in San Antonio, Texas—our house was flooded! Cathy was in charge of the house while we were away, but she was a schoolteacher, so was away from the house a good part of the day. In order to keep our new German Shepherd puppy from chewing up everything while Cathy was at school, she usually enclosed the puppy in the main bathroom, along with food and water and a few toys until she could get back home. That day, however, even though the puppy had plenty of food and water, apparently she did not have enough entertainment, because when Cathy got home, she found a good portion of the house flooded, and a really scared and completely drenched puppy.

Some time during her confinement in the bathroom, the puppy had chewed a hole in the water line that goes to the toilet, and water was still spraying wildly when Cathy arrived. (Incidentally, from that day forward, that dog never wanted to play in the rain or mud.)

Of course, there was nothing we could do from Japan, but Cathy wanted us to know what had happened and to tell us she had a tentative plan in place, but needed either our approval to go ahead or an alternative solution.

My mind was "flooded" with the problems that could come with the "flood" at home, but it was time to share the "it is well" testimony. I could almost hear those same words again, "Is it still well?" As I prayed, the Lord reminded me not only of His faithfulness in the past, but that He was still in control right then. It was OK—He **would** work everything out and bring good out of this experience, too. Besides, now, just minutes after the emergency phone call, I had another opportunity to "faith it" publicly, and God used that fresh "flood" experience as well as the "broken foot" testimony to declare His great faithfulness.

Did God work it all out for good? Indeed, He did! At first, things looked pretty disastrous—the practically new, less than a year-old carpet in our house was completely ruined! It would have to be replaced, and yes, there would be a lot of inconvenience. But, God provided brand new carpet, of better quality than the one that was ruined by the flood. We even got to choose a better color—I never did like the color of the ruined carpet anyway! And that is just a sample of "good" things God does when He works all things together for good.

The story of that puppy didn't end with the flood. By the following year she had grown considerably, and was now a fairly big dog, and no longer chewed things up. However, she was still young and not yet completely disciplined. She had the freedom of going in and out of the house through her "doggie door" except when we did not want her outside for some reason—then we would close her special door. That, however, didn't stop her from **wanting** to go out.

One morning as I was preparing to water the back yard, since I didn't want the dog to interfere, I closed her special door. With the sprinkler in my left hand, I reasoned that if I sort of entwined her collar with my right hand, I could slowly back out of the patio door, while holding the dog back, and she would not get away from me and run outside. Only it didn't work that way—as soon as I opened the patio door, the dog shot through the door, taking me with her and landing me on the cement patio with a big thud! There I lay, with my hand still entwined in the dog's collar. She just stood there, looking down at me as if to say, "What in the world are you doing down there?"

This was another of those times that I just couldn't understand. My time alone with God in prayer and Bible reading that morning had been wonderful—I had truly turned everything over to God, and had specifically asked Him to order my steps and direct my paths. As I lay there on the patio praying, I couldn't understand why God would allow such "falling down" times. What possible good could come out of this?

I disengaged my hand from the dog's collar, and thought about my situation. At least I was **able** to think. I knew I was not dead or unconscious—that was a good thing. I knew that I was really injured—that was a bad thing! I couldn't move on my right side, but I had to do something, because no one would find me there for a long time. My husband was out of town, and our daughter, Cathy, wouldn't be home until after school that afternoon. There was just one thing to do—somehow I had to shift to my left side and get from the patio through the kitchen to the living room phone and call for help.

I asked God to help me get to the phone, and then, ever so slowly, shifted to my left side. Little by little I dragged myself through the patio door, across the kitchen floor, and into the living room, reached the phone, and pulled it down to my level, and called our daughter's school. She had not yet arrived, so I left a message—one I really hated to leave, but there was no other way to say it: "Please ask her to call home immediately— I have fallen, and can't get up!" In just a few minutes Cathy called, and I briefly related what had happened and asked her to come home as quickly as possible.

When she arrived, I was sitting on the floor, sort of halfway propped up against the couch. She asked if she should call

911. I told her not yet, but to call Dr. Wilson, (the one mentioned earlier in this chapter). Cathy called in the nick of time—it was Dr. Wilson's day off and he was just getting ready to go play golf. He very kindly postponed his game, and said we should meet him at the hospital as soon as possible.

For the second time, Cathy asked, "Now shall I call 911?" I'm a little embarrassed to tell this part because it sounds so vain, but I said, "Not yet—first bring me my make-up kit." She protested, but I insisted, "Cathy, I know how these things go—I will be **really** ugly for a long time, so I want to at least start out looking decent." I mentioned shaving my legs too, but Cathy really balked at that, and I acquiesced. She asked again (her exasperation was beginning to show)—"**Now**, can I call 911?" "Well," I answered, knowing that would be expensive, "all you really need to do is figure out a way to get me to the van, and you can drive me to the hospital." She did come up with a solution which sounded reasonable. We had two steno chairs that would roll. If we could get me into one chair by the couch, she could roll me to the front door, and then help me to the other chair that she could already have in place outside the door, and just roll me to the van. It sounded like a good plan, and it worked. Soon we were on our way to the hospital emergency room.

The doctor met us, and after examination and X-rays, told me that my hip was broken and would require surgery. He also said that if he were doing the surgery, he would not use pins or screws, but that he would do a partial hip replacement, because otherwise, the bone above the break would not get any blood, and in about a year, another surgery would be necessary.

My major concern was that with the insurance we had, we would have to pay 20% of all costs. The doctor's estimate for surgery was a minimum of $25,000. I knew we would have trouble coming up with even 20% of that. The alternative was to go the military hospital nearby, where the cost would be much less. But, would I have the same level of care? I asked God for wisdom, and then told the doctor of my concern. His reply brought great relief—what a blessing he was with his honesty and integrity! He was quite willing to do the surgery, but he assured me that the military facility had excellent surgeons and modern equipment, and he would not hesitate to send me there. He graciously arranged for an ambulance to take me to the military facility, and even called ahead and made special arrangements with the military hospital. Because of this really special blessing there was no waiting at the military hospital emergency room—they already had everything in place for me, including a private room!

After the military doctors took further X-rays and finished their examinations, they told me that surgery would be necessary (which I already knew), and that they thought it would be best to use pins. That bothered me, but there was nothing I could do. The doctors left the room for a few minutes, and I quickly prayed again, "But, God, that's not what Dr. Wilson said was best. I can't do anything about this, but You can, and I am asking you to tell the doctors what is best for me. Whatever way you choose, I accept—I am in your hands." Just then the doctors came back into the room. They had re-evaluated the situation, and felt that the bone above the break would not get any blood, which would complicate things more and require further surgery. They had decided that the best thing for me would be a partial hip replacement. What a confirmation! That was exactly what Dr. Wilson had said! If I had felt better, I might have even shouted, "Hooray!" I didn't do that, but I did really thank God!

The surgery went well, and God really blessed that time in the hospital. He even graced the window ledge in my room, completely filling it with beautiful and fragrant flowers from friends and relatives. Yes, there was pain, but my room was filled with the very presence of God. There was one particular day in the hospital like none I have ever experienced before or since—it was like being in a quiet and beautiful garden with my Heavenly Father. All day long I felt His wonderful love as He tenderly held me in His arms.

God doesn't always tell us **why** things happen as they do, and we don't always **see** the good that He brings (Romans 8:28), but we know He is forever faithful, and His Word will always and forever stand. Whatever happens, we just need to keep on trusting Him. Yes, we did keep the dog—we did forgive her, and she did become a loving companion and protector. Sure enough, we could say…it is well!

Was that the end of all our problems? Not hardly! About a year after my hip replacement, my husband, Don, was diagnosed with colon cancer, both in the colon and in the bone marrow, but not in the blood. We were told that as bad as that is, it could be worse. If a person has to have cancer, his is the best kind—it is very slow, and there is no pain. There is inconvenience and fatigue, but no pain. Chemotherapy and radiation have not been the best options since the cancer is so widespread. The doctors are checking periodically, and we're just taking things one day at a time. So far, we don't know the "why" of this either—but we still **do** know God is faithful and doesn't make any mistakes—He is in control, and, yes, it **is** well.

I've shared all this simply to say that **a major part of God's design for His children is His peace:** *"Peace I leave with you, my peace I give unto you, not as the world giveth, give I unto you.*

Let not your heart be troubled, neither let it be afraid." (John 14:27) *"These things I have spoken unto you, that in me ye might have peace. In the world ye shall have tribulation: but be of good cheer; I have overcome the world."* (John 16:33) I once heard a preacher say that when tribulations come, we just have to "tribulate" until they are past—perhaps that was just his way of saying, *"Trust in the Lord with all thine heart; and lean not unto thine own understanding. In all thy ways acknowledge Him, and He shall direct thy paths."* (Proverbs 3:5-6)

Peace is not the absence of troubles or trials in our lives, but rather, it is the presence and power of God in the midst of all those troubles and trials.

> *Peace is not the absence of troubles or trials in our lives, but rather, it is the presence and power of God in the midst of all those troubles and trials*

We have spent a lot of time on the subject of peace, because it is such an important part of God's design for every new creation in Him. We are given permanent peace **with** God (forgiveness of our sin) the moment we are born into His family. Now the peace **of** God is available, along with **freedom** to walk in His love, in real **beauty** and genuine **joy.** If you recall my earlier testimony about beauty—it is not the world's glamour and great looks that make us beautiful. It is *"Christ in you"* (Colossians 1:27). Some of the most gorgeous people I know are some of the most ordinary-looking to the rest of the world. But it is not what's "up front" that counts, it is what's "inside"—rather, "**Who** is inside" that counts. How liberating! God has given us beauty— from head to toe:

*"And let the **beauty** of the Lord our God be upon us..."* (Psalm 90:17)

*"...How **beautiful** are the feet of them that preach the gospel of peace, and bring glad tidings of good things!"* (Romans 10:15)

Beauty cannot bring real joy. Joy springs forth from the presence of Jesus in our lives. The world can lend us temporary happiness, but only God can give us real joy. Remember how Jesus encouraged his disciples? These are some of the words He spoke to them: *"...I will see you again, and your heart shall rejoice, and your **joy** no man taketh from you."* (John 16:22). Then, as Jesus prayed to God His Father: *"And now I come to Thee: and these things I speak in the world, that they might have my **joy** fulfilled in themselves."* (John 17:13). Not only did He pray this for his disciples, but for you and me in this present world: *"Neither pray I for these alone, but for them also which shall believe on me through their word."* (John 17:20)

There are lots of Scriptures that reveal the many wonderful blessings inherent in God's design for every new creation in Him. We have only scratched the surface! With a Bible and a good, exhaustive concordance, you can experience a personal in-depth study for yourself. Not only will you learn more about His "flight design" for us, but it will be quite obvious that it is in God's will and delight that we "fly" (live and walk) daily in the light of His great design.

Chapter 6
Butterfly Life—Flight Destination

Butterflies know their destination by instinct.

Butterflies are one of nature's greatest marvels. They know **exactly** where they are going by God-given instinct—they just do what God designed them for, and they get where they are supposed to go.

According to an article I read recently, the Monarch is one of the most amazing of all butterflies, migrating with an annual round-trip journey of up to 3000 miles! They have a definite destination, and they absolutely must make that trip.

We know by the voice of God.

We human beings (all who have been born into God's family) know our destination, both here and hereafter, **by the voice of God through the Spirit of God who indwells every believer:** *"But when the fullness of the time was come, God sent forth His Son, made of a woman, made under the law, To redeem them that were under the law, that we might receive the adoption of sons. And because ye are sons, **God hath sent forth the Spirit of His Son into your hearts.**" (Galatians 4:4-6)*

Every new creation in Christ knows his or her destination **by the voice of God through His Word, the Bible:** *"For I know the thoughts that I think toward you, saith the Lord, thoughts of peace, and not of evil, to give you an expected end."* (Jeremiah 29:11) *"Thy Word is a lamp unto my feet, and a light unto my path."* (Psalm 119:105) *"My sheep **hear my voice**, and I know them, and they follow me: And I give unto them eternal life; and they shall never perish, neither shall any man pluck them out of my hand."* (John 10:27-28)

So far, I have not heard God speak to me in an audible voice, though He could do that if He chose to. Sometimes He lifts the words right from the Scriptures and speaks them to me personally. Sometimes He speaks to me while I am in everyday conversation.

At times God has spoken to my mind, giving specific directions. One such time was while driving back home from ministry on the East Coast. Suddenly there was a loud screeching, and it seemed to be coming from somewhere near the front or under the van, sounding much like brakes do when worn, but the brakes had been repaired recently. The sound continued intermittently, so I stopped at a service station in Jacksonville, Forida, but the noise would not present itself. So I thought the whole thing must have been a fluke, and hoped it wouldn't happen again.

I drove on, praying as I went, and things seemed to be all right. Later, about 8:00 that evening, as I approached a Tallahassee exit, I thought about stopping for the night, but actually felt pretty good—maybe I would just keep driving a while longer. Suddenly, almost audibly, I heard the urgent words, "Take this exit!" I answered, "OK," and turned off immediately. The minute the van began to slow down, the screeching returned, more loudly than ever—so much so that people began turning to look.

Apparently I would have to find a place to stay that night since, obviously, there was a big problem with the van, and by then repair shops were closed. There was a motel immediately across from the exit, and though they probably had no vacancies by then, I figured I should try anyway. Not only did they have a room available to me for the night, but one of the clerks overheard my question, "Do you know of a reliable mechanic?" The clerk volunteered that she knew one of the three reliable and honest mechanics in town, and asked if I wanted his telephone number. Did I ever! I called right then, and the mechanic was actually there at his shop. He agreed that I could bring the van over in the morning and he would check it out.

The next morning when I got to the mechanic's shop, he took one listen, and said the problem was the rear U-joint. In less than an hour, and for under $30, he had replaced the U-joint, and we (the van and me) were ready to roll. We finished the trip safely, and never heard that screeching again. What an awesome God we serve! Not only would He not let me stop at the wrong place for the repair, but He specifically told me where to get off the Interstate, showed me where to stay for the night, and through a motel clerk, directed me to the right place to have the van repaired. God still speaks to His children, and He will order our steps and stops all along the way. We just need to listen for His voice, and then do what He says.

Every new creation in Christ has a destination while on this earth—we **are** going somewhere **in this life** (and the journey is part of the destination). Even more exciting—every new creation in Christ has an **eternal, permanent** destination: to be with our Lord, **in His actual presence forever!** *"For we know that if* *our earthly house of this tabernacle* (our earthly body) *were dissolved, we have a building of God, an house not made with hands, eternal in the heavens."* *(1 Corinthians 5:1)*

Enroute to that great, perfect, final, and eternal destination, God has for us a myriad of paths while we are on earth. Some of these paths are easy and beautiful, some are difficult and treacherous, and many of them are filled with surprises. One such time for me was in August of 1991. I had been invited to go with an evangelism team for ministry in Romania; however, I did not know I was going until almost the last minute, and by then, it was too late to make the same travel arrangements as the rest of the team. It was decided that I would make my own separate flight arrangements.

> *God has for us a myriad of paths while we are on earth. Some easy and beautiful, some difficult and treacherous, and many of them are filled with surprises*

I was scheduled to arrive at the Budapest, Hungary, airport where someone from the team would meet me. Then we would travel by car to Oradea, Romania.

It sounded like a good plan, and in fact everything worked beautifully all the way to the Budapest airport. I even zipped right through customs. I walked out into a large reception area that was absolutely filled with people. I looked around for the evangelist who was supposed to be there to meet me. I looked…and looked…and looked…and kept on looking. Not only did I **not** see that evangelist, but there was not one familiar face in the entire crowd.

My first impulse was to get scared, but I figured there would be time for that later on, so I kept on walking (and praying). I knew God didn't bring me this far to leave me, and I knew He had a plan—I just didn't know what it was. About that time, I noticed a young man motioning to me. I felt a little apprehensive, yet somehow compelled to meet him. The young man was holding a book. To my surprise, he opened the book, and pointed to my picture and my name. It just "so happened" that he had a copy of the directory of Texas Baptist Evangelists—my name and picture are in that book. On the front of the book was written the name of the evangelist who was supposed to meet me—this was obviously his book!

The young man, Julio, motioned for me to come with him, so we loaded my luggage into his car, and away we went. For a moment, I wondered about getting into a car with a man I had never met, in an unfamiliar land, but in my heart was the assurance that it would be OK—it would be safe for me to go with the bearer of the book.

We had an interesting journey, which included a short stop at a Gypsy Flea Market—those places have just about anything you can imagine, but they didn't have the part Julio needed for his car. I don't speak Romanian or Hungarian, and Julio didn't speak English, so communication was challenging. However, the Romanian and Portuguese languages are both Latin-based, so there are some similarities. I do speak Portuguese, so I was able to find Scriptures in Julio's Bible and we conversed that way—but I was careful not to point the Scriptures out to him when he was going around curves in the road. We crossed the border checkpoint with no difficulty and arrived successfully at our destination in Romania.

The question continued to occur to me—what if Julio had not had that book at the airport? That was a scary thought—

"what if's" usually are! But then I remembered another book—
"The Book of The Lamb," or the "Lamb's Book of Life." I call
that book "Heaven's Official Birth Registry." The only way to
get your name into that book is to be born into the Family of
God. The name of **every** new creation in Christ is in that book.
My name is in that book! Jesus put it there the day I asked Him
to forgive me, save me, and come into my life—the day I received
Him as my Savior and Lord.

The apostle John gives us some insight into this *Book of the
Lamb*. What happens to those whose names are not in the book?
*"And whosoever was not found written in the book of life was cast
into the lake of fire."* (Revelation 20:15)   In Chapter 21 of the
book of Revelation, not only do we read John's description of
Heaven, but also of those who will be accepted, and those who
will not be allowed to enter: *"And I John saw the holy city, new
Jerusalem…And I saw no temple therein: for the Lord God almighty
and the Lamb are the temple of it. And the city had no need of the
sun, neither of the moon to shine in it: for the glory of God did
lighten it, and the Lamb is the light thereof…And there shall in no
wise enter into it any thing that defileth, neither whatsoever worketh
abomination, or maketh a lie: but they which are written in the
Lamb's book of Life."* (Revelation 21:2, 22-23, 27)

The Lamb of God is, of course, God the Son, the Lord Jesus
Christ. There are many Scripture references in this regard, one
of which is the declaration in the first chapter of the book of
John:

*"The next day John seeth Jesus coming unto him, and saith,
Behold the Lamb of God, which taketh away the sin of the world."*
(John 1:29)

Lamb of God[3]

Immortal, Invisible, Eternal, come to earth
Through that simple, lowly, virgin birth,
Now in flesh for all the world to see—
What love, that God would come to you and me!

Eternity invaded time that day
When in a manger, God Almighty lay;
But, Man of Sorrows would become His name,
Yet, for this, Jesus Christ, Lamb of God, Messiah, came.

Ancient of Days, Creator, Diety!
And yet, He came to die for such as me!
All-Righteous God, according to His plan
Gave His life, to snatch from death, un-righteous man!

Oh, Lamb of God, my Savior, Lord, and King,
My ransomed soul can only shout and sing!
Now and forever, let your praises ring!
Oh, Lamb of God, forever shall your praises ring!

In the words of Oswald Chambers, "Jesus Christ was born *into* this world, *not from* it. He did not evolve out of history, He came into history from the outside. He is not man becoming God, but God incarnate, God coming into human flesh, coming into it from the outside...Just as our Lord came into human history from outside, so He must come into me from outside. Have I allowed my personal human life to become a 'Bethlehem' for the Son of God?" Has Jesus come into your heart?

Hold Him in my Heart[4]

This whole wide world could not contain His glory,
But Mary held the Son of God within her womb.
A manger held the King of all the ages,
A rugged cross then held Him, then a tomb.

Death held my Jesus just for one brief moment,
Payment was fully made for all our sin—
It was God's perfect plan for sinful fallen man
To be restored completely once again.

God so loved the world He gave His only Son,
It was according to His plan right from the start.
Jesus fully paid the cost when He hung upon the cross;
Now thank God, I can hold Him in my heart.
Oh praise the Lord—I hold Him in my heart.

What can wash away my sin? Nothing but the blood of Jesus! In the first chapter of the book of the Revelation, we are told that Jesus loved us and washed us from our sins in His own blood! Think of it—the **blood of God** given for you and me! See Acts 20:28—those of us who have been born into His family are referred to as the *"flock"* of God, *"the church of God, which He* *hath purchased with **His own blood**.*" Jesus said, *"I and my Father are one." John 10:30* Jesus claimed to be Who He is—God! He gave His life for you and me. He offered His own pure and perfect blood as the Lamb of God (Isaiah 53:5-7), the **only** acceptable sacrifice for our sins—but each one of us must **personally receive** Jesus Christ as Savior and Lord. He doesn't save us as a group, but individually—every name of every person who does receive Him is inscribed forever in God's "birth registry"—the Book of the Lamb.

The Book of the Lamb[5]

My name's written down in the Book of the Lamb,
Inscribed through the blood of the Great "I AM,"
Once and for all, by God's mighty hand,
My name's written down in the Book of the Lamb.

Jesus stepped down from His glory,
Took on the likeness of man.
The King of Kings and Lord of Lords
Laid down His life as a lamb.

It's done, it's already done!
Finished at Calvary that day!
It's done, it's already done,
He has taken my sin away!

He took all my pain and my sorrow,

The thorns, the nails meant for me.

Jesus conquered the cross and the darkness of hell,

He is risen! Redemption's complete!

When I come to the end of life's journey,

When I cross the boundary of time,

Jesus will say to the Father,

I know her, I bought her, she's mine!

My name's written down in the Book of the Lamb,

Inscribed through the blood of the Great "I AM,"

Once and for all, by God's mighty hand,

My name's written down in the Book of the Lamb!

Is your name in the Lamb's Book of Life? If not, you can come to Him right now, ask Him to forgive you and come into your life. Receive Him as your Savior, and He will give you new birth—you will become His new creation, and your name will forever be in His book! Incidentally, this is called the "second birth." Did you know there is also a "second death?" There is a first and second resurrection and a first and second death. It is not a riddle—it is the road to your eternal destination: **Born twice—die once! Born once— die twice!**

Born twice— die once! Born once—die twice!

Born Twice—Die Once! All who have been born twice,

once physically, and the second time spiritually (into God's family) will be a part of the "First Resurrection"—the resurrection of the saved dead. The physical death of all who have been born again is the **only** death they will suffer—and that physical death is, in fact, simply the doorway through which we pass from this physical life to be forever in the presence of Jesus Christ and God the Father. *"Blessed and holy is he that hath part in the first resurrection: on such the second death hath no power…" (Revelation 20:6)*

Born Once—Die Twice! All who have rejected Jesus Christ as their Savior have never been born into God's family, never been transformed into His new creation. **All** who have been born only once will die twice—at the moment of physical death, these souls pass into eternal hell forever, and there will come a day the bodies of these "lost" dead will be resurrected unto eternal death. This death is not annihilation, but a "continual dying forever"—dying every moment yet never able to die. It will be an eternity of torment, with perhaps the words of Jesus ringing incessantly, *"I never knew you." (Matthew 7:23)*

*"And the sea gave up the dead which were in it; and death and hell delivered up the dead which were in them…And death and hell were cast into the lake of fire. **This is the second death.** And whosoever was not found written in the book of life was cast into the lake of fire." (Revelation 20:13-15) "But the fearful, and unbelieving, and the abominable, and murderers, and whoremongers, and sorcerers, and idolaters, and all liars, shall have their part in the lake which burneth with fire and brimstone: **which is the second death." (Revelation 21:8)***

To understand the Second Death more fully, read Chapters 20 and 21 of the book of the Revelation. No question about it—those who have never been born into God's family will die twice—physically, and forever dying in torment throughout eternity (and eternity never ends).

How important is it **where** your name is recorded? A few years ago, our church choir made a recording. Just a few weeks before the recording sessions were to begin, the accident had occurred that resulted in my hip surgery. It followed that there would be a very long period of recovery. But in spite of the serious nature of that major surgery and tedious recovery, God enabled me to be at every rehearsal and at the recording sessions, too. I was there for every bit of it, even though I had to use a walker and a cane.

When the recording was released, and I read the list of all the choir participants, to my surprise my name was not on the list! I couldn't believe it! Even though it had been one of the most difficult and painful times of my life, I was there—yet my name was omitted! I felt hurt and offended. What is more, it never will be corrected—my name will never be on that CD. I **wanted** that acknowledgement! My name should have been there, because I **was** there, and at great sacrifice. My voice was a legitimate part of the recording. But, looking at the big picture, how important was that really? Not very—God knows I was faithful to be there for every rehearsal and the actual recording. What really matters is that my name is in the **Book of the Lamb**, and nothing or no one, including me, can ever change that!

Once born into God's family, you can never get "unborn" any more than a butterfly can return to its prior caterpillar state of being. God will never blot your name out of His book! *"He that overcometh, the same shall be clothed in white raiment; and I will not blot his name out of the book of life, but I will confess his name before my Father, and before His angels." (Revelation 3:5)*

"Blessed be the God and Father of our Lord Jesus Christ, which according to His abundant mercy hath begotten us again unto a

*lively hope by the resurrection of Jesus Christ from the dead, to an inheritance incorruptible and undefiled and that fadeth not away, reserved in Heaven for you, who are **kept** by the power of God through faith unto salvation ready to be revealed in the last time. (1 Peter 1:3-5)*

*"Now unto **Him** that is able to **keep** you from falling, and to present you faultless before the presence of His glory with exceeding joy, To the only wise God our Saviour, be glory and majesty, dominion and power, both now and ever. Amen." (Jude 24)*

Once born into God's family, you are KEPT by His mighty power—Hallelujah—What a Savior!

Kept⁶

It's so lonely in the valley,
And my pathway seems so dim,
But Jesus knows the way that I should take,
So I'll walk hand in hand with Him.

The darkest valley never was my choice,
I wanted lofty mountains bright,
But in the darkness I have learned to see
That Jesus is my only light.

Oh, I am kept in the Name of Jesus,
Kept in the power of His blood,
Kept in the palm of His nail-scarred hand,
Kept in the arms of God.

Jesus keeps me in the valleys,
Through each dark and lonely night,
He leads me gently by still waters,
And on up to the mountain heights.

However rough my way shall seem to grow,
However dim becomes my sight,
He keeps me safely in His loving hand,
And gives me peace and joy and light.

Yes, I am kept in the name of Jesus,
Kept in the power of His blood,
Kept in the palm of His mighty hand,
Kept in the arms of God!
Kept in the arms of God!

Webster's definition of "keep" is "to have and hold; to not let go...to protect and defend!" You **can't keep** something you **don't have.** If God doesn't **have** you, His promise to keep and not let go does not apply to you. One day your life on this earth will be over, and you will irreversibly enter your final eternal destination—either Heaven or Hell.

You have heard the question, "What's in a name?" I think the big question should be "**Where** is your name?" You can have your name in all the "Who's Who" books in the world, you can have your name in lights and on all the biggest marquees in the world, but unless your name is in the Lamb's Book of

Life, you will never make it to Heaven—that wonderful destination—an eternity of love, joy, peace, light, freedom, and blessings beyond imagination that God has provided and reserved for "whosoever will" receive Him.

Chapter 7
Butterfly Life—Flight Preparation

Perhaps you have heard this quote by coach John Wooden: "Failure to prepare is to prepare for failure!" Are you prepared for daily flight, right here, and right now? If God can prepare the little butterfly insect to fly, you can be sure He knows how to prepare us—He has already given us everything we need for fantastic flight, and all of that "everything" is in Him, through Jesus Christ His Son.

God prepares us for flight Through His Holy Spirit:

The Holy Spirit is our Teacher, Comforter, and Power of God. *"Now we have received not the spirit of the world, but the Spirit which is of God; that we might know the things that are freely given to us of God. Which things also we speak, not in the words which man's wisdom teacheth, but which the Holy Ghost teacheth..." (1 Corinthians 2:12-13)* We will not here attempt to make a complete study of the Holy Spirit, but will just highlight some of the wonderful ways He prepares us and enables us for this new-creation, "butterfly" life. Incidentally, taking

Failure to prepare is to prepare for failure!

-John Wooden

flight in our new "butterfly" life is often called "walking in the Spirit" in the Scriptures.

Some time ago I read about a seminary professor whose assignment for his class was for each student to write a paper giving his own testimony of how he came to know Jesus Christ. One young man, in giving his account, said that he acknowledged he was a sinner and that Jesus had taken his guilt—only, somehow, the young man's fingers got mixed up on the keyboard, and he typed a "q" instead of a "g". So, it came out this way: "…Jesus took my quilt…" When the professor read the paper and saw the mistake he smiled, and wrote a little note on the paper before handing it back to the student. The note said, "Don't worry, Jesus may have taken your quilt, but He has given you a Comforter!"

"But the Comforter, which is the Holy Ghost, whom the Father will send in my name, He shall teach you all things, and bring all things to your remembrance, whatsoever I have said unto you." (John 14:26)

Jesus said, *"And I will pray the Father, and He shall give you another Comforter, that He may abide with you forever; Even the Spirit of Truth; whom the world cannot receive, because it seeth Him not, neither knoweth Him; but ye know Him, for He dwelleth with you and shall be in you."* (John 14:16-17)

What a glorious truth that Jesus Christ lives within all who believe in Him: *"To whom God would make known what is the riches of the glory of this mystery among the Gentiles; which is Christ in you, the hope of glory."* (Colossians 1:27) It is indeed a mystery!

I don't understand how He lives in us, but God said it, and that settles it! The moment a person receives Christ and becomes a new creation, he or she is placed in Christ, and Jesus Christ (in the person of God the Holy Spirit) comes to live within that person. *"What, know ye not that your body is the temple of the Holy Ghost which is in you, which ye have of God..."* (1 Corinthians 6:19) *"...Now if any man have not the Spirit of Christ, he is none of His."* (Romans 8:9)

There will be other things you and I won't be able to understand on this earth, but God is God, and we are not! And God cannot lie! We can always trust His Word whether we understand it completely or not. The late Dr. Vance Havner has well said: "I don't understand electricity either, but I'm not going to sit around in the dark until I do."

The Holy Spirit works in and through us—He is our Helper:

*"Behold, God is mine **helper**."* (Psalm 54:4)

*"My **help** cometh from the Lord, which made heaven and earth."* (Psalm 124:8)

*"Likewise the Spirit also **helpeth** our infirmities; for we know not what we should pray for as we ought; but the Spirit itself* (Himself) *maketh intercession for us with groanings which cannot be uttered."* (Romans 8:26)

*"...for He hath said, I will never leave thee, nor forsake thee. So that we may boldly say, The Lord is my **helper**, and I will not fear what man shall do unto me."* (Hebrews 13:6)

"I can do all things through Christ which strengtheneth me." (Philippians 4:13)

One day when Thomas, one of our grandsons, was only about three years old, he rode home from church with me—just the two of us. Thomas always had a lot to say, and that day he told me all about the new basketball goal that was over their garage door. He was so excited. But I was puzzled—Thomas was very short, kind of built like a tank, but very short—so, I asked him, "Thomas, how do you play basketball—I mean, how do you get the ball in the basket?" Thomas looked at me as if I should surely already know—"Grandma," he replied, "I'm little, but my daddy is BIG, and he will lift me up and make me stronger!" What a great snapshot! It is a wonderful picture of exactly what God, our Father, will do for us!

*"Fear thou not; for I am with thee. Be not dismayed; for I am thy God. I will strengthen thee; yea, I will **help** thee; yea, I will uphold thee with the right hand of my righteousness." (Isaiah 41:10)*

"Now the God of hope fill you with all joy and peace in believing, that ye may abound in hope, through the power of the Holy Ghost." (Romans 15:13)

God prepares us for "flight" through His Word:

*"For all the promises of God in Him are **yea**, and in Him Amen, unto the glory of God by us." (2 Corinthians 1:2)* I know that the "yea" means "yes," but, I'd like to say it even more strongly:

"YEA! HOORAY! YIPPEE!" OK, so the last two word spellings may not be in every dictionary, but they **are** expressions of how Isaiah 41:10 and many other Scriptures speak, and even shout, to your heart and mine. Just think of it! The Awesome Almighty God has given us His Word (and He always keeps His Word). We don't have to (and we can't) make it on our own— He is our preparation! JEHOVAH-JIREH (Provider, the All-Sufficient One) has already provided all we need for successful flight—more details in Chapter 9, Flight Provisions.

Yes, God has already made preparation for us to be successful in this earthly, daily "flight." And He has offered to everyone the way to a successful FINAL FLIGHT from this earthly life into eternity. The Bible tells us that *"it is appointed unto men once to die, but after this the judgement." (Hebrews 9:27)* God's will is that every person repent and be saved, transformed, made new. The Lord *"is longsuffering to us-ward, not willing that any should perish, but that all should come to repentance."* (2 Peter 3:9)

> *God has given every individual a free will— a choice. We cannot and God will not override that personal choice.*

In more than 30 years of this ministry, many have heard the wonderful good news of Jesus Christ through Bible studies; teas and Coffee Cup ministries; "Butterfly Life in a Caterpillar World" Retreats and conferences; concerts; publications such as letters and the little book, *Where To Go When It Hurts;* and even personally in many different settings including travel, hotels, etc. I wish we could say that everyone to whom we have presented the Gospel responded with a hearty "Yes" to Jesus, but sometimes the answer has been "No." That is because no matter how much you or I long to see someone come to Jesus Christ and be saved, we cannot "make it happen," for God has given every individual a free will—a choice. We cannot and God will not override that personal choice.

There it is again—choice! Some years ago I visited with a very elderly lady in a nursing home in Pauls Valley, Oklahoma. Friends had visited her a number of times, and shared with her the love of Jesus, but she had not said "yes" to Jesus. My friends thought perhaps she would respond if someone different went to visit her, so they invited me to go with them.

When I was introduced to the little lady, I told her I was from Texas and would be giving a concert in the city of Pauls Valley. My heart went out to her. I wanted so much for her to know my Savior. As I attempted to tell her about Jesus, she said she couldn't listen to me because she had to watch her TV show. I tried desperately to explain that this was literally a matter of life and death, but she completely shut me out, and told me to go away. I did—I went out to the car and just cried. Why would anyone choose a TV program over eternal life?

Then there was 72-year-old Beryl—I met her on a plane— she cared nothing at all about Jesus. In her words, she was doing just fine without him. But, as Jon Moore, an evangelist friend of ours once said, "What good is the 'milk and honey' without the Bread of Life" (Jesus Christ)?

I met Laura on a flight to Australia. Apparently she was not the only one assigned to the seat next to mine, so there was a bit of confusion. However, the flight attendants finally got everything sorted out, and Laura not only won the seat—she gained something far better—new life in Jesus! When I shared the gospel with her and invited her to pray to receive Jesus Christ as her personal Savior, she immediately said, "Yes!" Right then and there on the plane, she prayed to receive Jesus Christ and was born into the family of God! What an awesome, loving God we serve! He will use all kinds of things, great and small, even something as insignificant as confusion over a seat assignment, to save a soul and change a life forever!

Way back in the Outback of Woomera, Australia, I invited a hotel clerk to come to the chapel on Sunday morning where I would be singing and sharing about Jesus. He quipped, "Not me, I'm a loser!" He did not know, nor did he even care to hear, that **he could become a winner**, forever! When I invited another clerk to come to the chapel, he responded, "Oh no, I'll be fast asleep!" If only he knew how great it would be to **really** wake up!

After checking in to a hotel in a northeastern city of the U.S., on the way to my assigned room, I handed a tract to a cleaning lady. On the front of the little tract are the words, "You Are Loved!" The little lady smiled broadly and thanked me very kindly. I told her that Jesus loved her, and asked if she knew Jesus as her Savior, and she responded, "not yet, but I want to, I'm trying." Since she was on duty at that time, I invited her to come back to my room later, and I would tell her more about how she could know Jesus. She agreed to come at 7:30 that evening. That little woman did come, and we talked and looked into the Scriptures, and there in my room she prayed to receive Jesus Christ as her Savior. The following night, she brought her husband to the concert, where I sang and shared about Jesus Christ, and when the invitation was given, the husband received Jesus Christ as his personal Savior.

God could have created each of us with automatic devices so that at whatever time He chose, He could activate those gadgets and we would instantly be saved, changed, transformed into wonderful new creations, but it wouldn't be because we wanted to—only because we had no other choice. Out of His great love for us, He allows us to choose, even if we choose wrong! He longs to shower His love and grace upon everyone, individually, personally—but not by force.

You can't fake real wings—either you do or do not have them, and it takes wings to fly. Wings only come to the caterpillar by the unique process of being transformed into a butterfly. When a human being is transformed into a new creation in Jesus Christ,

He not only gives us "wings," but **everything** we need to "fly right," now in this life, and then into eternity with Him. He is Jehovah-Jireh, Provider, our Sufficiency, our Source. *"Not that we are sufficient of ourselves to think anything as of ourselves; but our sufficiency is of God." (2 Corinthians 3:5)*

God prepares us for flight through the privilege of prayer:

In May of 1992, I went to Okinawa for ministry at the invitation of Chaplain Matsumoto. At that time many in that country were praying earnestly for revival, and there were some very strong Japanese evangelists seeking to win their people to Jesus, both on the mainland of Japan and in the islands.

One of these men was evangelist Tanaka, who had the privilege of meeting with Emperor Akihito once a year. It was a rare honor for anyone to have even one visit, but Tanaka had met with the emperor 15 times and had been invited to meet with him again. This almost sounds like the apostle Paul's meetings with King Agrippa (see the 25th and 26th chapters of Acts). In fact, at one point, King Agrippa said to Paul, *"Almost thou persuadest me to be a Christian." (Acts 26:27)*

Evangelist Tanaka was scheduled to visit with the emperor on the second day of August. At Chaplain Matsumoto's request, I gave evangelist Tanaka a cassette copy of our *Kept* recording, a gift from this ministry that he could present to the emperor at their August meeting. We prayed that God would use that music along with Tanaka's witness to touch and turn the heart of the emperor and his wife, Michiko, and subsequently, Japan.

I could not go personally to meet the Emperor and deliver the gift cassette recording—there had to be a "go-between" to get the message of Jesus Christ (through the media of song) to him. In a sense, that is the case for all who would come to God.

Jesus said, *"I am the way, the truth, and the life: no man cometh unto the Father, but by Me." (John 14:6)* **Jesus Christ is our "go-between!"** *"For there is* **one** *God, and* **one** *mediator between God and man, the man Christ Jesus." (1 Timothy 2:5)*

On the day Jesus was crucified, when He uttered the words, *"It is finished" (John 19:30)*, the veil of the temple was literally ripped in two from top to bottom (Matthew 27:51, Luke 23:45), an act which said to the world, "whosoever will believe in Him" can now personally come into the very presence of God. Jesus Christ has opened the door—He **is** the door, and whoever has received Him as Savior and Lord can enter into the very throne room of Almighty God. He welcomes us freely and lovingly invites us to walk and talk with Him. He hears us and speaks to us. We need no longer be strangers and foreigners, separated from God.

"For through Him (Jesus Christ) *we both have access by one Spirit unto the Father. Now therefore ye are* **no more strangers and foreigners**, *but fellow citizens with the saints, and of the household of God." (Ephesians 2:18-19)*

"Let us therefore come boldly unto the throne of grace, that we may obtain mercy, and find grace to help in time of need." (Hebrews 4:16)

Our Heavenly Father, Himself, invites us to pray to Him: *"Call unto me, and I will answer thee, and show thee great and mighty things which thou knowest not." (Jeremiah 33:3)*

If you are yet unprepared for flight—if you haven't found the God who loves you, who will forgive you and give you a brand new life, if you really want to know Him, then seek Him:

"...your heart shall live that seek God." (Psalm 69:32)

"JESUS CZEKA"—these are the words on a poster that hangs on my office wall. This announcement was one of many that were used in Poland to notify people of our evangelistic meetings to be held in their local area. On the blue background of the poster is a blood-splattered cross, and in big white letters the words "JEZUS CZEKA"—Polish for "JESUS WAITS."

If you are reading this right now, then you have a chance. If you have never asked Jesus to forgive you, if you have not received Him as your Savior and Lord—if at this moment there is even a tiny tug at your heart, then Jesus is still waiting for you. How much longer will He wait?

Perhaps not at all. While writing this very page, I received a phone call, informing me of the death of a 46 year old friend. You may have 10 seconds, 10 minutes, 10 months, 10 years—or, your next breath may be your last.

Are you ready?

Are you prepared for daily flight?

Are you prepared for the final flight?

If the answer to these three questions is no, then seek Him now!

"Seek ye the Lord while He may be found, call ye upon Him while He is near." (Isaiah 55:6)

PRAY to God now! Ask Him to forgive you, then open the door of your life, and receive Jesus Christ as your Lord and Savior. This is a prayer He will always hear and answer—He will come into your life to stay, forever, and… NOW—you are prepared for flight!

Part II

The Butterfly Life—
How To Wing It

The Butterfly Life—
How To Wing It

W e have taken the seven previous chapters to explain the importance, indeed the absolute necessity of transformation God's way. You may have heard about the butterfly life weight loss program that is supposed to bring about a "new you." The real "new you" has absolutely nothing to do with physical weight loss—it has everything to do with a new nature! Just as the little caterpillar can never fly unless it is first changed into a butterfly with wings, so it is with you and me—we can never experience butterfly life until and unless we have been transformed into a new creature in Christ by receiving Him as our Savior.

When the little caterpillar becomes a new creature—a butterfly, it is **not** transferred to a different, perfect earthly world, but it **is** given wings, and a different view of the same world. That is precisely what happens to those who have been born into God's family. We have been given a new nature—a spiritual nature, and in a sense, "wings!" And, while we are not taken out of this present world until our fleshly bodies die, we most certainly are given the right equipment for a successful "flight" and a much better view of this present world while we are here!

It follows then, that in our earthly flight we need to learn to "wing it" in all kinds of circumstances. I've been learning a long time, and have not yet mastered this "Butterfly Life," but I am beginning to understand that as the Lord Jesus grows me in Him He is mastering me, ordering my steps and setting me free to fly. My personal "flight lessons" within the pages that follow are written with the hope that they will provide new insight and encouragement for the "flight of your life."

Chapter 8
Flight Control

The Power Available to You and Me

"I can do all things through Christ which strengtheneth me."
(Philippians 4:13)

> Not, I can do a **few**...
>
> Not, I can do **some**...
>
> Not even, I can **do a lot of**...
>
> But, I can do **all**...

What wonderful words of assurance! Of course, as has already been stressed, the first and most vital issue is to get connected (be changed into that new creation by being born into God's family). There **is** no power otherwise! Once connected, the power is there...always!

When I go overseas in ministry, I usually bring a portable sound system along. This small PA unit not only works with electricity, but it also has a built-in battery. What a great feature—it allows this compact little system to work whether there is electricity available or not!

During a mission trip to Africa, God gave me an opportunity to sing for a Sunday morning worship service at Parklands Baptist Church in Nairobi, Kenya. Not all the churches in Africa have electrical power, but this church did, and once my little PA sound system was plugged in and working, there was good sound and amplification. I was in the middle of a song, however, when the electrical power suddenly went off. Instantly, God reminded me that I had only to reach to the back of the PA and flip the switch that would access the internal battery—the power that was already there—I hardly missed a beat!

When things suddenly stop working in the life of God's child,

Within every believer dwells the Power of God — the Holy Spirit

Jesus **never** does—**He is there**, and His power is on the ready, always! You have only to access the inner power—not **your** inner power, but the power of God, the Holy Spirit, who lives within you. The mighty power of God is limitless and infinite. It is resurrection power— the very same power that raised Jesus from the dead!

Within **every** believer dwells the Power of God—the Holy Spirit. How sad to say that I did not know that for a long time. I must have heard that message at some time during my life, but somehow missed it—maybe I was listening without really hearing. I had been a Christian for 30 years and was working hard on my "super-Christian" image, trying to measure up—to be all I thought God wanted me to be, and everything people expected of me. The harder I worked, the more miserable I became inside. I knew there was something wrong, but didn't know what it was or how to fix it. I couldn't tell anybody—they would be so disappointed. I couldn't let people know what a big failure I was—I just had to keep on smiling and trying to look good on the outside, regardless of the way I felt on the inside, thinking that sooner or later I would surely work through it all.

Jesus said, *"I am come that they might have life, and that they might have it more abundantly."* *(John 10:10)* I had about decided that the Christian life was, after all, pain and hardship, and that the abundant life Jesus promised must surely be the "Pie-in-the-sky-when-you-die-by-and-by" life, and would only be mine when I got to Heaven. I figured that until then, I would just have to endure, rather than enjoy, my salvation, and I kept on working harder. I was a part of everything in the church that I could be. Since I grew up in a preacher's family, I knew how to do a lot of things in the church. I had been attending church since nine months before I was born. When we were young, my sisters and I sang together as a gospel trio. After we all married and left home, I continued singing in church, both solo as well as in choir. I even directed a church choir for a while.

I read my Bible every night—if I didn't, I couldn't check that little square on Sunday night that said I was a daily Bible reader, and that would be bad for my reputation. I prayed every night—though I often drifted off to sleep while praying. I did all the things a Christian worker is supposed to do—I was trying to be a perfect "**do**er," desperately trying to hold up that super-Christian image. The harder I worked, the heavier that image became. Incidentally, I have deliberately and liberally used the personal pronoun "I" because I thought it was all up to me. I was trying to work **for** God, instead of allowing **Him** to work through me.

Don't misunderstand—God **does** want us busy and active in a local body of believers, and on a regular basis—" *Not forsaking the assembling of ourselves together....*" *(Hebrews 10:25)* He **does** want us to be "*not hearers only,*" but also "*doers of the Word*" *(James 1:22)*. But, when we depend upon the energy of the flesh instead of the Holy Spirit, our deeds are actually works of the flesh, and ultimately there **will** come a time when we simply can't go on, and the super-Christian image we worked so hard to build up will come crashing down around us. Though it may not have been evident to those around me, that is precisely where I was headed!

Public music ministry was not even my idea—it was my husband's suggestion. He sensed there was something wrong—something missing. He thought I seemed somewhat unfulfilled. He didn't know it, and I didn't know it, but he "hit the nail right on the head!" To be "unfulfilled" is to be "un-filled-full." That is what I was, only I didn't know it.

> *To be "unfulfilled" is to be "un-filled-full." That is what I was, only I didn't know it*

In Ephesians 5:18, it is written: "*be filled with the Spirit.*" I didn't know what that meant, but if anybody was filled (whatever that was), I thought it must be me since I had been a Christian so long. Longevity, tenure, meant something in the military and in the post office, so maybe that applied here, I thought. In Colossians 1:27, it is written: "*Christ in you, the hope of glory.*" I remember talking with a Christian friend, who remarked to me, "Think of it—Christ in me—Christ in you! Isn't that wonderful!" Of course, I replied, "Oh yes, yes!" But,

I didn't have a clue what she was talking about. Yes, I was a child of God, a new creation—I had been born into God's family many years prior to that, and I had a great Christian reputation—but, I was woefully ignorant of some very important truths.

As I contemplated music ministry, I couldn't imagine that anyone would want to hear an alto like me, but then there was George Beverly Shea—he had low voice and was a very well-known bass soloist with the Billy Graham Evangelistic Association. Maybe there was hope for me after all. In April of 1974 I began a public music ministry, Sacred Music, Inc. I loved it! I have always loved singing about Jesus, and still do. However, this did not fix my "inside" problem. I thought perhaps I should give it a little more time—just stay with it a while longer. So I did, but things only got worse—I became more and more miserable inside. Still, nobody knew except me...and God.

After a few months, I finally came to the place that I could not go on. Still, I couldn't tell anyone, not even my husband. Now I realize that God was bringing me to the place of utter desperation, to the end of myself and all my resources, with no one to turn to...except Himself. That night after singing, I went home, walked into the bedroom, and closed the door, and fell on my knees. I cried out to God: "Oh God, if this is all there is to the Christian life, I don't want to live anymore—please, take me home to heaven to be with you, and would you do it now." Nothing happened—there was nothing but silence. I cried out even more desperately, "God, if you can't change my life, there is no hope for me." Still silence.

I had only one prayer left, "Oh God—help me!" I think God had been waiting for a long time to hear that particular prayer, because for the first time in a **long** time I came to Him without a single suggestion of what I wanted Him to do and how I wanted Him to do it. Dr. Vance Havner used to say, "You can't appreciate Jesus as all you want until He's all you've got." Jesus was all I had that night—but He was all I needed!

At that moment, when I knew I had utterly failed and was at the absolute end of myself, and all I could do was to cry out to God for help, He heard my cry. There were no bells, whistles, or sirens, no lightning flashes or visions of angels, but in my heart was the calm assurance that Almighty God, my Heavenly Father, had heard and **would** do something, though what or when He did not say. That very night He began, literally, working Psalm 40:1-3 in my life and ministry.

"I waited patiently for the Lord; and He inclined unto me, and heard my cry. He brought me up also out of an horrible pit, out of the miry clay, and set my feet upon a rock, and established my goings. And He hath put a new song in my mouth, even praise unto our God; many shall see it, and fear, and shall trust in the Lord." (Psalm 40:1-3)

A few weeks later, God put me in a revival meeting in our city—my part was to sing three songs prior to the evening message. When the evangelist stood to speak, and announced his topic, "The Spirit-Controlled Life," I began to feel very uncomfortable. I had always associated the Holy Spirit with strange behavior, and since I didn't want to be weird or make a spectacle of myself, I had altogether avoided the subject of the Holy Spirit. I was seated way up close to the front of the auditorium, and it would have been very rude to get up and leave, so I figured I would just have to suffer through that message. I have never suffered so much in all my life! Though I had never met nor even heard of that evangelist before, he seemed to know every secret detail of my life and being! I thought

God must have told him everything about me!

The evangelist began with Ephesians 5:18 ("...*Be filled with the Spirit*"), and then proceeded to explain what that meant. I don't know what God did in the life of anyone else that evening, but I do know that on that particular night through that particular evangelist, God spoke directly and specifically to me. While I won't attempt to tell you everything the evangelist said, I will try to give you the essence of it.

The evangelist said that if we are going to be filled with the Spirit, we must be empty of self, which simply means—give God everything, and start by giving Him your sin (that is confession/acknowledgement of specific sin). Yes, Christians do sin, and sin always separates—it separates the lost ones from God eternally. (The lost are the caterpillar-types—those who have never been transformed into new creations by believing on Jesus Christ and trusting Him to save them). Sin **cannot** separate the child of God (the believer/new creation) from God **eternally**, but sin **can** separate us from **fellowship** with God in this earthly life. Jesus said He would never leave us or forsake us, and He cannot and will not break His word. Even when we sin God is still with us, but fellowship with Him has been broken, and the **sense** of His presence is gone.

The only way to restore fellowship is to go to God in prayer, confess our sins, and accept God's forgiveness. The evangelist said to be specific and **name** those sins. All at once, it was like God pulled back a great curtain and showed me my own heart and the things that were wrong—things that I had refused to acknowledge as sin. I had always prayed, "Lord, forgive me of all my sins," but suddenly it was clear that I had been using that prayer as a sort of covering blanket, hoping God would not see the things I wanted to hide. But He sees our hearts—He knows every tiny detail of our lives. When we confess our sins, we are not informing God of anything—we are acknowledging that which He already knows. We are agreeing with God that we are wrong and He is right, and we are repenting—making that "you-turn" and walking back toward Him.

"If we confess our sins, He is faithful and just to forgive our sins, and to cleanse us from all unrighteousness." (1 John 1:9)

When we confess our sins (acknowledge those sins and agree with God that we have sinned), He forgives us and makes us perfectly clean. And when God forgives, He forgets. Those sins are buried in the deepest sea: *"Thou wilt cast all their sins into the depths of the sea." (Micah 7:19)* Those sins are removed as far as the east is from the west (and they never meet): *"As far as the east is from the west, so far hath He removed our transgressions from us." (Psalm 103:12)* We never have to confess those sins ever again (unless we commit those same sins again). *"Now ye are clean through the word which I have spoken unto you." (John 15:3)* Hallelujah!

Clean, perfectly clean! But, the evangelist said, sin always wants to come back—how can we deal with that? He said that every sin we commit comes out of one of five major areas of our lives: Attitudes, Desires, Decisions, Possessions, and Money. Remember, to be filled with the Spirit means to give God **everything**—allow Him to take **total** control. The evangelist said that when we have given God our sins, the next step is to give Him those five major areas of our lives. It is helpful to pray aloud as you yield every area, again being specific, naming each one. Give to Him your:

      Attitudes

      Desires

      Decisions

Possessions

Money

Ask God to take absolute control of every area of your life and every fiber of your being—ask Him to fill you with His Holy Spirit. When you are in the right position (empty of self), and ask according to His will (Ephesians 5:18 tells us to be filled with His Spirit), then on the authority of God's Word, you can absolutely know that He answers that prayer—He will fill you then and there with His Spirit:

"And this is the confidence that we have in Him, that, if we ask anything according to His will, He heareth us; And if we know that He hear us, whatsoever we ask, we know that we have the petitions that we desired of Him." (1 John 5:14-15)

"For God, who commanded the light to shine out of darkness, hath shined in our hearts, to give the light of the knowledge of the glory of God in the face of Jesus Christ. But we have this treasure in earthen vessels, that the excellency of the power may be of God, and not of us." (2 Corinthians 4:6-7)

*God the Holy Spirit is not an ethereal, wispy, floating, spook-type thing, but a **Person**—God the Holy Spirit—Christ in you!*

The moment we are saved by trusting in the Lord Jesus Christ as Savior—in that very instant, God the Holy Spirit comes to live within us. And from that moment on, He is with us all the way to eternity. God the Holy Spirit is not an ethereal, wispy, floating, spook-type thing, but a **Person**—God the Holy Spirit— Christ in you! God the Holy Spirit is the Person and Power of

God, and is resident in every new creation. Spend time alone with Him every day, preferably beginning your day with Him, giving everything over to Him and asking Him to take control. Whether you have been a Christian for many years, or only minutes, **He is present** in your life—invite Him to be **President** of your life, now, and every day, every moment of the day.

God continues to teach me this vital principle through many ordinary things, one of which has been the ministry van (the same one mentioned earlier) that we lovingly called, "Old Sweetness." That old van was always coming up with new problems, much like we humans do. One day, out of the clear blue sky with no rain in sight, her windshield wipers just started going, and the wiper switch was in the "off" position. I thought maybe that it was just a fluke that hopefully would not happen again, but it did! From that day forward, if the key was in the ignition and in the "on" position, the wipers wiped. It didn't matter whether the engine was on or off, or if it was raining or not—the wipers never stopped. Now that's all right if it is raining, but on a sunny summer day in Texas, it's a bit embarrassing for the wipers to be going like mad when I'm stopped for a traffic signal, and I'm trying to look normal.

Knowing this particular problem would be expensive to repair, we continued to put up with it, hoping that somehow the wipers would one day stop as suddenly as they had begun. But that was just not to be! They actually did stop once, in the straight-up position! I never realized how hard it would be to look around those wipers stuck right in my direct line of vision! I was kind of glad when they started wiping again!

We tolerated that "wiping" inconvenience for about 6 months, until one day a friend told me he thought he could fix it—and he did! This man could fix almost anything—in fact, whatever the problem was, if he couldn't fix it, then it probably couldn't be done! He installed an inline fuse, and ran a line from the fuse box (which was way up underneath the dashboard, and nearly impossible to get to), to a toggle switch that he had positioned on the dash in such a way that it was within easy reach. Now the van had a master switch—all I had to do was to flip that switch, and Old Sweetness would not "wipe" unless I wanted her to.

I was elated! How good of my Heavenly Father to send this very talented friend to fix the problem! Even as I was praising and thanking God, He spoke to my heart: "Betty, you are like that van sometimes—you just "wipe"—you just do your own thing, and you don't even ask if it is My will." How true! How often I have gone **my** way. Oh, how important, how critical, each day, to give everything back to God, and ask Him to take control of everything I am and have, can become and can obtain. He is the Great Shepherd—He knows precisely how to direct my way, thus preventing me, just like that old van, from "wiping" at the wrong time.

From the day the master switch was installed in the van, we operated the windshield wipers by way of that switch, and that old van was well behaved! She never wiped unless I told her to. One day, after about two years of great performance, I was thinking about the way Old Sweetness used to wipe without permission, and about how well she was doing now. I wondered what she would do if I turned off the master switch and went back to the way it used to be.

Had she learned her lesson? She was doing fine now—was it just a matter of needing a lot of practice in the right direction? Curiosity got the best of me—I had to check it out. I got in the van, turned off the master switch, made sure the old on/off wiper switch was off like it used to be, then turned the key and started the van, and you know what happened? You guessed it! Without hesitation the windshield wipers started going like mad! "Well, I'll be," I said right out loud. "You would have thought that after all that time, after all that practice, she would have learned by now how to get it right!"

And God spoke to my heart again, "Betty, you're like that. No matter how long you have been a Christian, and no matter how long you have been obedient, unless you give me the master switch every day of your life, you can go back to the old ways, in a heartbeat!"

That's true! You can be an obedient Christian for two days, two years or two decades, or any amount of time, but the moment you turn off the master switch and try to do His will your way, you will be out of control, and headed right back to a caterpillar kind of living. Only as we yield control to the Holy Spirit and allow God to do **His will, His way,** can we live the butterfly life, one that pleases Him and fills our flight with His freedom and joy.

We don't much hear God's voice, but we keep on trying to do God's will…

I am convinced there are a lot of Christians who, like I was, are desperately trying to live up to that super-Christian image—trying to do all the right things, but in the energy of the flesh. This is always the path to failure and desperation. For most of us, it is only when we reach "the end of our rope" that we are finally willing to let God do what only He can—live the Christian life through us. Until we reach that point, we don't much hear God's voice, but we keep on trying to do God's will… our way.

"I am crucified with Christ; nevertheless I live; yet not I, but Christ liveth in me; and the life which I now live in the flesh I live by the faith of the Son of God, who loved me and gave Himself for me." (Galatians 2:20)

A lady once asked Dr. Vance Havner if God has "favorites." He wisely answered, "No ma'am, God does not have favorites, but He **does** have **intimates**." The choice is yours. If you would be an "intimate," it will take time—time alone with God, daily giving Him total control of everything you are and everything you have, and daily praying, seeking His face, and reading His Word, the Bible.

As you continue to search the Scriptures, you will learn more and more about flight control for the "Butterfly Life." Like my experience with the the telephone system I wrote about earlier, you will be absolutely amazed at the things you will discover when you:

Read the directions!

Heed the directions!

And, even, memorize the directions!

There may be times when a printed copy of the Bible is not readily available, but the Word of God is desperately needed. If it has been hidden in the heart, then the Spirit of God can bring it to mind instantly.

There will still be times when we fail, when we have grabbed control for ourselves. When that happens, we mustn't wait a second, but instantly stop, confess our sins, give everything back to God, and ask Him to take control again. The power of God (the Holy Spirit) did not leave when we sinned. He is still there, but only as He is in control is His power truly active in and through us, and as we have already pointed out, He will only take control (fill us with His Spirit) when we ask Him to.

"Let us therefore come boldly unto the throne of grace, that we may obtain mercy, and find grace to help in time of need." (Hebrews 4:16)

"Let the wicked forsake his way, and the unrighteous man his thoughts: and let him return unto the LORD, and He will have mercy upon him; and to our God, for He will abundantly pardon." (Isaiah 55:7)

God has promised to forgive, to **abundantly** pardon, and what He has promised He will always do:

"God is faithful, by whom ye were called unto the fellowship of His Son, Jesus Christ our Lord." (1 Corinthians 1:9)

"Faithful is He that calleth you, who also will do it." (1 Thessalonians 5:24)

Forever Faithful

All of Thy paths are mercy and truth,
And all of Thy statutes are right,
Thy wonderful Word is steadfast and sure,
Thy love is my song in the night.

Lead me in Thy truth, O Lord,
Teach me Thy paths, Thy ways;
Oh God of my salvation,
On Thee do I wait all the day.

Thus will I bless Thee while I shall live,
Christ Jesus, forever the same!
The One Who is forever faithful—
I will lift up my hands in Thy name!

I know in my flesh dwells no good thing,
At times I see nothing but failure,
But I thank my God, my Redeemer, Forgiver,
He who called me is faithful forever!

(Source—KJV Bible: Psalm 25:10; Psalm 19:8; 1 Peter 1:25; Psalm 42:8; Psalm 25:4-5; Psalm 63:4; Hebrews 13:8; 1 Corinthians 1:9; 1 Thessalonians 5:24)

Ultimately, successful flight will never be achieved by our own manipulations—it can only be accomplished when we are totally yielded to the Master Controller. *"For it is God which worketh in you both to will and to do of His good pleasure." (Philippians 2:13)*

Chapter 9
Flight Provision

The Provision Available to You and Me

God has promised to supply all our needs: *"But my God shall supply all your needs according to His riches in glory by Christ Jesus." (Philippians 4:19 emphasis, mine.)* Notice, again, that little word "all."

Not, **a few, some, many, or even most** of our needs—God said that He would provide ALL of our needs!

Time after time after time, in over 30 years of traveling all over the world, sharing the wonderful good news of the Lord Jesus Christ, God has never failed to supply ALL of our needs. He has not always supplied my needs the way I expected, but then, God's ways are not our ways: *"For my thoughts are not your thoughts, neither are your ways my ways, saith the Lord. For as the heavens are higher than the earth, so are my ways higher than your ways, and my thoughts than your thoughts." (Isaiah 55:8-9)* Our earthly vision is very limited, but God sees, all at once, our entire lives—from beginning to end and everything in between. Nothing ever surprises our Heavenly Father!

The summer ministry tour of 1981 had been planned and numerous hurdles already cleared, but then came the "biggie"— worldwide airline and transportation strikes! There could be many delays and problems. This would prove interesting since I was traveling from San Antonio, Texas, to Spain, Italy, Germany, the Netherlands, Norway, back to Germany, and then back to San Antonio.

He has not always supplied my needs the way I expected, but then, God's ways are not our ways

Not only would the actual flights prove challenging, but maneuvering of my luggage might be really interesting. I was not traveling light, since I was bringing recordings, tracts, and booklets for new believers. Except for being a little inconvenient, however, I thought it would all work out, since at the beginning, I claimed the extra baggage and paid the necessary extra fees.

The first shock came the day I was to leave Madrid, Spain for the next ministry stop in Italy. A chaplain friend took me to the airport, and thankfully, stayed with me until he was sure everything was all right. When we arrived at the check-in counter, I was told I would have to pay an additional $203 for excess baggage. It didn't matter that I had already paid excess baggage fees in New York—this was a different plane. I did not have $203 in cash, and a check was not acceptable. However, the chaplain just "happened" to have his rent money in his pocket, in cash. He suggested that he pay the fees, and I could give him a personal check in exchange. I gratefully accepted his offer, and I thanked God for His great provision through that very kind chaplain.

But the story doesn't end there. Just the day before, because of the airline strikes, I had changed my 7:30 p.m. connecting flight from Rome to Venice for an earlier flight, just in case there was a transportation problem in Rome. I reasoned that if something happened to that 7:30 flight, then I would be unable to leave Rome until the following day, and that would not be a good thing. Now, however, because of airline strikes in Spain, my plane was late leaving Madrid, and for the same reason, the new connecting flight from Rome to Venice was cancelled.

Upon arrival in Rome, I was informed that I could **try** to get on standby for the 7:30 flight—the last evening flight to Venice that day, and the same one I had cancelled! There was already a long, long list on standby—oh boy, trouble was not only on the way, it was there! Then came the good news and the bad news. The good news was that the clerk who made the schedule change the day before had failed to cancel my 7:30 flight reservation, so I already had a confirmed reservation on the only available flight from Rome to Venice! Thanks be to God!

The bad news was that there would be excess baggage fees to pay, **again**! It didn't matter that I had paid twice already—now I would have to pay again! I was told that I would have to pay every time I changed planes throughout the entire tour! At that point I asked the agent at the counter, "Would you please excuse me a moment? I'll be right back."

I went immediately to the ladies' lounge, looked around and saw no one there. Then I turned my face upward and asked aloud, "God, are you here?" (I **knew** He was there, even though things were going wrong). "Lord, I know you're here, even though I don't feel like it at the moment, and I know You know all about these problems—none of this is a surprise to You. So, I'm claiming your Word right now—You said You would never leave me, and You said you would supply all my needs according to your riches in glory by Christ Jesus, so here I am. You sent me on this tour—I am yours—this tour is yours. I **need** You, and I believe You to work everything out. Thank You, Lord, for hearing me, and for loving me—I believe you, Jesus."

Then I went back to deal with the excess baggage problem— the agent said my cost would be $53—all I had in cash was $60. That would leave me only $7! I started to get concerned, but remembered that God said He would supply **all** my needs, so, obviously, He knew $7 was all the cash I would need between Rome and Venice. Besides, what financial needs could I have on the plane? God gave me perfect peace. Upon my arrival in Venice, friends from Aviano Air Base met me, and we traveled by car to Aviano for the next concert and ministry. Not only did I still have the $7, but God also supplied additional funds at Aviano. Every time I had a need, God was already there with the supply.

The purpose and reason God allowed this European concert and ministry tour was to share the gospel of the Lord Jesus Christ, but I believe God also wanted to demonstrate His perfect provision, protection, and peace, all of which negate the need to panic. How great is our God! There is none like Him! He is perfect in all His ways—throughout the tour the Lord Jesus touched hearts and lives, and many responded. Some of the testimonies were:

"I've been looking for answers—tonight I found them!"

"God sent you here for me."

"That's exactly what I needed."

"I've been lazy in my Christian life—I've been letting things slide—now I see there's got to be some changes—I need to let

Jesus be **Lord** of my life!"

"I saw Jesus tonight."

"I have never heard the gospel so clearly in all my life."

We do not always have the privilege of seeing or hearing all that God accomplishes through this and other ministries, but we do have the assurance that His Word will achieve all He sends it to do:

"For as the rain cometh down, and the snow from heaven, and returneth not thither, but watereth the earth and maketh it bring forth and bud, that it may give seed to the sower, and bread to the eater; So shall My word be that goeth forth out of My mouth: It shall not return unto Me void, but it shall accomplish that which I please, and it shall prosper in the thing whereunto I sent it." (Isaiah 55:10-11)

In continuing the tour, from Italy I would be flying to Germany, so the excess baggage problem could easily reappear. However, God already had the solution—it "just so happened" that the chaplain at Aviano was going to be traveling by car to Germany at just the right time, and he offered to take some of my supplies with him so I wouldn't have to pay any more fees. Since I had one more stop in Italy we would arrive in Germany at about the same time. From then on, as I distributed more and more of the materials, I no longer had "excess baggage."

Travel plans continued to fluctuate throughout the tour. But always, God was already there and had a plan in place to meet every challenge. There was a little Italian lady named Lucia, whom the Lord wanted me to see, but once again the strikes had shut down just about every form of public transportation, and I needed a way to get from Aviano to her little town of Brescia. Miraculously God provided a ride by car with one of our military personnel who just "happened" to be going that way, then a taxi right to Lucia's front door, and another taxi to the airport in Milan where I would depart for Germany.

From Italy to Germany to Norway, back to Germany and the Netherlands, from the beginning to the end of the tour God always made provision for everything I needed just when I needed it.

Many years later Don and I were given the opportunity for another ministry tour to Italy. At that time the most practical mode of transportation was by car, so we rented a car in Rome, and thus began another travel challenge.

When we traveled from Rome to Naples, we decided not to take the very expensive toll-type autoestrada (similar to our U.S. Interstate highway system). Instead, we took a shortcut someone had told us about. But the roads were not clearly marked, and time after time, we were certain that we must have taken a wrong turn and were surely hopelessly lost. Each time that happened, we prayed aloud—"Oh God, we don't know where we are, but You do; please direct our path—show us where to go." And suddenly, we would see a rock or tree on the side of the road with the word "Napoli" painted on it. There were no arrows or mileage indicators, but God used that one word to let us know we were on the right track.

At last, we arrived in what we thought was Naples, but still couldn't be absolutely sure. We were looking for a particular street—if we could just find that street, it would lead us directly to the Agnano U.S. Naval Base in Naples, which was right where we wanted to be. Agnano was next on the ministry schedule. Again we prayed, "Oh God, we don't know where we are, but You do—please show us what to do." At that moment I looked up, and saw a name on a street sign—it was the one we were looking for! Our greatest need on that drive from Rome to Naples was **direction!** Maybe the need for direction in traveling seems a little insignificant to some, but it was a major necessity to us. Just as He promised, every time we called out to Him for help, our merciful Heavenly Father answered our need.

Ministry travels in the United States have been mostly by private vehicle, and much of this was in the van, Old Sweetness. There have been many needs associated with this van. Once, during the eighties, I was traveling in Northern California, and things had been going well. I was all set to "hit the road" early—I had three days to get to the next scheduled ministry in Clovis, New Mexico. Just as I started to get into the van, I noticed a puddle of water forming on the ground underneath the radiator. I guess "OH, NO!" is a natural reaction when you're looking at a leaky radiator at 6:15 in the morning in a small town, with 2000 miles of mountains and desert ahead. Still, I knew that God would take care of the problem. I was certain He wanted me in New Mexico for those two Sunday ministries, and He would get me there somehow.

I prayed as I drove to a service station, hoping the problem would be an easy one to fix—maybe just a loose connection. On close examination, it was easy to see the problem was **not** simple—it was definitely the radiator itself! I followed directions to a radiator shop, and began to wait patiently for the shop to open. The doubts rushed in like a flood...was I in the right

Just as He promised, every time we called out to Him for help, our merciful Heavenly Father answered our need

place?...should I have gone to some other shop?...would they do a good job?...would I get to Clovis on time? ...would I have enough money?...and on and on. I began to pray again—I **had** to hear from God!

"I sought the Lord, and He heard me, and delivered me from all my fears." (Psalm 34:4) And you know how He did it—how He delivered me from all my fears? Through His Word! As I prayed, my eyes fell upon a little 3x5 card that "just happened" to be there in the van. It read: *"Wait on the Lord; be of good courage, and He shall strengthen your heart; wait, I say, on the Lord." (Psalm 27:14)*

As clearly as if I had heard God's audible voice—I was to **wait**—I was in the right place—I just needed to wait. So, I answered, "Yes, Lord," and I waited. When the shop opened, the mechanic determined that the radiator could not be repaired. I would make it no farther without a new radiator. Small towns do not often have a wide selection of radiators. We could order one from the nearest big town, and it would arrive the following day, but I did not have a day to spare.

To make a long story short, as I continued to pray, and the mechanic tried to find a radiator, it somehow came to his attention that they had a radiator in the shop that had been special ordered, but after it arrived the customer had changed his mind, so they still had the radiator—and, you guessed right— it was the exact size I needed for the van! When it was time to pay the bill, the mechanic's comment was something like, "Lady, you made out like a bandit!" I assured him, however, that I really didn't think that was the case. God knew I would need a radiator and when I would need it, so He ordered it ahead of time, in someone else's name. And the cost of the radiator? Precisely the amount of the love offering the church had given me the night before—to the penny!

Not only did God meet my specific needs for the radiator just at the right time, but He also led me to talk to a man there at the shop, a man who needed to know about Jesus. In fact, this may have been the primary reason for my being there at that particular time and place. God is Sovereign! He never wastes circumstances—He permits them...He engineers them...He uses them all. Although my travel had been delayed, God used even that for my good. It had been raining most of the morning, but by the time the van was ready, the sun was shining, and the road crews had cleared away the mud slides in the mountains, and I drove through with ease, and without delay to the inland highway. Truly, there is none like our God—exalted in majesty, yet merciful, loving, caring for, and supplying every need even for one of the least of His children. Isn't HE wonderful!

It seems that limited funds have always been a problem in this ministry, but God never fails to make a way for all that He calls us to do. There have been many times we did not have money for airline tickets. The first opportunity I had for ministry in Australia was one of those times. In fact, Australia had been on my mind for two years when, one day, our pastor announced that a team from our church would be going to Australia in partnership missions, and any who would like to go could participate. My heart said, "Yes, Yes, Yes!" But, my mind said, "How?" Whoever wanted to be a part of the Australia mission team would be required to pay their own way, and it would cost $1800 per person. I had nothing—zero dollars!

The more I thought and prayed about this mission, the more I felt impressed to go—yet there were so many questions: Don could not go because of his job situation—was it all right for me to go without him? And what about the money? Was this all my idea, or was it really God's will? Was I once again trying to do God's will my way? And what if God said no—could I thank Him for a "no" as well as a "yes"? How could I find the answers? The only answer I could find was to pray and…wait. I love to pray, but I hate to wait! Yet, waiting is so often God's way. That same Scripture kept coming back to me: *"Wait on the Lord; be of good courage, and He shall strengthen thine heart; wait, I say, on the Lord." (Psalm 27:14)*

> *I love to pray, but I hate to wait! Yet, waiting is so often God's way*

So, I waited…and waited…and waited…and nothing happened! I was just about ready to give up—only one day left to make the initial deposit and confirm; otherwise, the decision would be made automatically—I would **not** be going to Australia with the team.

Now, it was the **last** day to say yes—in fact, it was later than that—just two hours from the deadline! And I still didn't have the deposit of $600! But, I couldn't get Australia off my mind. If I just knew for sure that God would have me go, then I could believe Him to provide the deposit, even though it had to be within two hours. I asked Don what he thought, and because he was going through a time of employment uncertainty and discouragement, his response was, "Honey, all I can see right now is dollar signs hitting me over the head! I can't tell you what to do—you'll have to do what you feel God tells you to do. I'll pray for you, and support you whatever way He leads."

There was no question about it—what I really needed was a word from God! As I prayed earnestly for that word—for direction and wisdom, there came to my mind a possible source for the deposit, but at the same time came the question, "What if the rest of the money doesn't come in?" The entire balance—**all** the money would have to turned in within 30 days of the deposit. I wasn't quite sure—was God saying, "Yes, just trust me," or was I trying to **make** it happen? Faith or presumption— which was it?

In desperation, I asked God to speak to me from His Word. Rather than go to a familiar passage of Scripture, I felt strangely compelled to continue in 2 Chronicles where I had been reading for several days. As I began in the 25th chapter, these words seemed to leap off the page and land right in my heart: *"…The Lord is able to give thee much more than this." (2 Chronicles 25:9)*

My answer! I just knew it. Though these words were directed to King Amaziah long ago (at a time when he was obviously worried about money), I knew God was speaking the same word, right now, to me. Not only would He provide the deposit I needed, but everything else as well.

I could, and would trust everything to my loving Father. Words cannot express all my feelings just then. My soul was singing in praise and thanksgiving, excitement and anticipation, joy, and delight…and peace!

There is no feeling like **knowing** God's will! Within those last two hours God did supply the $600 down-payment, and the full assurance that I was to be a part of that mission to Australia, and it was one of the most special and precious times in my life and ministry. At this writing, God is still bringing forth fruit from that mission to Australia.

There have been other like challenges during the course of this ministry. One of those times I was uncertain whether God would have me accept an invitation to go to Poland with the

Tom Popelka evangelistic team. Once again, the strong desire was there, but not the funds. At last I gave up trying to figure it out—I "cast all my cares" on Him, and believed Him to show me His will.

*"Trust in the Lord and do good; so shalt thou dwell in the land, and verily thou shalt be fed. **Delight thyself also in the Lord; and He shall give thee the desires of thine heart.** Commit thy way unto the Lord; trust also in Him; and He shall bring it to pass."* (Psalm 37:3-5)

Talk about flight provision! When this scripture says He will give us the desires of our heart—the meaning is greater than we realize. While it does mean that He will give me what I want, first and foremost it means that when I delight in Him, He will put the right desire (His) in my heart and then grant that desire to me. Awesome, isn't it!

As I prayed, surrendering all to Him, acknowledging that I would be OK to go or not to go, and giving Him thanks for whichever way He wanted me to go, the burden was lifted. Again, I asked God to speak to me from His Word, and again, He led me to that same Scripture in 2 Chronicles 25:9, assuring me that not only was He able to supply **much more** than I needed, but that it was His will for me to be a part of that particular team, at that particular time, for evangelism in Poland—the very crusade we spoke of in Chapter five of this book. I repeat, there is no feeling like **knowing** God's will!

The ministry continues to be challenging, and even more so as I get older, but God continues to supply every need regardless of the size or kind. Whatever stage of life we are in, the only way to face these issues, **always**, is give our needs to Him—lay them **all** at His feet, daily, and ask Him to take total control. Our loving Heavenly Father will **always** meet **all** of our needs.

He never promised to supply "all our greeds," however, so it is incredibly important that we earnestly examine our motives and desires to know whether they are His, ours, or one and the same.

Sometimes God uses **angels** to supply our needs. You may say what you will, but I know for a fact that it is true—there are times that He does send His angels to minister to us. Because of the nature of my husband's employment, there have been many times he could not accompany me in ministry and travel. There are probably more times that angels have been dispatched for my aid than I can imagine, but I do know about two distinct occasions.

> *It is incredibly important that we earnestly examine our motives and desires to know whether they are His, ours, or one and the same*

One such occasion was during the European concert tour, at the time of the worldwide transportation strikes mentioned earlier. I was scheduled to fly from Germany to Norway for ministry at the Oslo Air Force Station and the American Lutheran Church in Oslo. The chaplain from the Air Force station met me at the airport and we proceeded to his car, loaded my luggage, and everything was going fine, except…the car would not start.

We looked up and there, all of a sudden, a man was standing beside the car, asking the chaplain if he needed help. The man was of dark complexion, perhaps of a Middle East nationality. He was dressed casually, and **he was holding tools in his hands!** Instantly I thought this might be a set-up of some kind.

The chaplain opened the hood of the car, and the stranger fiddled around for a bit under the hood, and then asked the chaplain to try to start the car. The car started on the first try! I still did not trust the stranger completely, thinking that now he might want an outrageous sum of money or something. The chaplain politely thanked the stranger and asked, "How much do I owe you?" The stranger refused to take any money at all. As we drove away, the man was standing on a street corner, but even as I watched, suddenly he was no longer there. An angel? I think so.

Some eight years later, I was driving in Kansas on an interstate highway near Topeka. I wasn't sure about which exit to take and wondered if I had already missed it, so I pulled over to the shoulder of the highway so I could look at my map. The highway was fairly straight at that point, and I could see for quite a distance—there were no cars in sight behind me, so I thought it would be all right to stop for a few moments. As I reached for my map, I glanced in the rearview mirror, and to my complete surprise, pulling up behind me was the most beautiful, sparkling white patrol car I have ever seen in my life.

An officer was getting out of the car and heading my way. Never in my life have I seen an officer like that one—his uniform was perfectly fit with just the right creases—his whole grooming was absolutely stunning! He walked up to the van, and I rolled down the window—I hadn't done anything wrong, so I didn't know why he was there. The officer asked if there was a problem, and I told him that I had stopped to look at the map because I was unsure of the exit I needed to take to get to a particular area of Topeka. He told me that it was the very next exit, and warned me that this was a dangerous place to stop, that I should move on immediately. I thanked him and moved on. I looked back, and he and the patrol car were gone! I did take the next exit and had no trouble finding the way to my destination.

Neither of these situations were desperate, but in both cases there was a need, and I believe God sent his angels to do his bidding—to meet those particular needs. God can choose any number of ways to supply our needs—it doesn't have to be through angels, but it certainly can be.

"Are they (angels) *not all ministering spirits, sent forth to minister for them who shall be heirs of salvation?"* (Hebrews 2:14)

"And He (Jesus) *was there in the wilderness forty days, tempted of Satan; and was with the wild beasts; and the angels ministered unto Him."* (Mark 1:13)

"And there appeared an angel unto Him from heaven, strengthening Him." (Luke 22:43)

I believe God delights in surprising us. And I believe His Word—He promised to supply **all** our needs, and He can do it any way He chooses!

Not so incidentally, even the conjunctive names of God reveal not only His attributes, but also give assurance of His perfect provision for **everything** we could ever need. Some years ago in a Texas Bible Conference, Jack Taylor preached a wonderful message on this very subject, explaining the meaning of those precious names of our great God. As I was driving home from the conference, thinking about the wonderful truths in that message, God gave me a song. I had to find a place to pull over and stop so I could write down the words. This is the song of assurance He gave:

Jehovah My All [7]

Jehovah-Jireh, Provider, my Sufficiency, my Source.
Jehovah-Rophe, my Healer, my Physician, my Health.
Jehovah-Nissi, my Victory, God of all power and might,
Jehovah-M'Kaddesh, my Holiness, my Sanctity, my Light!

Jehovah-Raah, my Shepherd,
Jehovah-Shalom, my Peace,
Jehovah-Shammah, Omnipresent,
Jehovah-Tsidkenu, my Righteousness.
Lord God Almighty, Jehovah, my ALL!

HE IS:
    El Elyon—Most High God!
    El Shaddai—All-sufficient One!
    Elohim—Great Creator!
    Adonai—Lord and Master!
    El Roi—The God Who sees!
    He is Lord God Almighty,
    Jehovah—my All!

"Blessed be the Lord, who daily loadeth us with benefits, even the God of our salvation. Selah." (Psalm 68:19)
"Bless the Lord, O my soul, and all that is within me, bless his

holy name. Bless the Lord, O my soul, and forget not all his benefits: Who forgiveth all thine iniquities; Who healeth all thy diseases; Who redeemeth thy life from destruction; Who crowneth thee with lovingkindness and tender mercies; Who satisfieth thy mouth with good things; so that thy youth is renewed like the eagle's." (Psalm 103:1-5)

Chapter 10
Flight Priorities

The Call of God

God calls us to come

If we would achieve successful "flight," we must first answer the call of God to come to Him. He calls us to come for peace, comfort, joy, direction, instruction, strength—for everything we need, and when we do come we get all this and more. But we don't usually get these things in a hurry. Indeed, we often miss some of God's best blessings because we don't take the time to come aside with Him. Dr. Vance Havner used to say that if we don't come apart with Jesus, then we'll just plain come apart!

We live in such a fast and busy world, and sometimes get so caught up in that hasty kind of life, that we forget how to really live. And if we are not really living the "butterfly life," it is difficult to help anyone else learn to live it. If that's where you are right now, or if that's where you're headed, slow down—in fact, stop—and spend some time alone with Jesus and listen.

Not only will He give you sure direction for your life and ministry, but He will also prepare you for all that He has planned for you. And, just in case you grow weary in "flight," remember, with arms open wide He calls you to come unto Him. He follows that call with His promise: *"Come unto me, all ye that labor and are heavy laden, and I will give you rest."* *(Matthew 11:28)*

In his wonderful devotional book, *My Utmost for His Highest*, Oswald Chambers has given some great insight into this promise of rest. Here is just a portion of what he said:

> Have you ever come to Jesus? Watch the stubbornness of your heart, you will do anything rather than the one simple childlike thing—"Come unto Me."…At the most unexpected moments there is the whisper of the Lord— "Come unto Me," and you are drawn immediately. Personal contact with Jesus alters everything…The attitude of coming is that the will resolutely lets go of everything and deliberately commits all to Him. "…and I will give you rest," i.e., I will stay you. Not—I will put you to bed and hold your hand and sing you to sleep; but—I will get you out of bed, out of the languor and exhaustion, out of the state of being half dead while you are alive; I will imbue you with the spirit of life, and you will be stayed by the perfection of vital activity.

When we learn to come to Jesus all the time, the most wonderful thing happens—not only do we experience extreme joy, pleasure and satisfaction, but He shows us the best direction—His path.

"Thou wilt show me the path of life; in Thy presence is fullness of joy; at Thy right hand there are pleasures for evermore." *(Psalm 16:11)*

God Calls Us to Flight

The butterfly obeys the call to flight by God-given instinct. That is the new nature of this little creature—it cannot help but fly! With brand new wings, this new creature is not only capable and ready, but obedient to fly—just what God designed the butterfly to do!

In a sense, we are like the butterfly. At the very moment that we are born into the family of God by receiving Jesus Christ as our Savior, God miraculously transforms us into a new creation, giving us a new nature and spiritual wings! *"Therefore if any man be in Christ, he is a new creature: Old things are passed away; behold, all things are become new."* (2 Corinthians 5:17)

As already mentioned in a previous chapter, however, we have something the butterfly does not have—choice! The butterfly obeys the call to flight by instinct. The child of God obeys, or fails to obey, by choice, and that is in God's design for humanity. He could have made us to be robots, so that at the right moment in time He could push the right button, and we would do exactly as He directed. But God gave us choice. He will never force us to obey, even though the consequences of our disobedience may be devastating. It is true that He will sometimes bring pressure into our lives to "encourage" us to make the right choices. Still, we can (and sometimes do) choose not to obey.

God the Holy Spirit indwells every believer in Christ. It is God the Holy Spirit who gives us the ability and freedom to "fly." Of course, it would be absurd to think that God is calling us to flap our arms and literally fly. Obviously, God's call to "flight" for His children is His call to the way of life that places total trust in Him. The more we rely upon God, the more He produces in the life of the believer the fruit of His Spirit: love, joy, peace, long-suffering, gentleness, goodness, faith, meekness, self-control (see Galatians 5:22-23). The result for the child of God is a free and "abundant" life! This is not a "care-free," undisciplined life—it is rather a "casting our care on Him," a "yielded, obedient to Him" life.

There is something in the nature of the butterfly that must answer the call to fly, as well as to find just the right flowers, and to migrate at just the right time. There is something in all of nature that must respond to the call that complements its specific design. Probably everybody has read or heard the story of the ugly duckling that really didn't know his true identity until one day that urge within was so compelling that he could not help but join the swans. To his great surprise, the ugly duckling discovered that he was not a duck at all, but was truly a beautiful swan.

You may have also heard the story of the young wild goose that joined a bunch of turkeys on the ground below, just to see what it was like. He continued to hang around with them, and before long he began to act just like them. Soon he no longer took flight up high in the heavens. From time to time flocks of geese would fly far above, and something inside that young goose made him want to join them, but he felt sure he could never fly like that—he had been too long with the turkeys on the ground.

One day a large flock of geese flew by, honking loudly, and something began to happen within the heart of that wild goose on the ground. Suddenly, he had an overwhelming desire to mount up and join those geese and their chorus. But he was afraid—it had been so long—would his wings even work? The flock of geese way up in the air would soon be out of sight. It had to be now! With all his might, the young goose began to flap his wings, and slowly began to rise, and then he mounted up into the air, and soon was united with the flock of geese in the sky. At last, the once "earth-bound" goose knew who he really was and where he was really meant to be.

The moral of that story is, of course, that if you live with turkeys you will behave like them and cannot experience the joy of being who you were created to be. The wild goose **did not become** a turkey—he just acted like one. Even though you and I have been born into God's family and are new creatures in Christ, sadly we sometimes choose to live like turkeys…or caterpillars…when we could be, and ought to be, enjoying our new life in Christ. Now that God the Holy Spirit lives within us, there is His continual call, and the strong compelling desire within us to answer His call to "come up higher."

> *If God has given you some special work to do that frightens you, it's your responsibility to jump at it. It's up to the Lord to see you through.*
>
> *-Dr. R. W. DeHaan*

When God calls you to come, calls you to flight, don't be afraid. Dr. R. W. DeHaan has well said: "If God has given you some special work to do that frightens you, it's your responsibility to jump at it. It's up to the Lord to see you through. As you faithfully do your part, He will do His part." That's it—jump at it!

"…arise, go over this Jordan, thou, and all this people, unto the land which I do give to them, even to the children of Israel…I will not fail thee nor forsake thee…Have not I commanded thee? Be strong and of a good courage; be not afraid, neither be thou dismayed; for the Lord thy God is with thee whithersoever thou goest." (Joshua 1:2,5,9)

If we are available and listening we can hear God's call, and we can respond as Isaiah did: *"Here am I, send me."* *(Isaiah 6:8)*

Why is it that, even though we hear God's call, we sometimes do not obey? Perhaps the greatest reason is fear. Though it should not be the case, one of the hardest things for a believer to do is to continually surrender to our Heavenly Father. It seems kind of scary to give Him free reign. We should be praying, "Father, here I am—I give everything back to You—everything I am, everything I have, everything I can become, and everything I can obtain. Please take absolute control of my entire being— mind, body, soul and spirit." That is the kind of prayer that God will always answer—but that means asking God to do whatever He wants in my life and being...**without my instruction or supervision.**

For a long time I was afraid to pray that prayer—until the night I finally came to the end of "me." God had to bring me to the place of sheer desperation so that I would finally be willing to yield completely to Him—no matter what His will turned out to be.

I had been afraid to give God total control because of the "what-ifs." Like, what if God makes me give up something I want to keep? Or what if He makes me go where I don't want to go? It was kind of like that goose/turkey situation—something inside wanted to respond to the call of God (really, it was not some thing, but some One—the Holy Spirit). But, I was fearful. Secretly I was afraid He might send me to Africa where I would die in poverty as a missionary.

To my utter surprise, when at last I came to the place of real surrender so that He could do whatever He wanted with my life, He began to change my thinking and my life. A funny thing happened—a strange desire began to grow within me—a longing in my heart to go to Africa to share the gospel. That desire continued to grow stronger as time went by, but I wasn't sure whether I was just dreaming about it or if it was a genuine call from the Father. The only thing I knew to do was to give that desire to God and ask Him to show me what to do. I prayed that if this was not His idea He would take that longing away, but if it truly was His desire that He would keep it before me and bring it to pass.

As I prayed, the desire for ministry in Africa not only remained in my thoughts and my heart, but continued to increase in intensity. Where once I feared God would send me to Africa, now I really **wanted** to go. I prayed for such an opportunity for two years, and God granted that desire of my heart.

When we give Him everything, sometimes our deepest fears are the very arenas of God's blessings! But this is only discovered by faith—by yielding completely to God and trusting His wisdom, direction and provision. Our Heavenly Father is absolutely faithful. He is perfect and righteous in all His ways. I am finding that when I truly surrender to God, then I am in the **center** of His will, and there is absolutely no better place to be, no matter **where** in the world that is! I have tried the "edges of His will," and didn't find it very satisfying. Now I know that in the center of His will is the "flight" of my life!

The Edges of His Will

I searched for one to love me,
Hold and cover me with care,
Looked for one to fill my longings,
Seeking, finding no one there.

But there was One Who was waiting
While I searched so desperately
For acceptance and approval,
Looking for a "place for me."

All along there was One waiting,
Wanting all my needs to fill.
It was Jesus—He was waiting
Just for me to choose His will.

So long I lived around the edges,
Walking there so foolishly,
Till I heard the voice of Jesus
Calling softly, "Come to me."

"Come to me," He whispers gently,
"Come to me.
I will fill your every longing,
If you'll only come to me.

If by faith you'll leave the edges
For the center of My will,
Yield each day to me completely,
All your being I will fill.

Don't be content with just the edges
When my best I offer you.
Choose the center of My will—
What I promise I will do."

Joyful life to us He offers—
Every longing He'll fulfill.
He only waits for us to choose
The very center of His will.

God Commissions us to Flight

Although God sends all butterflies to flowers, He does not send all butterflies to the same kind of flower. Different species may enjoy the same or a variety of flowers, but each butterfly instinctively, in obedience to God's individual design, goes to exactly the right flower! And as he goes where God sends him, the little butterfly is itself nourished, and at the same time naturally pollinates the flowers to which he goes, ultimately bringing more flowers to life.

God not only calls His children to flight, but He also commissions us as well—He has reasons for us to fly. He puts His Spirit within us so that we can know Him and make Him known to others. Someone has said it like this:

Jesus Christ gave His life for us,
In order that He might give His life to us,
So that He might live His life through us!

The child of God is commissioned (sent) by God that He might, through us, offer life to others. And, God uses all kinds of situations to do just that. He never wastes circumstances! Sometimes when God sends us, we don't initially have a clue about what we are on the way to do. Several years ago, there was just such an occasion in my life. I was experiencing symptoms that specifically pointed to heart problems, and after failing a stress test, it was decided that I should have a heart catherization procedure.

When I asked God for a word from Him, I expected more than just one—I thought it would at least be a sentence! God literally gave me one word, but in that word He spoke volumes!

This has become a rather commonplace procedure these days, but it is still a little scary—especially when you read of all the possible side-effects and problems, such as... "death"!

The day for the catherization procedure arrived, and I was ready to go to the hospital. As I prayed and read the Scriptures, I knew I was in God's hands, but the thought occurred to me that none of us have any guarantees about the length of our lives on this earth. I was not expecting to die that day, but still I realized that things go wrong sometimes—this could possibly be my last day on earth. Either way I would be OK. If I died I would go to heaven forever, otherwise there was still a lot for me to do on Earth. I just wanted to hear from God, so I asked Him to speak to me, to give me a word—would I live or die? Sometimes God speaks to me through Scripture, sometimes through my husband and family, and sometimes He just speaks to my mind. I listened for His voice as I read my Bible, and the Scripture was good, but the special word I had asked for was not there.

I really thought that God would speak, but it was time to leave for the hospital, and His message had not come. As I gathered my things and started to walk out of the room, my eyes were drawn to a calendar by the door. As I focused on the date, April 24, there was **one word** printed on that square—the word was **"Passover."** When I asked God for a word from Him, I expected more than just one—I thought it would at least be a sentence! God literally gave me one word, but in that word He spoke volumes!

The account of the first "Passover" has been recorded in the twelfth chapter of Exodus. If you have read that chapter, then you know what "Passover" is and what it meant to the Israelites. When God spoke "Passover" to my heart, I knew He was telling me that:

- Just as the death angel passed over all those who had the blood of the sacrificed lamb on the sides and at the top of the door posts of their dwelling places, and death did not enter those homes, and;

- Just as the blood of Jesus has been placed over the doorpost of my heart (and all who have received Him as Savior and Lord), and I have been passed from death unto life, eternally;

- God would pass over me at that time—I would not die physically that day!

What an awesome word! I got the message, and it filled me with unbelievable joy! Most people do live through heart catherization procedures, but there are risk factors. Now I knew

God would bring me through just fine. I couldn't help rejoicing all the way to the hospital. Since I had to be awake throughout the procedure, I hardly stopped talking—I shared the gospel with everyone who would listen. When the test was completed, the doctor said my heart was "perfect!" I honestly think God healed me the moment He spoke the "Passover" word to me.

But the story doesn't end there. I was required to lie flat and still for eight hours after the catherization procedure, so, obviously, once they put me in a room, I wouldn't be going anywhere for a while. In the bed next to mine there was a lady named Velma. I wanted to meet her, but since I could not get up and go to her, she came to me, and we began to talk. I told her about asking God for a word that morning, and the wonderful word He had given me. I also told her that if God had said He was taking me to heaven it would have been OK with me—I could find great joy in that, but I was glad He had given me a little longer on Earth since there must be some unfinished business here for me.

About that time a nurse came into the room. She scolded Velma and told her to get into her bed and lie down. It was then I learned that Velma's heart was 95% blocked and she was not supposed to be up at all. She went back and got into her bed, but we continued to talk. With such a serious heart condition, Velma was in great danger. I asked her that supposing she never made it out of the hospital alive, did she know for certain that she had eternal life and that she would go to heaven when she died. Although she had attended church since she was a little girl, she wasn't sure if she would go to heaven and was really eager to hear how she could know for certain.

I carefully explained that we are all sinners, and that the Bible says the wages of sin is death (eternal separation from God), but the gift of God is eternal life through Jesus Christ our Lord. If she believed Jesus was the Son of God and that he died on the cross for her sin, was buried, rose again, and lives today, He would forgive her and give her new life if she would ask Him and personally receive Him as her Savior. I reminded her that *"God so loved the world* (that's us) *that He gave His only begotten Son* (Jesus) *that whosoever believeth in Him should not perish, but have everlasting life." (John 3:16)* It was just at this point that a nurse came to move Velma to another room. She begged the nurse to give her just ten more minutes. Reluctantly, the nurse agreed and left the room.

I continued by telling Velma she only had to pray—to ask Jesus to forgive her, and He would. Then if she would open the door of her life and invite Him to come in, He would do that, and when she received Him into her life she would, in that moment, be born into God's family. I asked if she had ever prayed a prayer like that, and she said she had not. When I asked if she would like to pray right then, she said, "Yes, I would." She bowed her head and in the simplest way acknowledged that she was a sinner, asked Jesus to forgive her, and placed her trust in Him as her personal Savior. She opened the door of her heart and asked Jesus to come in. She received Him, and was born into God's family—and became a new creation in Him. At that very moment the nurse returned and whisked Velma off to another room. I have never heard from her again, but I surely do expect to see her in Heaven!

God calls us to come, calls us to flight, then commissions us to go! Go ye...Go tell!

After His resurrection, and before He ascended back to the Father, Jesus commissioned his disciples, saying *"All power is given unto Me in heaven and in earth. Go ye therefore, and teach all nations, baptizing them in the name of the Father, and of the Son, and of the Holy Ghost: Teaching them to observe all things whatsoever I have commanded you; and lo, I am with you always, even unto the end of the world. Amen." (Matthew 28:18-20)*

According to Dr. W. A. Criswell in his commentary note on the above scripture, "The commission of Jesus was to the whole church in every age. The imperative word in the commission is 'teach all nations,' more literally rendered as 'make disciples.' However, the baptizing and teaching ministries have the force of a mandate because they follow logically the imperative 'make disciples.'"

> *God calls us to flight— commissions us, CO-missions us, we never have to go alone!*

It is God's will that none should perish, so He sends His children to shine His light in a dark world, so that the lost can see how to come to Him:

"But if our gospel be hid, it is hid to them that are lost; In whom the god of this world hath blinded the minds of them which believe not, lest the light of the glorious gospel of Christ, who is the image of God, should shine unto them." (2 Corinthians 4:3-4)

Jesus said, *"I am the light of the World: he that followeth me shall not walk in darkness, but shall have the light of life." (John 8:12)* Jesus also said, *"Ye are the light of the world..." (Matthew 5:14).* How can that be? How can Jesus say HE is the light, and also say that we are the light? The answer, of course, is found in Colossians 1:27, *"...Christ in you, the hope of glory."* Jesus Christ, who IS the light of the world, indwells every believer in the person of God the Holy Spirit, but He, the Light, only shines through as we allow Him to be in total control.

God calls us to flight—commissions us, CO-missions us (we never have to go alone). As we go where He leads and in the power of His Spirit, His light shines through us, bringing life and light to others. God may not let us know all the details of our "flight plan," but our responsibility is to come to Him, trust and obey Him, and leave all the results with Him. And His results are awesome!

We do live in a dark world! This was so obvious when I was in Japan for ministry. At one point I visited one of the gardens where there were many idols—gods of the Japanese people. I noticed with interest that on one of idols someone had placed a bib (yes, a bib like a baby uses), and there was food set in front of the idol (as if a piece of stone could eat). *"If therefore the light that is in thee be darkness, how great is that darkness."* (Matthew 6:23)

"Let your light so shine before men, that they may see your good works, and glorify your Father which is in heaven." (Matthew 5:16)

The Light of Jesus

Blinded minds begin to see
And night turns into day
As the Light of Jesus shines—
The Life, the Truth, the Way!

There have been many times in the course of this ministry that we have witnessed the miracle of darkened hearts becoming light. When God called me to go on mission to China, I was caught by surprise during a phone conversation with a close friend, Pam. She had just received an opportunity to go with a mission group to China, but it would cost $2000, and she had to have $1048 of that amount for airfare within five days! She asked me to pray for a miracle for these funds, so I prayed with her right then. Personally, I had never had the slightest desire to go to China, but while praying, God seemed to be speaking to me—that I should go to China on that same mission trip. (Now, this would require another miracle, or three: one, that the missionaries would agree to adding one more to the team; two, that the travel agency could even get me booked on the same flights with the team; and three—I would need a financial miracle as well.)

Was God truly speaking to me? Was this His desire, or mine, or one and the same? It is not a good thing to be outside of His will, especially in China! That night as Don and I prayed together, we asked God to show us what He wanted. We specifically asked that He would give us His answer through the team leader on the following day. The next day, the team leader called, and the answer was, "yes!" Yes, I could go—there was room for me on the team, and yes they could still get booking for me on the same flights as the rest of the team—two miracles at once!

Now for the next miracle—the financial one. That night, as Don and I prayed together again, we asked God to supply the necessary $2000, and particularly the $1048 for airfare that was needed immediately—in three days. And, **Praise the Lord!** The next morning (Friday) He placed the airfare in my hands! Late that same morning, the team leader called saying that the travel agency needed the money **that very day** instead of Monday. The money was already in my hands—God's provision is **perfect!** Not so incidentally, on the same day God provided the funds for me, He had also already provided airfare for Pam. And He supplied all the rest of the money, when it was needed, for both of us to go to China.

Neither time nor space will permit a detailed account of this mission, and names have been changed to protect real identities, since there is still much persecution of Christians in that part of the world. The night we arrived in China I met and visited personally with two special young university students, Allison and Leslie. They spoke English fairly well, so we were able to communicate, and we agreed to get together as their school schedule would permit. Later in the week I called both girls and we agreed to meet downtown.

In the early mornings our team walked in the park, meeting people and sharing the good news at every opportunity, including singing my song, "Butterfly Life in a Caterpillar World," which is the gospel in a nutshell (or should I say a cocoon)? One morning, Wendy (one of our team members) came my way along with two Chinese girls who wanted to become believers. We prayed together right there on the spot, and both girls received Jesus Christ as their Savior.

The same afternoon, I met Allison (mentioned above) downtown, and after we shopped for a short time, she returned with me to my hotel room. Pam was there too, and as we visited together, Allison began to make some revealing comments that indicated she was close to being a believer but not really there yet, so we began to ask questions. While I was explaining how to be born into God's family, Pam was silently praying. Later we discovered that, at the very same time, Celia, another of our team, was in her hotel room, on her knees in fervent prayer, and she didn't even know for whom, but God had called her to prayer, and as she and Pam were praying, God was working in Allison's heart and life.

I asked Allison if she had ever prayed to God, acknowledging that she was a sinner, confessing that Jesus Christ died for her sins, was buried, rose again and lives today. Had she ever asked Him to forgive her and come into her life—had she opened the door of her life and invited Him in, and received Him? She had not. The good and glorious news is that, right then and right there in the hotel room, she did pray and receive Jesus Christ as her Savior and Lord. At that moment Allison was born into the family of the living God! I will always remember what she said: "I was just waiting for the chance!"

The very next day, Allison was baptized. She said it was the most wonderful day of her life! How we rejoiced! I honestly believe that Allison is the main reason God sent me to China.

One evening in the same city I met another young woman. She didn't have an English name, but wanted one, so I gave her mine. She said she knew about Jesus, and her boyfriend was a believer, but she had not made that commitment for herself yet—she wanted to wait.

To my surprise, the next evening, Betty came to my hotel room, saying she was **ready** to become a believer, and then and there, she prayed to receive Jesus Christ. Hallelujah! What a Savior!

Our teams visited in several university classrooms, where I had the joy of sharing my "Butterfly Life..." song, and this led quite naturally to an explanation of the new kind of life found in Christ.

My friend, John, often followed up with a gift for each student, a commemorative coin (the new Texas quarter), further opening the door to explain about new life in Christ—the "gift of God"—"*For by grace are ye saved through faith; and that not of yourselves; it is the gift of God.*" *(Ephesians 2:8)* A gift can be offered all day long, but it isn't yours until you receive it. We are saved only by **receiving** God's gift, the Lord Jesus Christ.

Another day as we were prayer-walking in a cultural park, I stopped to rest awhile. As I sat praying silently, a young Chinese man two seats away suddenly spoke to me. "Hello!" he said. "Oh, you speak English," I responded, and a conversation began. When our team leader, Kevin, walked by, I called out to him, "I would like for you to meet someone." In a few moments, I introduced him to Chet. As they visited together, others of our team and I prayed. Though Chet did not make a decision at that time, I cannot help but believe that this was a divine appointment. Many are praying for him, and we believe that Chet will come to know Jesus Christ, the true and living God, as His Savior and Lord.

> *I am brought to tears to think that you, a grandma, would leave your home and family and everything and come to China for me!*

On the night Allison was born into the family of God, she said something I will never forget: "I am brought to tears to think that you, a grandma, would leave your home and family and everything and come to China for **me**!" Yes, it was a sacrifice—it was very hard physically, but there is ONE who made a far greater sacrifice—JESUS CHRIST, the Son of God! He left His Father and all the glories of Heaven, stepped down into this world, took on human flesh, lived a sinless life, then suffered and died on the cross—for **me**—for **you**—and for **whosoever** will call upon His name. JESUS made the ultimate sacrifice! And because He arose from the dead and lives today, He has promised that we shall live also! (John 14:19)

Over the years there have been many other times that God has said, "go," and wherever that was, even in the smallest places, He has given His light. One small place was Scotland, Arkansas—the little town where I was first born. Early in this ministry a desire began to grow within me to go back there, and it wasn't long before God opened the door for me to sing and share at the Scotland Baptist Church.

On arrival in Scotland, I drove to the little town square and then visited the general store. There I met an 88-year-old man— he was the only one old enough to have known my family back at the time of my birth. As we visited, I was surprised that the old man did not know Jesus, and I shared the gospel with him. My heart was broken when he did not respond to my invitation to come to Jesus. There was nothing I could do—I could not make him open his heart—he would have to do that for himself.

My heart was heavy as I left the store, but when I walked outside, who should come driving up but my Sunday School teacher, Helen Cade! By a strange "coincidence" she had come from San Antonio to that same little town in Arkansas to visit some of her family. When I introduced Helen to the old man she also shared the gospel of Jesus with him, and with that second chance He said "yes," and received Jesus Christ as his Savior. I don't know all of God's purposes for sending me (and Helen) to Scotland, Arkansas, but I do know that a great big part of His plan was to reach that 88-year-old man before it was forever too late.

One Sunday in San Antonio, I sang and spoke at the Little Church at La Villita downtown. A dear little Spanish lady came to me after the service and through an interpreter, told me that even though I sang and spoke in English, she heard it in Spanish! I don't know how God did that, but once again, He calls us to be faithful to do what He directs us to do, and He will miraculously shine through us according to His will.

During my first ministry tour to Japan, there were many opportunities to share the gospel, not only on the mainland but also on the island of Okinawa. The presentation I gave in the Sunday morning service at Kanto Plains Baptist Church in Tokyo was in English, but thanks be to God, there was a fine young man who translated everything into the Japanese language, and by way of special headphones, English and Japanese were heard simultaneously. What a special service! Some said, "You don't know how much I needed this!" God knew! He touched many hearts and lives in Japan, and also blessed me with new friends and Christian family everywhere he sent me.

When I arrived at the Naha, Okinawa airport, the first person I met was Eiko Shima Bukuro. She was sent to find me there. This lovely Okinawan lady was not only very helpful, but she became very precious to me. She spoke to me in English, "Sister Betty Moni?" Then she introduced herself and took me to meet Chaplain Matsumoto and the others who were waiting for me.

One of the scheduled ministry stops was at Kadena Air Base, and God's timing was incredible! Unbeknown to us when the trip was planned, there was to be a major inspection and a military exercise, each requiring 12-hour shifts for military personnel, during the same period of time I was to be in Okinawa. Nothing ever surprises or flusters God! The inspection finished the day before I arrived, and the military exercise began the day before I left. Isn't it amazing? God set this ministry visit right smack in between those two critical times—not a day too soon nor a day too late.

While in Okinawa there were opportunities of ministry in local churches as well as in the military arena, and God continued to bless in many ways. For most of the local ministries, my witness in song and testimony had to be translated, and Eiko was right there beside me to interpret. What a blessing! And, it was a special blessing to be in her church, Miyazato Linjin Kyokai. I will always remember the prayer of one youth, "I thank you Lord that you are not a scary God." Probably one of the most humbling experiences I've ever known was listening as a young Japanese woman prayed, with Eiko-san translating softly to me at the same time. As her words reached my ears and my heart, I could not hold back the tears, "Thank you God for Betty Moni; she teach us so many things—she teach us to pray..." To God be the glory—how I thank Him for what HE has done!

A number of years later, during another ministry tour to Japan, I was invited by the Atsugi Naval Base Chapel to present a "Butterfly Life in a Caterpillar World" women's retreat at Ashigara. At the close of the retreat, a precious young Japanese woman wrote this note to me: "I was so much blessed in Atsugi Airbase Women's Retreat where you ministered (to) us. I was the lady who had bad nightmares. God kept His promise like He said in the Bible. He saved me. Now Jesus is my Savior and is in me. Your songs are always, each time I listen, (a) blessing to me. Thank you so much again." Our loving and merciful God had completely released that precious woman—only HE can really set us free! Praise be to our great God for what HE has done!

Overseas ministry has always been a challenge, and as mentioned before, for many years because of my husband's job, he could not accompany me. I have often been asked "Did you come all by yourself?" I always found great pleasure in answering "Oh no, God is with me!" Almost invariably the next question would be something like, "Oh yes, I know, but I mean don't you have anyone else, a human being...?" And, my response was always "The God of all the universe, the One who made everything is with me—do I need anyone else? And, of course they had to admit, "Well, no, I guess not!"

One particular American lady that I met at an airport in Germany was using her vacation to visit Europe, but she was extremely fearful of traveling "alone," especially when faced with delays and changes. She even wrote me a letter when she returned to America, telling me of her fears, and how she remembered my testimony about not being alone because God is always with me, and she exclaimed, "If Betty Moni can do it, so can I!" What she meant was that **anybody** who chooses to can completely trust the God who will never leave us or forsake us. We can do whatever He tells us to do and go wherever He sends us without fear.

When I wanted to take a trip to Georgia to see our beautiful newborn grandson, Daniel, God turned it into a ministry tour, with that little personal visit on the side. There was a full schedule except for one Sunday. I felt certain there should be some ministry opportunity somewhere close for that day, but no doors were opening, and I didn't have a clue where God wanted me to be. On impulse, I stopped at a Christian book store in the area. I asked if they could recommend a church I might contact, and they gave me a couple of names. One of those churches extended the invitation to be with them in ministry for that Sunday, and they welcomed me with open arms.

After that Sunday service, several people told me that God had spoken to them specifically, and one in particular said,

"Thank you so much for coming—you answered six things in my life tonight. God sent you here for me!" Though she did not tell me the questions for which she been seeking answers, God knew both the questions and the answers, and used that service to respond to everything that was troubling her. I believe that lady is the reason God closed all other doors of opportunity and waited until the "last minute" to show me where He wanted me to be for that open Sunday—so that I would be in the right place at the right time for the right plan.

When God sent me to Fort Wainwright, Alaska, in ministry, a special lady named Rose came to me after the service with tears in her eyes. She, too, said, "God sent you here for me." The same thing has happened all over the world. While I don't get to hear about all that He does in the hearts and lives of all the people God sends this ministry to, I am sure there are times when the main reason He dispatches me to a particular place is in response to the cry of just one who is desperate for Him.

"The Lord is nigh unto all them that call upon Him, to all that call upon Him in truth. He will fulfill the desire of them that fear Him; He also will hear their cry, and will save them. (Psalm 145:18-19)

The call to completion

Within the commission to go, we can't forget there is the call not only to go, but also to finish, and **finish well!** Our earthly "flight" has also been referred to as a "race to be run." So, for a successful "flight" with a magnificent finish, we must **fly—run to win!**

For a successful "flight" with a magnificent finish, we must fly—run to win!

"Know ye not that they which run in a race run all, but one

receiveth the prize? So run, that ye may obtain." (1 Corinthians 9:24)

Though I am not an avid sports fan, I do like to watch our grandsons and the San Antonio Spurs play basketball. Does it matter who wins? You bet it does! Sometimes the goals seem impossible, especially when the referees make wrong judgments and unfair calls, but that's not the time to give up. Quitters don't win, and winners don't quit! Maybe a time-out is needed so the coach can change strategies and encourage, or even strongly reprimand, but the whole idea is to **win** the game! In a world full of changing values the idea of winning may not always be popular—you might even be called "too competitive!" Funny thing—in every challenge or game there **is** competition, and the end results will reveal, of all things, winners and losers! I like what Dr. David Jeremiah of Turning Point Ministries said— "I work hard at winning!"

"I therefore so run, not as uncertainly; so fight I, not as one that beateth the air; But I keep under my body, and bring it into subjection, lest that by any means, when I have preached to others, I myself should be a castaway." (1 Corinthians 9:26-27)

By using the term "castaway," Paul did not mean he could lose his salvation, but rather than he could be disqualified to run the race—he could be put "on the shelf." I am reminded of a Christian lady I met many years ago. She said, "I knew God had given me a voice to sing, and that He wanted me to sing for Him, but I refused—now my voice is cracked and weak. How I wish I had been obedient to God—now I can no longer sing." That lady did not lose eternal life, but she did lose her ability to sing.

Incidentally, for an example of a real winner, see the 14th chapter of Joshua and read about Caleb. He was the kind of guy that would not be sidelined or "shelved." Caleb was 85 years old when he declared, *"Now, therefore give me this mountain…" (Joshua 14:12)*, and he got it—he took it! *"Hebron therefore became the inheritance of Caleb…because that he wholly followed the Lord God of Israel." (Joshua 14:14)*

The Christian life is not a 100-yard dash—it is a marathon! There will always be obstacles, which make it easy to think of quitting. I like the story Chuck Swindoll related about the movie star Charleton Heston and filmmaker Cecil B. DeMille. It is a true story about the making of the film, *Ben Hur*. What most of us may not know is that DeMille wanted Heston (not a stuntman) to actually drive the chariot. This was not just any chariot—it was the kind with four horses abreast! Heston did learn to drive the chariot, and when DeMille asked him if he was ready, he responded, "I'm ready, but I'm not sure I can win." DeMille's reply was, **"You just stay in the race—I'll make sure you win!"** I think I get the picture: It is our responsibility to run the race the best we know how, and trust God for the victory. *"…We are more than conquerors through Him that loved us." (Romans 8:37)*

The major theme of the Billy Graham Amsterdam 2000 Conference was: **Who** evangelists are; **why** we are evangelists; **what** our message is based upon: the Bible; **Who** we represent— the Lord Jesus Christ; and **how** we represent Him—in the power of the Holy Spirit and bathed in prayer. Technically, those principles apply to every Christian, for that is how we run the race in this life.

Have you or I mastered the "running" of the race God has given us? It could be we were running well, and then stumbled and fell. The apostle Paul wrote this to the churches of Galatia: *"Ye did run well; who did hinder you that ye should not obey the truth?" (Galatians 5:7)*

Everybody stumbles and falls at one time or another, but that is not the time to give up. We just need to get up, receive God's forgiveness, get back to running, and let Him master the race. For the right motivation to stay in the race all the way to the finish line, no matter what we face along the course, we must:

Run with focus—keep our eyes and our minds on Jesus:

"...Looking unto Jesus, the author and finisher of our faith; who for the joy that was set before Him endured the cross, despising the shame, and is set down at the right hand of the throne of God. For consider Him that endured such contradiction of sinners against Him, lest ye be wearied and faint in your minds." (Hebrews 12:2-3)

Run with purpose and patience—run to win:

"...Let us lay aside every weight, and the sin which so easily doth beset us, and let us run with patience the race that is set before us. (Hebrews 12:1)

Run with zeal and with trust in God—to the finish:

"But none of these things move me, neither count I my life dear unto myself, so that I might finish my course with joy, and the ministry, which I have received of the Lord Jesus, to testify the gospel of the grace of God." (Acts 20:24)

I Will Go

Like a fire that won't stop burning,
Like a dream that will not die,
Like a circle never ending,
Like a stream that won't run dry,

Is His call to share the story—
Jesus lives and reigns on high!
I must answer to His calling—
I will go, Lord, here am I.

"But it is good for me to draw near to God: I have put my trust in the Lord God, that I may declare all Thy works." (Psalm 73:28)

Chapter 11
Flight Precision

Perfect Life?   Perfect Flight?

Even though the caterpillar has been permanently changed into a butterfly, it **can** crawl. Although crawling is not nearly as satisfying, and it leads to a "low" view, it is still within the butterfly's capabilities to crawl.

It is also possible for a New Creation in Christ to "crawl" (go back to "low living"). This does not mean that person is no longer saved, because when we are born into God's family by His Spirit, we cannot be unborn any more than a butterfly can go back to being a caterpillar. It is a permanent change. But again, we have a choice in the way we live. We can live like who we are by allowing God to be in control, or we can let "self" have its way.   We all make this choice daily, even "minute-ly."

From many personal experiences, I believe one of the biggest problems in the life of the believer is our attempt to do God's will our own way.   Remember "Old Sweetness," the ministry van I mentioned earlier? God has taught me a lot of things through that old gal, one of which was: "High mileage doesn't mean that God can't use you anymore!" (Think about that if you are a senior citizen, or somewhere close.) When the mileage on the van was nearing 100,000, there were some signs that things were not working as well as they used to, so I began to pray for a new van. But, we didn't get one.

At 125,000 miles, I thought I had better get more serious about a new van, so again I prayed, and explained to God that it wasn't a matter of vanity—I only wanted a new van so I could be sure to get where I needed to go in ministry. And, of course, since Don couldn't go with me most of the time, God surely wouldn't want the van to break down on the way somewhere

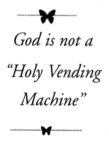

God is not a "Holy Vending Machine"

with no one there to fix it. I had also heard that if you needed and wanted something that you could just "name it and claim it" in Jesus' name, and you would receive it. So, I named it, claimed it, and asked for a new van in Jesus' name, but I didn't get it.

I should stop to point out that God is not a "Holy Vending Machine," where we can just drop in our little prayer (just put in our order) in the name of Jesus and get exactly what we asked for. Nobody can **order** God Almighty to do anything, not even in the name of Jesus.

Back to my request for the new van, however—although my need was legitimate and unselfish, and my motive was right, my problem was that I did not ask God for **His will.** I assumed that it must be His will since it was so practical in my own thinking. It had not occurred to me that God might choose a different way, which in fact, He did. He chose to keep that van going and going and going, so long in fact, that the life of that van became a tremendous testimony to the power of God. Almost everywhere I went, people would ask first about the van—was she still going? My father-in-law said he had never heard of a gasoline engine lasting that long without an overhaul. At 225,000 miles, she was still going, and we had never had anything done to the engine. My answer was always, "The only explanation for that van is God!"

Was the van perfect? Of course not! Maintenance had to be performed from time to time, new tires were needed periodically, and sometimes there were problems that required repairs. But, truly, the only explanation for the life of that van was God!

At 325,000 miles, Old Sweetness did have a "heart" problem, so we arranged for her to have a heart transplant—a new engine. Only, the new one was actually a rebuilt engine, and had a few problems of its own right from the start. Old Sweetness was not too happy with her new/rebuilt heart, but she still faithfully did her job until at 350,000 miles, another vehicle plowed into the right front wheel and did irreparable damage. So ended the life of that faithful partner in ministry.

Some vehicles are faster than others, some are better looking, and some have lots of extra features, but none of these things matter if the vehicle isn't there when you want to use it

Old Sweetness was not perfect, but she was available. She never went anywhere on her own—she always waited in the driveway until I got in and directed her where I wanted to go. She wasn't perfect, but she was available! Availability—that is one of the key words in "flight precision." Some vehicles are faster than others, some are better looking, and some have lots of extra features, but none of these things matter if the vehicle isn't there when you want to use it.

Butterflies are not all alike. While their basic design is the same, there are many differences, for example: shape, size, color. Some are much more brilliant in color, while others are intentionally less colorful in order to blend in with their surroundings. People are all different, too. Though there are similarities in every human being—some more than others—we are not all the same; but we who are children of God are all part of the same body, the body of believers, also referred to as the body of Christ. And each one of us has a special place in that body:

"For as the body is one, and hath many members, and all the members of that one body, being many, are one body, so also is Christ.

For by one Spirit are we all baptized into one body, whether we be Jews or Gentiles, whether we be bond or free; and have been all made to drink into one Spirit.

For the body is not one member, but many.

If the foot shall say, Because I am not the hand, I am not of the body, is it therefore not of the body?

And if the ear shall say, Because I am not the eye, I am not of the body; is it therefore not of the body?

If the whole body were an eye, where were the hearing? If the whole body were hearing, where were the smelling?

But now hath God set the members every one of them in the body, as it hath pleased him.

And if they were all one member, where were the body?

But now are they many members, yet but one body.

And the eye cannot say unto the hand, I have no need of thee: nor again the head to the feet, I have no need of you.

Nay, much more those members of the body, which seem to be more feeble, are necessary:

And those members of the body, which we think to be less honourable, upon these we bestow more abundant honour; and our uncomely parts have more abundant comeliness.

For our comely parts have no need: but God hath tempered the body together, having given more abundant honour to that part which lacked:

That there should be no schism in the body; but that the members should have the same care one for another.

And whether one member suffer, all the members suffer with it; or one member be honoured, all the members rejoice with it.

Now ye are the body of Christ, and members in particular." (1 Corinthians 12:12-27)

Every member of His body is of great value to God—He loves you as if you were His only child. He loves each of us, individually, in that very same way, and all at the same time. Too often we assess our own personal value according to the world's standards. Sometimes we think that because we are not as brilliant or beautiful as others, we are not important. Or, if a career has not turned out like we hoped or expected, we feel like failures, but God sees far beyond our present. He sees the big picture and the greater plan that we cannot yet even begin to fathom. Regardless of where you are right now, or how insignifica t you may feel, take heart in knowing that, as my friend, Jo \uth once said, God will never love you any more than He (es right now, and He will never love you any less. *"I have love thee with an everlasting love…" (Jeremiah 31:3)*

I nev realized until about four years before my mother went home t Heaven that at one time she had felt very insignificant and u mportant. In June of 1984 my mother accompanied me (a short ministry tour. As we traveled, I began to ask que ions about the early years when she and dad were first m ried, and about my childhood. I knew that mother loved to ay the violin, and that she was very good at it, but I didn't know that she had wanted to be a concert violinist—it was her dream. But before that could happen she met my dad, fell madly in love with him, and gave up her dream of a career as a violinist to become the wife of a preacher. Of course, she did play her violin for revival meetings and churches, and she also sang in the choir—she had a beautiful alto voice.

Life was not easy for my mother. She told me that once she became very ill—too sick to go with Daddy for a revival meeting he was to preach, so she stayed at home. Every passing day she grew more ill, and there was no way to reach Daddy to let him know. Finally, in desperation she cried out to God, "Oh, God, I am so sick, and I can't get well. I'm no good to anybody this way. I can't help my husband. I can't help myself. Why don't you just take me home to Heaven." She went on to say, "Then all of a sudden, God assured me that I would be all right, and He gave me a vision. All around me, and as far as I could see, were people, people, people—all kinds, all nationalities, in every direction for as far as I could see—people! And then the vision ended, and I began to get better." My mother had not realized she was pregnant and was suffering a miscarriage. She said that when she was growing up mothers didn't tell their daughters much about sex and child-bearing or she might have known what was happening.

She went on to say that she had thought about that vision from time to time, and always wondered about the multitude of people, who they were, and what they represented. "I never have understood the meaning of that vision," she said. But in that instant it seemed clear to me. I replied, "Mother, I think I know what it means—I think I know who those people are. If God had answered your prayer and taken you home to Heaven when you asked Him to, I wouldn't be here today, but I **am** here, and God has placed me in this ministry to tell people about Him. He has sent me to people of all nationalities all over the world, and many have heard the good news of Jesus Christ, and they have told others. Many more will hear about Jesus, because you lived." And she said, "Why, I never thought about that." She was just doing her job, teaching her daughters, being a good pastor's wife, loving and caring and blessing family and friends. An insignificant, unimportant life? No way!

No life is an accident! Each one is in God's plan! One day I was at a local hospital visiting with a lady who had just had a miscarriage. In my attempts to comfort her, I assured her that her baby was in Heaven, and reminded her of the account in the Scriptures about David and the baby that was born to him and Bathsheba (who was Uriah's wife). You can read the entire story in 2 Samuel, chapter 12, but, in short, after David and Bathsheba sinned, a son was born

No life is an accident! Each one is in God's plan!

to them. The prophet Nathan told David that even though God had forgiven him, the child would die. The child became ill, and David fasted and prayed, and asked God to spare the life of the child.

"And it came to pass on the seventh day that the child died. And the servants of David feared to tell him that the child was dead; for they said, Behold, while the child was yet alive, we spake unto him, and he would not hearken unto our voice; how will he then vex himself, if we tell him that the child is dead? But when David saw that his servants whispered, David perceived that the child was dead; therefore David said unto his servants, Is the child dead? And they said, He is dead." (2 Samuel 12:18-19)

Then David did the strangest thing: He *"arose from the earth, and washed, and anointed himself, and changed his apparel, and came into the house of the Lord and worshiped; then he came to his own house; and when he required, they set bread before him, and he did eat."* (2 Samuel 12:20)

The servants were puzzled, and this was King David's response, *"While the child was yet alive, I fasted and wept; for I said, Who can tell whether God will be gracious to me, that the child may live? But now he is dead, wherefore should I fast?* ***I shall go to him, but he shall not return to me."*** (2 Samuel 12:22-23)

As I shared this account with the lady in the hospital, I told her that I, too, have a child in Heaven because I had a miscarriage very early in my second pregnancy. Though I had been pregnant only six weeks, I knew that I had carried a real person, who is now really in Heaven, that I will really meet one day. As I left the hospital, I realized that I had been mis-introducing our family for some time by saying we have four children. We really have **five** children—one just got to Heaven before the rest of us.

The more I thought about our child in Heaven, the more I realized why I felt such a loss when that little one departed. In Psalm 139, God clearly shows us that these little ones are not "blobs of tissue"—they are real people from the moment of conception: *"Thou hast covered me in my mother's womb. I will praise Thee, for I am fearfully and wonderfully made... Thine eyes did see my substance, yet being unperfect; and in Thy book all my members were written, which in continuance were fashioned, when as yet there was none of them."* (Psalm 139:13-14,16)

While reading Jack Hayford's book, *I'll Hold You In Heaven*, God began to give me the words to a song, and then later the music to that song, *Little One*. If you have lost a child, whether by miscarriage, still birth, or even abortion, perhaps this song will minister to you. Remember, you haven't lost anything if you know where it is—your "little ones" are safe in the arms of Jesus. You will hold your little one(s) in Heaven one day if you have been born into God's family by receiving Jesus Christ as your Savior.

Little One[8]

Little one, I wanted you,
I miss you so today.
You were here so briefly,
Why could you not have stayed?

Oh, little one, I wanted you,
I don't know what went wrong,

But I know you're in Heaven,
And I sing to you this song:

Little one, I never got to hold your hand,
Little one, I never saw you smile,
But, little one, I'll hold you close in Heaven one day.
So, little one, just wait a little while.

No life is an accident,
Each one is in God's plan.
Every child within the womb
Is formed by God's own hand.

To let this little one be born?
The choice is not our own,
For only God gives life and breath—
It is His right alone.

You made the wrong decision
For the child that was within.
Ask Jesus to forgive you
And cleanse you from your sin.

That is why He came to earth,
He died that you might live.
Receive Him as your Savior.
To you this song He'll give:

Little one, I never got to hold your hand,

Little one, I never saw you smile,

But, little one, I'll hold you close in Heaven one day,

So, little one, just wait a little while.

Oh, little one, just wait a little while.

The first time I shared this song publicly was during a ministry tour in Puerto Rico for a chapel women's meeting at the Roosevelt Roads Naval Station. Later that afternoon, the chaplain called and told me his phone had been "ringing off the wall"—calls from women whose hearts had been broken through the loss of a child. There is not only assurance in this song to comfort those who have lost their little ones, but there is also another message the whole world needs to hear: "Yes, abortion is sin, but as bad as it is, it is not the unpardonable sin. God can and will forgive you if you will turn to Him, repent of your sin, and receive His forgiveness."

About six months after returning from Puerto Rico, God gave me an opportunity to present the "Butterfly Life in a Caterpillar World" ministry in a retreat setting near San Antonio. Immediately after a session in which I shared the *Little One* song and testimony, a precious young woman came to me with tears streaming down her face—tears of joy! She related to me that 12 years ago she and her husband had decided that a child would be inconvenient for them, so they agreed upon an abortion, but they never told anyone. She had been carrying the horrible guilt of that abortion for 12 years! She didn't think she could ever be forgiven, but that day she acknowledged her sin and accepted God's forgiveness, and she was finally free! She was going home to tell her husband how he, too, could be forgiven and set free!

---✹---

God loves us enough to take us just as we are, but He loves us too much to leave us that way

---✹---

Who among us has never failed? No one! Who among us always gets everything right, every time? Not a single one of us! God loves us enough to take us just as we are, but He loves us too much to leave us that way. He will use all kinds of circumstances to grow us in Him, to enable us to live the "butterfly" life, and bring us unspeakable joy!

"Commit thy works unto the Lord, and thy thoughts shall be established." (Proverbs 16:3)

"Trust in the Lord, and do good; so shalt thou dwell in the land, and verily, thou shalt be fed.

Delight thyself also in the Lord; and He shall give thee the desires of thine heart.

Commit thy way unto the Lord; trust also in Him; and He shall bring it to pass." (Psalm 37:3-5)

Perfect life? Perfect flight? Maybe not yet, but as the old saying goes, practice makes perfect! So spend time alone with God every day—practice living in His presence and His presence living in you. Some time ago I saw a highway sign in Portland, Maine with these words: "Take time, before time takes you!" Take time to talk with the Father, ask Him to fill you with His Spirit and take total control of your life, and then let Him do it!

Time—Alone With God

There are times when winds of circumstance
Just press me to the max,
And with these raging winds inside,
My mind cannot relax.

One voice says, "Why not just give up?
It isn't worth the fight!"
But deep inside, another speaks,
"Stand tall in Jesus' might!"

I was not designed to bear
Such pressure in my heart,
If I don't come apart with God,
I'll surely come apart!

So, when He calls me early,
In the stillness of the morn,
I stop and listen for His voice—
New hope within is born.

He soothes my spirit, calms my fears,
And speaks right through His Word.
What a precious gift of love from Him—
Time, alone with God!

"Cause me to hear thy loving-kindness in the morning, for in Thee do I trust; cause me to know the way wherein I should walk; for I lift up my soul unto Thee." (Psalm 143:8)

Chapter 12
Flight Protection and Precautions

Having "wings," guarantees that my life will be free of problems, troubles, and sorrows—right? NOT! We still live in a caterpillar world (a fallen world) after all. Even though we are new creations in Christ, things will not always go smoothly for us. But we can take heart in the fact that God has provided protection for our "earthly flight."

Even the little butterfly has protection. One of its most obvious safeguards is its very appearance—God has provided a camouflage covering (garment). God has provided special protection for us, too—it is the "whole armor of God":

"Wherefore take unto you the whole armor of God, that ye may be able to withstand in the evil day, and having done all, to stand.

Stand therefore, having your loins girt about with truth, and having on the breastplate of righteousness;

And your feet shod with the preparation of the gospel of peace;

Above all, taking the shield of faith, wherewith ye may be able to quench all the fiery darts of the wicked.

And take the helmet of salvation, and the sword of the Spirit, which is the Word of God." (Ephesians 6:13-17)

This great protection is continually available to every child of God. In order to do what God has designed us for, we just need to use what we have already been given. I am embarrassed to give this illustration, but it fits. Some 10 years ago, one of our daughters gave me some beautiful fabric of my favorite colors to make a new dress for me. We purchased a pattern and thread, and I put fabric and everything carefully away in a drawer. At this writing, it is all still in the drawer!

Our intentions were good, but we never got around to actually doing anything with those lovely materials that would have made a beautiful dress that I could have been enjoying for years. If only we had appropriated, or used, the materials that were already purchased and in my possession! But, we kept waiting for the "right time." We sometimes do that spiritually—we put things off, thinking we will get to them later. God has already provided protection for every believer—it is in our possession—it is our responsibility to avail ourselves of what is already ours.

Another very effective defense for the butterfly is its God-given diet. The life of the Monarch butterfly was described in a recent magazine article. The story of the migration of the Monarch population to and from their winter havens is very fascinating. How do these little creatures know what to do, and when? Once again, they simply obey as God designed them.

On their way back from "wintering," they may travel 1,000 miles or more, at cruising speeds of 10 miles per hour. They travel through wind and rain, crossing every kind of terrain, and along their way, each female butterfly will lay hundreds of eggs, one at a time, on young milkweed plants. The larvae will feed only on one particular genus of milkweed. Incidentally, this unique characteristic is responsible for the Monarch nickname, the "milkweed butterfly."

It has been discovered that certain species of milkweed produce a poisonous substance, which not only can be accumulated by the larvae, but also carried over during metamorphosis into the adult butterfly life. Hence, if the Monarch becomes a bird's lunch, the milkweed poison kicks in and causes the bird to be sick enough to vomit. Consequently, the bird learns not to eat black and orange butterflies. This amazing protective measure keeps the Monarch population from being exterminated!

The Monarch butterfly is protected by what he feeds on! We are also protected by what God has given us to feed on— His Word—the Bible! His Word is the **Sword of the Spirit.**

From the moment God placed me in the music ministry, He gave me a very strong desire to use the Bible—not just to reference certain passages, but to quote or read Scriptures during concert presentations. Part of this inspiration came through other music evangelists that I had observed as they read Scripture during their testimony or before their message in song. I felt certain that God wanted me to use His Word in much the same way, but there was a problem. I would be holding a microphone in one hand, so in order to hold a Bible in the other, the Bible would need to be small in size so that I could manage it one-handed. Therein lay the problem—my eyes were already changing requiring me to hold printed text farther away, but

> *The Monarch butterfly is protected by what he feeds on! We are also protected by what God has given us to feed on— His Word—the Bible!*

that made the print too small to see without glasses. However, glasses bothered me because I really wanted to make eye contact with people, but looking back and forth meant moving my head up and down a lot, and that was disconcerting to me and probably to others as well.

What to do? I thought perhaps if I could just get a large print Bible, maybe that would solve the problem. So, I bought one with the biggest print I could find; however,when I tried to use it during a concert, there were even more problems. The Bible was about the size of a Sears Roebuck catalog or the San Antonio Yellow Pages—much too heavy to hold in one hand, and so big there was no good place to put it in order to use it easily. This would never do.

As I prayed the thought came to me that since God is the Great Physician, I could just ask Him to heal my eyes so that I could read the tiny print of the little Bible, and that would solve the problem. So I earnestly prayed that God would fix my eyes, but it didn't happen.

Again I prayed, "God, I know You want me to use Your Word for these concert presentations, so if I can't use this huge Bible, and You are not going to change my vision so that I can see the print on the small one, there is only one thing to do—I will just have to memorize Scriptures. But memorizing isn't easy for me, I can't do it—You will have to help me." Memorizing Scriptures wasn't easy—I had to go over and over and over them time after time, but as I prayed for God's help and continued to repeat the Scriptures, success finally came and those words were locked in memory.

I began to see that this was what God had wanted all along, because when our minds dwell on His Word and we hide it in our hearts, then the Holy Spirit can bring His words to our conscious thoughts in a flash! Yes, God did indeed want me to use His Word in concert and other presentations, but He also wanted me to **know** it in my heart. There will be times for all of us when a printed copy of the Bible is not readily available but we really need a word from God. When His Word is in our hearts and minds, it is also on the tips of our tongues and we can speak it. Yes, **the Bible is the Sword of the Spirit,** but if we only carry it in our hands it is like a sword sheathed. The Sword of the Spirit is the mighty Word of God, and it is most powerful when spoken or read aloud.

When we know and purposely use the Scriptures, the enemy is repelled. When Jesus was tempted by the devil after 40 days in the wilderness, three specific times He answered the devil by declaring *"It is written…"*, and He quoted the very words of Deuteronomy 8:3; 6:13, and 6:16. You can read all about it in the fourth chapter of Luke.

The devil's deceptive words are no match for the Word of God, but he continues to try to fool believers into thinking that we are powerless. We have been redeemed through the blood of Jesus Christ, and made alive in Him. Nothing—no enemy (person or power), can ever change that! The transformation has been performed by God in the life of every believer, and it is totally irreversible. *"Verily, verily, I say unto you, He that heareth my word, and believeth on Him that sent Me, **hath** everlasting life; and shall not come into condemnation; but **is passed from death unto life.**" (John 5:24)*

Precautions—Warning! Warning! Warning!

As God's new creations (His children), we need His protection, because as long as we live in this "caterpillar" world, we will **always** have enemies—three major enemies in particular:

The World

The Flesh

The Devil

The World

When we speak of the world as an enemy, we are not referring to this round ball of earth we live on—we are talking about world systems—the ways of the world. As long as we live on this earth we will be **in** the world, but we must not be **of** the world.

"And be not conformed to this world; but be ye transformed by the renewing of your mind, that ye may prove what is that good, and acceptable, and perfect, will of God." (Romans 12:2)

So, how do we renew our minds?

By spending time alone with God, in prayer, praise, worship, and thanksgiving.

By spending time reading and studying God's Word, and committing it to memory.

By spending time with other believers in a local church on a regular basis, worshipping and praising God together, learning through Bible studies, and listening to the Word of God preached and taught by Pastors and Evangelists.

The Flesh

When we speak of the enemy of "flesh," we are referring to "fleshly patterns," i.e., our selfish human nature and all its manifestations. When we are born into God's family we become new creatures, but we still have old fleshly patterns that must, by an act of our will, be yielded to God's control if we would overcome those old patterns.

Surely everyone has heard the quip, "We are our own worst enemies!" Walt Kelly may not have realized how accurate he was when his cartoon character, "Pogo," looking in the mirror, announced, "We have met the enemy and he is us."

Pride and forgetfulness are two of our biggest "flesh" problems. Both are so subtle, and so effective in keeping us from walking closely with our Heavenly Father. In the matter of pride, Dr. C. H. Spurgeon said that we need to be broken every two or three weeks or we will even get proud of being broken! And regarding forgetfulness, we sometimes forget some of the most important principles of this new life we have been given.

Even though I know **who** I am in Him, on occasion I have forgotten **whose** I am, and sometimes I have had to learn things I thought I knew…like an experience during my first time in Australia. I went there on a mission trip with a team from our church. We left San Antonio, Texas at the peak of a hot and dry summertime with daily temperatures of 98-100 degrees. The seasons in Melbourne, Australia are exactly opposite from ours, so we arrived there in mid-winter. Since we knew in advance that it would be very cold, I planned ahead as best I could, taking along a heavy coat, a warm dress, several pairs of slacks, some long underwear, and some sweaters that I had borrowed from a friend.

It was indeed cold, windy, and rainy when we arrived in Melbourne. The first Sunday we were there found us somewhat shocked by the severity of the weather. We understood that the heat in the church was in the floor, but my feet never found it! (Many years later, we learned that while the heat was indeed in the floor, during the time of that visit the heating system was broken!) I was excited about singing for both morning and evening services, but at the same time wondered if I would be warm enough. Would I be able to sing if my teeth were chattering and my legs shaking from the cold?

The morning service went fine, but in the evening I was truly dreading taking my coat off. Not only was I sure I would be very uncomfortable with that heavy garment on—I also thought it would be terribly rude to sing before all those people with my coat on. That, of course, was pride (which I didn't recognize until later.) So, I kept my coat on until the last second, and then got up and sang. As soon as I finished singing, I sat down and quickly put my coat on again. My feet were still cold, but at least I wasn't shivering.

It follows that on Monday morning I was still concerned about being warm enough to sing—after all, I had only one warm dress, and I would be singing three times a day for morning, afternoon and evening meetings, all week long. The slacks were fine for the morning and afternoon meetings, and I could use my long underwear and sweaters along with the slacks, but the evening evangelistic meetings would be held in the church, and I have always felt that dresses or skirts and blouses were much more appropriate when singing in the worship center of a church. How would I stay warm? That was one of my biggest concerns as I went to God in prayer that Monday morning.

During the time in Melbourne I was staying in the home of an Australian family, Gerry and Chris and their children. Australians don't heat their homes the way we do in America, so my room felt quite chilly to me that morning. I sat praying, wrapped up in every blanket I could find. Since I know God cares about everything that concerns me, I had no problem taking my needs to Him, including the need for warmth.

As I prayed, it occurred to me that if I just had a navy blue skirt, I could mix and match the skirt with the sweaters I had brought—I would be warm enough to sing, I wouldn't have to wear the same and only warm dress for every service, and I wouldn't look boring. So, I asked God to provide me with a navy blue skirt that day. I asked Him to give me a little time to go shopping and for a bargain since I didn't have very much money. In that moment I felt His blessed assurance all over me! I just knew God had heard and was going to answer my prayer.

Sure enough, after our morning meeting, one of the ladies just happened to offer to take those of us who wanted to go—shopping! We wouldn't have much time, but that should be no problem, I thought—God not only invented time—He controls it as well! He could find me a navy blue skirt in five minutes or less if He wanted to. So, I was the first to raise my hand—yes, I definitely wanted to go shopping!

We arrived at the shopping mall, and since we had a very limited amount of time, it was agreed that we would all go our separate ways and meet back together in one hour at one particular spot. I was so excited—I could hardly wait to see the skirt that I knew God had for me. So, I shopped, and shopped, and shopped, and shopped…and I did not find a navy blue skirt. I couldn't believe it! Either the stores did not have navy blue, or the price was out of sight, or the fabric was too lightweight, or the style was all wrong. Suddenly, the hour was up! I cannot tell you how disappointed I felt—had I missed God? Hadn't He assured me that He had heard and answered my prayer? I didn't understand at all.

As we left the shopping center, the others were all talking and laughing and enjoying the ride back, and I was scrunched down in the back seat. No one noticed that I was very quiet…and depressed. I was carrying on a conversation, silently, with God—only I was doing all the talking. I was not angry, but I was deeply disappointed and puzzled—let's face it, I was smack-dab in the middle of a serious "pity party."

> *Everything you have is borrowed! You are not your own—you are bought with a price!*

"God," I complained, "I only asked for one thing—just one navy blue skirt—that's not much to ask. You own the cattle on a thousand hills so one navy blue skirt is no problem to you—I don't understand! I just knew you would give me a navy blue skirt today. Besides, the only reason I'm here is that **You** sent me. I didn't have any money—and **You** provided every penny to get me here, or I wouldn't even **be** in Australia. And, besides all that, You know that I had to **borrow** all those sweaters just to have something warm to wear with the pants…"

God is so good! He didn't get angry with me—He just let me pour out my heart to Him, and when I finally stopped talking, He lovingly and tenderly spoke to my heart: "Betty, everything you have is **borrowed**! You are not your own—you are **bought** with a price!" Those very words are written in 1 Corinthians 6:19-20: *"What? Know ye not that your body is the temple of the Holy Ghost (Holy Spirit) which is in you, which ye have of God, and ye are not your own? For ye are **bought** with a price; therefore glorify God in your body and in your spirit, which are God's."*

How can I express the shame I felt? It was true—**everything** I have **is** borrowed—even the very air I breathe! I felt lower than the floorboards of the vehicle I was riding in! The Lord had brought me to Australia to tell the people about Him, and I had forgotten one of His most important principles—ownership!

"Oh Father," I wept, "I am so sorry—how could I have forgotten? Please forgive me; I don't need a navy blue skirt, another dress, or anything—I will wear the same dress every meeting, every day!

It doesn't matter—just please don't take the sense of Your presence from me—I want **You** more than anything!" I knew that He, Himself, would never leave me, but I also knew that my fellowship with Him had been broken, and the sense of His presence was gone.

When I confessed my sin and acknowledged my desperate need for Him, I was assured of His forgiveness, and the most unusual thing occurred. A warm glow seemed to flow completely over me, from the top of my head to the tips of my toes. That particular experience had never happened to me before, it hasn't happened since, and may never happen again, but that day, in a little corner of the back seat of the car, unknown to anyone else around, God blessed me with an amazing evidence of restoration and the awesome sense of His presence.

At about eleven o'clock that same evening, I was getting ready for bed, thinking about all that had happened, still a bit puzzled about the assurance I had felt in my early morning prayer time, and the way things had turned out. But, it didn't matter any more. I was so thankful and satisfied that God had restored the joy of my salvation and refocused my thinking.

As I walked toward my room, Chris appeared before me. She was holding up for me to see—a navy blue skirt! She said, "Betty, do you think this would fit you? I had forgotten all about it, but a few weeks ago I thought I needed a new skirt, and I bought this one. I haven't worn it, and you are welcome to borrow it if you would like." (Did you notice the word, "borrow?") I started to protest, but stopped instantly, knowing that **this** was God's specific answer to my prayer of that morning.

I thanked Chris. I didn't have to try on the skirt—I knew it would fit, but I tried it on anyway and was not one bit surprised—it was perfect! If I had gone to a clothing store and had measurements taken, I could not have gotten a better fit! It was not only the right size—even the shade and style were just right. I had **not** missed God! He **had** answered my prayer—just not the way **I** thought He would. His way was better! It always is!

A couple of days later, I had an unexpected 45 minutes to shop. I wanted some souvenirs for my grandchildren, so was not even looking for anything for myself. But then, I "just happened" to notice a sale rack, and right there in plain sight was a black skirt that looked to be my size. The sale price was $4. I had $4. The skirt fit, and I bought it and used it, along with the navy blue skirt and the one warm dress, and that was all I needed for the rest of the time in Australia.

When I left Melbourne, I returned the navy blue skirt to Chris and also gave her the black skirt, along with my thanks and appreciation. Above all, I thanked our gracious and loving Heavenly Father, not only for providing the clothing, but also for re-teaching me one the most important principles of the Christian (butterfly) life—not only **who** I am in Christ, but **whose** I am—HIS!

Protection against Pride and Forgetfulness—Humility

Sometimes we forget that our confidence is in the Lord, not

in our flesh. In those times, we need to "lower our wings" (humble ourselves before the Lord), yield to Him, and be filled with His Spirit. *"Humble yourselves in the sight of the Lord, and He shall lift you up." (James 4:10)*

Many heroes of the faith are some of the most humble people the world has known. Anne Graham Lotz, daughter of the well-known Dr. Billy Graham, is considered to be one of the best evangelistic speakers of our time. She gave her testimony during one of the sessions at Amsterdam 2000 Conference. She said many good things, but some of the most impressive were the following comments (though not precise quotes).

The heart of her message was "Such as I have, I give…" She referred to the third chapter of Acts, where, as Peter and John went to the temple to pray, they encountered a lame man who sat at the gate of the temple, asking for alms. *"Then Peter said, Silver and gold have I none; but such as I have give I thee: In the name of Jesus Christ of Nazareth rise up and walk." (Acts 3:6)* The "rest of the story" is recorded in verses 7-11—the lame man did rise and walk! *"All the people saw him walking and praising God." (Acts 3:9)*

"Such as I have, I give…" Anne went on to say that we must **first** give what we have to God, and **then** give to the world the gospel. I was struck by her humility. In her personal testimony, Anne does not claim greatness, but says that she has a **little** time, a **little** talent, and a **little** money, and she just gives it all back to God. He takes that which we yield to Him and uses it according to His will, and somehow multiplies all that we give to Him. Without Him, we can do **nothing**! (John 15:5) But, we **can** do **all** things through Christ who strengthens us. (Philippians 4:13) When we humble ourselves and give "such as we have" and "such as we are" back to God **first**, HE will live through us in such a way that we really can **then** give to the world the gospel.

There is another precaution along this line—it is a warning about what could happen if we do not humble ourselves and yield, give ourselves back to God, and allow Him to take control. God is patient—the Bible says He is long-suffering. But if I, His child, have sin in my life and continue to refuse to confess and repent—if I willfully refuse to surrender to God, not only will I have nothing to give to others, but the time may even come that God will put me on the shelf permanently. If that happened, although I would not lose my salvation, I surely would lose my usefulness to Him. I could never really "fly" again!

These must have been the same kind of thoughts that prompted the Apostle Paul to write: *"But I keep under my body, and bring it into subjection: lest that by any means, when I have preached to others, I myself should be a castaway." (1 Corinthians 9:27)* In *The Criswell Study Bible*, Dr. W. A. Criswell has commented on this passage and the word, castaway—"This final word is *adokimos*, suggesting the idea of 'disapproval.' Paul does not fear the loss of salvation, but rather the loss of his work and influence as a minister of Christ."

There are many ways to be "sidelined," or "castaway," and Paul could not stand the thought of dropping out of the race or being disqualified to run. He was determined to be truly disciplined in the "race of life," and he did in fact, run the race in such a way that near the close of his life on earth he could, and did, say to Timothy:

"I have fought a good fight, I have finished my course, I have kept the faith: Henceforth there is laid up for me a crown of righteousness, which the Lord, the righteous judge, shall give me at that day; and not to me only, but unto all them also that love His

appearing." (2 Timothy 4:7-8)

In order to say, as Paul did, that we have fought, finished, and "faithed" a good fight, we need to be ADVD:

Attentive   — To hear God's direction.

Diligent   — To heed God's direction.

Vigilant   — To keep from being drawn away from God's direction, and

Determined — To follow God's direction at all costs.

Our third major enemy is The Devil (Satan).

From his beginning, Satan wanted to have something, do something, and be something apart from God—in fact, he wanted to be God himself! (Isaiah 14:12-14)   He is called, among other names, Satan, and the Adversary, and he has been active in this world since the Garden of Eden, trying to persuade mankind to act independently of God.

He is the god (little "g") of this worldly secular order. His primary purpose is to blind men and women so they will not be saved by Jesus.

"But if our gospel be hid, it is hid to them that are lost; In whom the god of this world hath blinded the minds of them which believe not, lest the light of the glorious gospel of Christ, who is the image of God, should shine unto them." (2 Corinthians 4:3-4)

The devil wants to divert man's worship from God to anything he can, but ultimately to Satan himself. Satan is unseen and unconventional. He deceives, denounces, disturbs, distracts, divides, discourages, delays, and destroys in his attempts to divert both non-believers and believers from God. Furthermore, the devil wants to keep believers ignorant of who we are and what we have in Jesus.

Although the devil was defeated at the cross, he is still trying to convince the world that he is all powerful. He does have power, but he is **not** all-powerful. He has many tricks and wears many faces. We **cannot isolate** ourselves or our children, but we **can insulate** ourselves with the Word of God and His Spirit Who indwells every believer. We have the wonderful assurance in 1 John 4:4, that greater is He that is in us than he (the devil) that is in the world!

As Christ's return draws ever nearer with each passing day, the devil tries harder and harder to deceive and destroy, and he still uses the same old tools because they still work. In 2 Corinthians 2:11 the Apostle Paul declares that we are not ignorant of the devil's devices (tools). Some of those major tools are:

> Doubt
>
> Deception
>
> Fear
>
> Worry and Anxiety

Doubt—Did God really say…? Satan has used this one as far back as the Garden of Eden: *"Now the serpent was more subtile than any beast of the field which the Lord God had made. And he said unto the woman, Yea, hath God said, Ye shall not eat of every tree of the garden?" (Genesis 3:1)* Satan still employs the tool of doubt to bring us to defeat.

Protection from Doubt—the Word of God. We will always find the truth in the Scriptures. God cannot and will not lie. The moment doubt comes to the door of our minds, we must not open the door, instead we should answer with the Word of God.

Deception—Satan sometimes appears as an angel of light: *"For* *such are false apostles, deceitful workers, transforming themselves into the apostles of Christ. And no marvel; for Satan himself is transformed into an angel of light."* (2 Corinthians 11:13-14)

Protection from Deception—Again, the Word of God.

Plastic apples can look very real, but they are totally inedible! Satan is the great counterfeiter, and he can make things look genuine, when they are absolutely fake.

Bank trainees are taught how to spot counterfeit money by studying the real, genuine currency. When they know exactly what the real $100 bill looks like, the phony is much easier to detect. So it is with the Word of God—when we know what **He** says, we are much less likely to be deceived.

Fear—This is one of the devil's favorite tools, because it can utterly immobilize people—stop us dead in our tracks!

Protection from Fear—Not only the Word of God, but also His name.

In His Word, He tells us, "Fear not!" He declares to us over again and again that He is with us, and He will never leave us or forsake us.

And, He has given us His **name**—there is power in the name of Jesus. For just one example, remember Acts 3:6 that we have already referenced—Peter declared, *"In the **name** of Jesus Christ of Nazareth rise up and walk."* Jesus is not a "genie in a bottle." The name of Jesus is not a magic charm to be used at any whim, but when we use the authority of His name **within God's will**, His awesome power is known and shown.

Some time ago in a Bible study meeting, I heard the testimony of a friend who had inadvertently surprised an intruder in her home. When she asked him who he was and what he wanted, he said nothing, but his menacing movements made clear that his intentions were anything but good. At once, my friend remembered the name of Jesus—she looked the intruder straight in the eye and shouted, "By the authority in the name of the Lord Jesus Christ, get away from me and leave me alone!" Instantly, the man fell backward in a heap on the floor. My friend called the police, and they took the man away. It was later learned that this man had no history of fainting or seizures of any kind. My friend was supernaturally rescued—in the name of Jesus!

I thought about the testimony of my friend, and wondered to myself that if something similar ever happened to me, would I have the presence of mind to remember to specifically resist evil in the power of Jesus' name? Months went by, and those thoughts sort of drifted into my mental file cabinet.

One particularly gorgeous South Texas day I decided to go for a walk, but as things turned out, it was a longer walk than I had planned. On my way back home I chose a short cut—bad idea! Just as I rounded a corner, I noticed five big dogs. I have always heard that if you ignore animals they won't usually bother you—the key words are "won't usually."

I kept on walking, ignoring the dogs the best I could, and praying, but they were getting closer, especially the big white one. Thinking maybe I could scare them away, I looked around for some rocks or anything I could throw at the dogs. The only objects on the ground were a few very small pebbles, but few and small were better than none, so I picked them up and threw them, pretending they were big. That didn't work, and the dogs were gaining ground.

Suddenly I remembered the testimony of my friend when she was in trouble with the intruder. I prayed for God's help, and then turned and looked the big white dog right in the eyes and shouted, "By the authority in the name of the Lord Jesus Christ, get away from me and leave me alone!" To my utter amazement, the dog stopped, whimpered, and turned and walked away—and the rest of the dogs followed him. You can think what you will, but I know God rescued me that day by the authority in His powerful name!

Some battles in life are unavoidable, but we don't necessarily have to run—we can face our foe in the name of the Lord, for not only does He have all authority, HE is Jehovah-Nissi, Victorious Warrior, God of all power and might!

Worry and Anxiety—Another handy tool of the devil. I have heard that most of us spend a lot of time worrying about things that never happen. The "what ifs" and "if onlys" can drive us nuts!

This little excerpt about worry is from *God's Little Devotional Book for Women*:

Worry is like a rocking chair: It gives you something to do, but doesn't get you anywhere.

People who continually worry about every detail of their lives are like a patient in a mental hospital who stood with her ear pressed against the wall.

"What are you doing?" an attendant asked with curiosity.

"Shhh" the woman whispered, beckoning to the attendant to join her at the wall.

The attendant pressed her ear to the wall and stood there for several moments listening intently. "I can't hear anything," she said.

"No," the patient replied with a furrowed brow. "It's been like that all day!"

Some worry about what might be said. Others worry about what hasn't been said. Some worry about what might happen. Others worry about what hasn't happened which should have happened by now. Others worry about their future while others fret over the consequences of their past.

We were created to live abundant lives in our mind, our body, and our spirit. Like a flower we were meant to blossom, not to wither on the vine. Put Jesus in charge of your worries today and walk in newness of life!

Worry is the exact opposite of faith—it is impossible to worry and "faith it" at the same time. Anxiety is the "twin sister" of worry, and they are both akin to fear.

Protection from worry and anxiety—the Word of God, Prayer, and Keeping our Minds Focused on the LORD:

"Be careful (full of care, anxious or worried) *for nothing, but in every thing by prayer and supplication with thanksgiving let your requests be made known unto God.*

And the peace of God, which passeth all understanding, shall keep your hearts and minds through Christ Jesus.

Finally, brethren, whatsoever things are true, whatsoever things are honest, whatsoever things are just, whatsoever things are pure, whatsoever things are lovely, whatsoever things are of good report; if there be any virtue, and if there be any praise, think on these things." (Philippians 4:6-8)

God also sends angels for our physical protection. We are never to worship or to be preoccupied with angels, but we can certainly thank God for sending them.

There have been many authenticated and amazing accounts of angel-protection and deliverance. For instance, just recall what happened in the lives of King Hezekiah, the prophet Isaiah, and the people of Judah when their enemy was not only threatening, but altogether capable of, the annihilation of the people of God. Hezekiah and his people made ready for battle, and:

"...Hezekiah the king, and the prophet Isaiah...prayed and cried to heaven. And **the Lord sent an angel**, which cut off all the mighty men of valour, and the leaders and captains in the camp of the king of Assyria. So he returned with shame of face to his own land. And, when he was come into the house of his god, they that came forth of his own bowels slew him there with the sword." (2 Chronicles 32:20-21)

"Thus the Lord saved Hezekiah and the inhabitants of Jerusalem from the hand of Sennacherib the king of Assyria, and from the hand of all others, and guided them on every side." (2 Chronicles 32:22)

For another fascinating true account of God's angelic intervention, read the story of Elisha in the sixth chapter of Second Kings. The king of Syria had sent spies to find Elisha's whereabouts. Upon discovering that Elisha was in Dothan, the king immediately dispatched horses, chariots and a great host that surrounded the city of Dothan. It looked like there was no way out!

"And when the servant of the man of God was risen early, and gone forth, behold a host compassed the city both with horses and chariots. And his servant said unto him, Alas, my master! How shall we do? And he answered, Fear not; for they that be with us are more than they that be with them. And Elisha prayed, and said, Lord, I pray Thee, open his eyes, that he may see. And the Lord opened the eyes of the young man; and he saw; **and, behold, the mountain was full of horses and chariots of fire round about Elisha.**" (2 Kings 6:15-17)

While you may or may not have been aware of such angel-intervention by personal experience, we have it on the best authority, the Word of God, that angels do exist and that they do minister to His children.

"For He shall give His angels charge over thee, to keep thee in all thy ways. They shall bear thee up in their hands, lest thou dash thy foot against a stone." (Psalm 91:11)

The bottom line is that when God saves us ("births" us unto His family, and makes us new creations in Him), we still live on this earth, (a "caterpillar" world), and we will face difficulties and troubles as long as we are here. However, **not only has God given us precautions** for our earthly "flight," **He has provided His perfect protection** for each and every one of us. We need only appropriate what is already ours.

Chapter 13
How To Wing It—
When You Don't Understand (But, God...)

Brother Lee Patton, a pastor friend of ours, is also a very talented artist, particularly in chalk-art. Every year at our annual ministry banquet, Brother Lee draws a beautiful picture right before our eyes. He uses special chalks of all colors, some of which have a fluorescent quality that allows him to draw a picture we cannot see—maybe I had better explain that.

Brother Lee prepares the background of the picture before he brings it to our banquet. Using the special chalk that can only be seen in special lighting, He skillfully draws the "hidden" picture, which appears to be simply a background of sky and clouds. At the banquet, that is what is visible to us at first sight. Then Brother Lee begins to draw, adding to and changing the scene while we watch. It is amazing the way he brings all the colors together with just the right strokes in just the right places to create an absolutely beautiful picture.

But that picture is only part of the finished product. Brother Lee also comes equipped with special lighting, and that lighting changes everything! As he adjusts the lights in different intensities, the "hidden" picture comes into view. And how beautiful it is! But we cannot see the complete picture until Brother Lee shines those special lights upon it.

Our "butterfly" flight in this "caterpillar world" is a lot like those chalk drawings. The complete picture is not obvious until God gives His illumination. We will not always understand the "hidden" parts of our earthly journey, and God may or may not reveal them to us during this lifetime. We often protest—"But, God..," and then we question, or give our excuses. Some of our most frequent quandaries and questions during our earthly journeys are, very simply:

WHY?

WHY ME?

WHY THIS?

WHY NOW?

WHY?

But, God...Why ? Why do I have to be left behind?

That was my cry when our ministry team was leaving Romania. We had experienced God's blessing and power in many ways during that mission effort, and now it was time to return home. The group would go first to Budapest, Hungary, where we would stay overnight, and then fly back to the U.S. the next day. But the bad news was that they did not have a hotel room for me in Budapest, so I wouldn't be going with them. What a blow!

I waved goodbye to the team as they boarded the bus and left me standing there. I would be going to Budapest the next day, by car. I felt so alone. It was hard to keep the tears back. And, the "what-if's" just seemed to bombard my mind. As I prayed that night before going to bed, I was still crying out, "Why, God? I'm lonely and worried...and scared." Ultimately, I knew the only thing to do was just give the whole thing, including myself, to God, and "trust in the Lord," just as His Word says. I didn't sleep much that night—how glad I was to see morning arrive!

God never makes any mistakes—later that day I began to understand. I was to be accompanied by Elizabeth Tson, wife of Joseph Tson. The Tsons were well-known Romanian Christians. They were supposed to catch a flight out on the same day that I was to leave, but they were being watched by the Romanian government. Although initially unknown to me, since it was easier to cross the border in the company of an American citizen, it had been decided that I should be the one to stay behind so Elizabeth could go with me.

Our car went directly to the border guard station, passing long lines of people on foot who were waiting to cross. We accomplished the crossing into Hungary in good time, and made it to Budapest and to our respective flights as scheduled. Now I see that I was chosen to help Elizabeth, and I thank our great and all-wise God for that special privilege.

WHY ME?

But, God...why me? I am not qualified—that was my response when God called me into the music ministry. I am small and ordinary, and I'm an alto, and the most successful soloists are sopranos. I had been singing all my life, but had no professional training other than two or three voice lessons when I thought I was a soprano. Then I read:

"But God hath chosen the foolish things of the world to confound the wise; and God hath chosen the weak things of the world to confound the things which are mighty;

And base things of the world, and things which are despised, hath God chosen, yea, and things which are not, to bring to nought things that are:

That no flesh should glory in His presence.

But of Him are ye in Christ Jesus, who of God is made unto us wisdom, and righteousness, and sanctification, and redemption:

That, according as it is written, 'He that glorieth, let him glory in the Lord." *(1 Corinthians 1:27-31)*

Come to think of it, when God commissioned Moses to deliver the children of Israel from Egyptian bondage, he felt much the same way:

"Faithful is He that calleth you, who will also do it."

1 Thessalonians 5:24

"And Moses said unto the Lord, O my Lord, I am not eloquent, neither heretofore, nor since Thou has spoken unto Thy servant: but I am slow of speech, and of a slow tongue."

And the Lord said unto him, Who hath made man's mouth? Or who maketh the dumb, or deaf, or the seeing, or the blind? Have not I the Lord?

Now therefore go, and I will be with thy mouth, and teach thee what thou shalt say." *(Exodus 4:10-12)*

Evidently, Moses was not chosen because of his qualifications, but God **did** choose him, and it was in His plan to work through Moses. God promised to be with him, and that would be enough! If He has called you or me, will He not do the same for us? Absolutely!

"God is faithful, by whom ye were called unto the fellowship of His Son Jesus Christ our Lord." (1 Corinthians 1:9)

"Faithful is He that calleth you, who will also do it." (1 Thessalonians 5:24)

But, God...I'm scared! Although I used to sing with my sisters when we were growing up, and over the years had sung solos in churches, I was still nervous about singing and being in front of people. When God called me into the music ministry, my heart wanted to say "Yes!"—but with my mouth, I protested, "I'm scared!" But, God was prepared for that response, and again, spoke to me through His Word:

"For God hath not given us the spirit of fear; but of power, and of love, and of a sound mind." (2 Timothy 1:7)

To this day when I am preparing to sing and speak, fear still knocks at the door of my heart, but when I answer the door with the wonderful word of God, fear is turned away.

But, God...I can't sing without crying—what about the tears? Although I had been singing solos in church, it seemed that the more I thought about the lyrics I was singing, the more emotionally involved I became, so that even though I might do all right for part of the song, by the time I reached the last chorus the tears were uncontrollable. One former pastor even went so far as to ask, "Betty, would you cry us a special on Sunday?"

If tears were a big problem for just one song, I could only imagine what it would be like to try to give a whole concert.

God knows and cares about our tears—the Psalmist cried out to Him, *"Put Thou my tears into Thy bottle."* *(Psalm 56:8)* I prayed, "God, I know tears are a language You understand, but nobody wants to listen to 45 minutes of them!"

I didn't ask God to take away my tears because I had heard about people who prayed like that, and their tears did go away, but so did the tenderness of their hearts, and I didn't want that to happen to me. The only thing to do was to lay the whole problem at Jesus' feet. I told Him I wanted to be obedient—I wanted to be in the music ministry, but I could not manage the tears, and I did not know what to do or even what to pray.

God answered my dilemma through a friend who suggested that the next time when I pray before singing, I should try asking God to **lend** my tears temporarily to someone else. I have been praying that way ever since, and God has loaned my tears over and over again.

In over 30 years of ministry there have been some public tears, but they didn't end the message, and God enabled me to continue and complete those presentations. Over the years only a very few songs were unfinished because of tears, and usually at the end of a concert or speaking ministry I get the tears back.

It was surprising sometimes, the people that God chose to "borrow" my tears. Once, when I was giving a concert presentation at the chapel at Luke Air Force Base, there was present a visiting chaplain from another base. He stopped to talk with me after the service. He said that something happened that he just couldn't explain—he was not an emotional type person, but he wept the entire service. This chaplain was seven feet tall (they called him "Big John")! I just smiled and said, "Praise God—he loaned my tears to a giant!" Of course, I explained to the chaplain about my prayer asking God to lend my tears. Maybe they were his, and maybe they were mine, or a combination of the two; nonetheless, the chaplain seemed somewhat relieved.

There are still times when it suits God's will to use my tears, and when that is His choice, He enables me to sing **through** the tears. Before singing and speaking I still pray that God will lend my tears, but I am also learning to pray "nevertheless, do what is best—Thy will be done."

Evangelist John Bunyan Wilder was, physically, a very tall, big, and strong man, yet, he wept all through his sermons. He said that he wished he could learn to preach instead of cry. But, when that big man stood, weeping, as he shared the Gospel, every heart was touched. Tears are not so bad—they don't necessarily hinder a ministry. We just have to yield the tears, along with every other part of us, to God.

We just have to yield the tears, along with every other part of us, to God.

"They that sow in tears shall reap in joy. He that goeth forth and weepeth, bearing precious seed, shall doubtless come again with rejoicing, bringing his sheaves with him." (Psalm 126:5-6)

WHY THIS?

But, God...we're ready to go home—why this? Why the delay? Why the change? Through many years of ministry God has proven faithful—always! Yet, sometimes I still protest, "But, God..."—especially when He changes my plans.

Sometimes God changes our plans not only for our

protection, but also in order to express His extravagant love for us.

On our way home from ministry in Hawaii, Don and I were somewhat settled in reasonably good seats on the aircraft, just waiting for the plane to take off. But we didn't go, and we didn't go, and then we still didn't go. From time to time, there would be an announcement, giving us the status—the technicians were working on some sort of mechanical problem. That was a real comfort!

Eventually, after we had been sitting on the plane going nowhere for a little over two hours, the announcement came over the intercom that the problem was not fixed, the plane would not be going, and that everyone would have to get off the plane, reclaim our baggage, and proceed to the ticket counter to be re-routed. Oh boy!

Sometimes God changes our plans not only for our protection, but also in order to express His extravagant love for us

Don went to the baggage claim area, and I went to stand in line at the ticket counter. About 15 minutes later an airline representative announced to us that the plane we just left would, in fact, be going after all, and that we should hurry back to the plane. Sure enough, when I got back to the downstairs baggage area, Don had already taken our luggage off the carousel. Back to the ticket counter we went, rechecked the bags, and once again proceeded to the security check station. We were hurrying as fast as possible, especially since we had just heard another announcement that we had only 18 minutes to get back to the plane. But there was only one security station open, and a long,

long line of people—the minutes were slipping away quickly.

We finally got through security and all the way into the corridor between the gate and the plane door, when suddenly the crew closed the plane door. They would not let anyone else on or off. Apparently a union official had said they could wait no longer or their flight crew would be flying illegally, or something like that—it had something to do with the length of time the same crew could be on duty. Well, consequently, we, along with about 35 others, were left behind.

At least Don and I were together—there were two couples that we know of that were separated—one on the plane, and the other left behind. Well, the plane door was closed, we weren't on the plane, and there was nothing we could do to change that.

Incidentally, there will be another flight one day when God calls all those who are His to Himself. *"Then shall be two in the field; the one shall be taken, and the other left... Watch therefore; for ye know not what hour your Lord doth come... be ye also ready; for in such an hour as ye think not, the Son of man cometh."* *(Matthew 24:40,42,44)* That separation will be permanent. For those that are left behind there will be no "next flight"—no "re-routing." Are you ready?

But back to the airport in Hawaii—we waved goodbye to our luggage as it was being reloaded on the plane we were **not** on. We then got in line to see what would happen next. I must admit, it was a little tiresome running back and forth between the plane and the ticket counter, but we knew there must surely be a reason for all of this. Although my eyes couldn't see "why this, why now, why me," my heart still knew that God was in control. To quote Oswald Chambers, "You may not know what you are going to do; you only know that God knows what He is going to do."

We were in line a long time, but overhearing some of the conversations ahead of us brought first a smile, and then soft laughter—I was beginning to get the picture. God provided another flight for the following morning, and since we couldn't get a flight out until then, He also provided hotel accommodations for our overnight stay, and not just any hotel— it was the Hilton Hawaiian Village!

And the room God provided was not just any room. Our voucher said a maximum of $85 room rate—but we were given the Molokai Suite on the 17th floor, which rented for, not $85, but $850 per night! God knew we could not pay for such expensive accommodations, so He just "gifted" us with a sweet taste of His loving extravagance! We could not have paid, and didn't have to pay the cost—it was all gratis, including dinner, breakfast, and taxi to and from the airport.

In addition, we were given a $200 voucher toward a future flight. All this, to us, had been a fresh reminder of God's greatest extravagance—He spared no expense when He sent His only begotten Son (not a cheap imitation, but Himself, God Incarnate)—the best He could give, so you and I could be forever forgiven—eternally His! And this great salvation is free to all— costly indeed, but paid in full by the priceless blood of Jesus.

"For by grace are ye saved through faith, and that not of yourselves; it is the gift of God." (Ephesians 2:8) Have you received the Lord Jesus Christ, God's most extravagant gift of all?

Not only did God shower us with His lavish provision, but He also sheltered us in more ways than one. We learned that when the flight we missed landed in San Francisco, rains there had been so heavy that freeways were flooded, and local travel was horrendous! It would have been impossible for our relatives to get there to pick us up, and we would have had to spend a very long time at the San Francisco airport—overnight most likely—and that would have been nothing like the Hawaiian Hilton!

But, God...why this? Why do I have to endure such unbearable conditions? Not all our problems turn out as well as the Hawaiian Hilton. Not every "why" is answered in this lifetime. Early in this ministry, I was invited to sing

Not every "why" is answered in this lifetime

at a Retreat Center in another state. The setting was out in the country with facilities nowhere near the elegance of that Hawaiian hotel. In fact, I was shocked at the accommodations that had been arranged for me. Not only was I to sleep in a rather small, run-down mobile home on the retreat grounds sort of removed from everything else, but at the same time the weather was positively dreadful, complete with very strong winds and extremely heavy rains.

It was also very cold that night with no heat in the room, and the bed was absolutely the lumpiest I have ever experienced in all my life. When I finally found a position to lie in that might possibly work, the roof started leaking directly over the bed—talk about an incredibly wretched night! I was scheduled to sing the next day, and really needed sleep, but there wasn't a whole lot of sleep for me that night.

Of course, I prayed, but for whatever reason, that miserable "sleepless" experience was just something I had to endure. One thing for sure, it really made me thankful for the comfortable times. It also gave me fresh insight into "guest accommodations," and a real desire to provide comfort for those who come to visit in our home. From that time on, we have really endeavored to make convenience and comfort a top priority in providing for our guests. In fact, when we bought a new mattress for the bed in our guest room and a new sleeper-sofa, we first tried them out ourselves to be sure they would be comfortable.

But, God…why all the obstacles? Why this? Why the cancellation? Sometimes God changes our schedule in order to arrange a special meeting that He has planned, and there is no way we can know in advance to rearrange our schedules in order to accommodate His. Sometimes He even cancels a firm appointment so that He can move us into the right place at the right time.

When I received a concert cancellation from Barstow, California, just one day before my scheduled tour departure, doubts and anxieties began to multiply! There would be an entire Sunday open—too late to try to schedule anything else. I didn't know what God would do or how, but somehow I knew God still wanted me to go to Barstow. I **knew** God had a plan— I just **didn't know** what that plan was…yet.

The tour began as scheduled. After all, if Abraham could go out by faith, not knowing at all where he was going, at least I knew most of where I was going, so surely I could believe God not only for the entire tour, but also for a portion known only to Him.

After I arrived in Barstow, the Lord graciously gave me **three** opportunities of ministry that took the place of the **one** cancelled, keeping me in Southern California for that entire week. I began to see some of the reasons why God allowed the cancellation. One of those "replacement" commitments was to sing for a women's luncheon on a Saturday. God blessed that presentation with an overwhelming sense of His presence. After the luncheon, a young lady came to me just bursting with excitement. She was radiant as she referred to one of the songs I sang. She said, "I have been praying for a **year** that **someone** would sing **that** song in one of **these** meetings at **this** place, and **God** has answered my prayer!" That may seem like a little thing, but think about it—even though God had other purposes as well, He changed an entire week of the concert tour so He could answer one small desire and prayer of one woman!

But, God...it's not on my schedule—I don't have time! But it is on His schedule, and time is no problem to Him! Ministries are usually scheduled well in advance, but sometimes God suddenly interrupts our busy schedules and calls us to go somewhere when we least expect it. That was the case in 1990 when, at the last minute, I was asked to sing at the Bexar County Jail. Over the years God has given many opportunities for various prison ministries, but this one was not on my agenda. I had so much to do that I was reluctant to fit it in. It was, however, apparently in God's plan.

Changes and obstacles in our path may mean we need to detour—change our direction—but sometimes they are just a part of the journey

Not only was there an opportunity of ministry through song and testimony to the inmates, but God gave me the perfect opportunity to witness to one of the lady police officers. She received that witness right then and there, and accepted Jesus Christ as her Savior and Lord. Wow, what a joy to see this precious lady born into God's family!

Changes and obstacles in our path may mean we need to detour—change our direction—but sometimes they are just a part of the journey and our direction is right, so we just need to persevere—just keep going. God never promised this life and ministry would be easy (though it sometimes is), but He did promise He would always be with us. Remember what He promised Joshua?

"Have not I commanded thee? Be strong and of a good courage; be not afraid, neither be thou dismayed: for the Lord thy God is with thee whithersoever thou goest." (Joshua 1:9)

He is Here

Just because you cannot see Him
Does not mean God is not there.
Just because you hear no answer
Does not mean He doesn't care.

He said He'd never leave you,
So trust Him, don't despair.
Trust Him when you cannot see,
Keep going when the way's unclear.

For He's watching and He's listening,
And will hear your smallest plea.
He said He'd never leave you,
He is here for you and me!

WHY NOW?

But, God...why did you let this happen now? I don't know what to do! When we are in the center of His will and we know it and something drastic happens, we immediately question the timing—why did God let it happen now? We often have to make some major decisions quickly, and sometimes, quite honestly, we become unsure if we are "flying" in the right direction. Of course, the obvious answer is to go to the "Flight Controller"—our Heavenly Father. But sometimes we don't seem to get an answer. And then we wonder, "What if I make the wrong decision?"

I had just finished ministry in an evangelistic crusade in Salvador, Bahia, Brazil, and had arrived in Rio de Janiero for the second crusade, when my husband called to tell me that my dad had died, and that my family had scheduled the funeral in Fort Worth, Texas.

Brazil is a long way from Texas, and it was going to be impossible to get back in time for the funeral. I didn't know what to do. If I couldn't get back in time anyway, then maybe I should stay and finish the mission for which I came. My dad was a preacher, and that is what he would have done. But, maybe my family needed me. The doubts and questions were innumerable! My husband and I agreed that we would both pray about it, and he would call me back the next day.

I prayed, searched the Scriptures, and talked to my missionary friends, but I did not find an answer. The airline agent had indicated they had no flight that would get me back at the right time. So, as I prayed I made my commitment to the Father that, since I had no specific word from Him, I would stay and do the scheduled mission work in Brazil. When my husband called back, I told him that since God had not directed me otherwise, I thought He must want me to stay in Brazil.

I asked Don to tell my sisters that I would not be able to get there for the funeral. He said he would go along with my decision, but that I should know, from his phone conversations with my sisters, they would be very hurt and disappointed if I didn't get there. Perhaps I should pack up, go to the airport, and try, in person, to get an emergency flight. We agreed that I would follow that plan. It would take a miracle, but if God provided a flight that would get me there in time for the funeral, I would go—otherwise I would stay on mission in Brazil. We continued to pray.

Miracles, of course, are God's specialty—He gave me swift, confirmed passage all the way back to Fort Worth. Funny thing, Don was driving from San Antonio to meet me at the Dallas/ Ft. Worth airport, and I got there before he did! When we arrived at my parents' home and walked in, my sisters said, "Betty, you're here! It's a miracle!"

Why was it so difficult to know God's will whether to return home for the funeral or not? I don't know, but, I suspect that part of the reason may have been to reassure us of God's great faithfulness. When we seek Him for His answer, and find no apparent response, and take the direction that to the best of our understanding seems to be right—if it is not God's will, He will intervene and redirect our path.

Many years later my sisters told me that when our dad died (though they did not tell Don or me at the time) that if I could not get home for the funeral, they would have changed the date of the funeral and had our dad's body held over until I could get back from Brazil. Since I did not know that, it would have been two weeks before I returned. How awful that would have been for my family! But God knew about the family's "Plan B", and in His mercy to everyone He redirected my path and sent me back at just the right time.

"But, God...I'm not left-handed!" That was the cry of my sister-in-law, Arlene, when she broke her right wrist. Although sometimes we act in such careless ways that it is no wonder we break things, there are times that accidents happen through no fault of our own. We know that God could keep these things from happening, yet sometimes He allows them to come into our lives. "How could this possibly be in God's will?" we ask. Although He may answer that question, He may not. God does not have to explain to us. He is sovereign, and His ways, His thoughts, and His purposes are higher than ours:

"For my thoughts are not your thoughts, neither are your ways my ways, saith the Lord. For as the heavens are higher than the earth, so are my ways higher than your ways, and my thoughts than your thoughts." (Isaiah 55:8-9)

I am reminded of our ministry tour to the UK in 2003, and a particular visit in the home of friends in Lochgelly, Scotland. As I stood looking out the window observing the skies, I commented to my Scottish friend, Clodagh, something about the weather, wondering if there would be rain. She responded, "Well, you get what comes!" How right she was! But the wonderful thing is that no matter what comes, GOD is absolutely sovereign, and nothing can touch any child of His without His permission or direction. During a season of great difficulty and many struggles, when God did not tell me "why," He gave me a song instead:

The Higher Purpose[9]

Child of God, when your world is falling apart,
And your mind cannot understand,
And things are just not turning out
The way that you had planned,
Remember all that comes into your life
Passes first through the Father's own hands.

So, look for the higher purpose,
For God is in control.
Submit your will to Jesus,
He'll give peace within your soul.

Well, the problem may still be there,
And the options may be few.
But the Father promised in His word
That He'd watch over you.
And in the power of His Spirit,
He will bring you safely through.

So, look for the higher purpose,
For God is in control.
Submit your will to Jesus,
He'll give peace within your soul.

Sometimes it takes a crisis in our lives
To cause our blind eyes to see.
We're thrust helplessly on God's mercy and love,
His grace and sovereignty.
But it's then we learn to trust Him,
It is then we're finally free.

So look for the higher purpose,
For God is in control.
Submit your will to Jesus.
He'll give peace within your soul.

Does this mean there will never be any more problems? Of course not! There will still be any number of things we cannot understand in this lifetime—accidents, illnesses, diseases, to name a few.

Why does God permit these things? Why did God allow the accident that broke my hip? It took an entire year to get over that surgery. Moreover, I was told that hip replacements like mine don't last, and when they wear out, "adjustments" have to be made—most likely more surgery.

Even the Apostle Paul had a "thorn in the flesh," and prayed three times that God would take it away from him, but God allowed the "thorn" to remain, and assured Paul that His grace was sufficient (2 Corinthians 12:9). Paul's response was:

"...Most gladly therefore will I rather glory in my infirmities, that the power of Christ may rest upon me. Therefore I take pleasure

in infirmities, in reproaches, in necessities, in persecutions, in distresses for Christ's sake; for when I am weak, then am I strong." (2 Corinthians 12:9-10) No question about it, God truly showed Himself strong through the life of Paul!

When the "why's" come, the only thing to do is take them to the Father in prayer. Though we may not see the answers every time, He **will** always answer:

The Answer

Sometimes God says "Yes"—
There's the answer right away.
Sometimes God says "No"—
We can only trust and pray.

Sometimes God says "Wait"—
And you will see My plan.
But sometimes there is a greater "Wait"—
Only in Heaven will we understand.

We must keep our faith in God
Each moment that we live,
For in His way and in His time
The answers He will give.

Why? Why me? Why this? Why now? WHY NOT?

When we don't know "why," and we're tempted to complain, "But, God…," this just could be another of those "hidden" pictures like the ones Brother Lee draws. Our only answer at the moment may be, "…*My grace is sufficient…*" *(2 Corinthians 12:9)* He will answer our prayers according to His will, in His way, and in His time. As one pastor has said: "With God, timing is more than time."

The point is, **God is sovereign**—He **always** will be! He will **always** hear His children, and He will **always** give what is best. So instead of asking, "Why," maybe the better response is, "Why not?" **Our God reigns!**

Chapter 14
How To Wing It—
When Surrounded

During its long flight to and from wintering, the little butterfly can often be surrounded by elements that could devastate him, but he continues his journey in spite of these things. During the lifetime of every new creation in Christ, there will be times when we are "surrounded" by problems that could not only affect, but actually terminate our flight. To name a few of those things that can surround us:

Deceptive Forces

Disruptive Forces

Destructive Forces

Discouragement

Disappointment

Despair

While our adversary, the devil, often employs many of these devices to get us off track, sometimes they are just part of life in a fallen world. Either way, for believers, *"...we know that all things work together for good to them that love God, to them who are the called according to His purpose." (Romans 8:28)*

Deceptive Forces

One of the biggest temptations in a music ministry (or any other) is the desire for acceptance and promotion of that ministry. The desire to share the gospel through a ministry such as Sacred Music, Inc. is legitimate, but we must be careful that it is Jesus Christ we want to promote and not our own personality or talent. In the early days of my involvement in the music ministry, I was invited by a well-known TV personality to sing at a large event.

It sounded like a great opportunity, and this ministry would get a lot of "free" publicity, but there was just one problem: the proceeds of the event would go to fund an unrighteous cause.

The Apostle Paul said, *"All things are lawful for me, but all things are not expedient..." (1 Corinthians 10:23)* Paul was legally free to do all things, but he did not want to do anything that would influence people in the wrong direction.

In any opportunity presented to us, we must examine our own motives, asking ourselves (and being honest with our answers), "Will this please and honor God, and will it be true to His principles?" If I were to sing at this particular event, there could be a great deal of public promotion for this ministry, but at the same time, I would be saying by my participation that this ministry (and I, personally) approved and supported the "cause" to which the proceeds of the event would go. Compromise may be all right in some instances, but never in Christian principles. I could not in good conscience support the cause which the event was promoting, and so declined the invitation to sing for that event. Did I "burn some bridges?"

Perhaps, and perhaps not, but God gave me the discernment to do what was right, and the results were up to Him.

We do not always recognize deception initially, of course, because, as Webster's Dictionary says, to "deceive" is to mislead by falsehood, to lead into error, to delude (mislead the mind or judgment). In other words, on the surface, something may look one way, but when inspected, it is quite another way. For example, a veneer finish on furniture can look like real wood, but when closely examined, the truth is, veneer is only a thin layer of material applied over another substance. Veneer is not genuine wood, it is an imitation. It only has the **appearance** of wood.

Deception is a lot like bait to a fish—it looks so good that it must be good, but it only takes one bite for the fish to realize it has been "hooked!"

There are other pitfalls in ministry, such as the temptation to change a schedule for the wrong reason. In the early years of this ministry, there was one specific instance where we were scheduled to be in a small church, but then received an invitation for the very same date, to minister in a much larger church. I took the "bait," and guess what—the larger church had to cancel.

Deception is a lot like bait to a fish—it looks so good that it must be good

Served me right! My motives were wrong. I was deceived by my own rationalization that if I took the bigger church, I could reach more people, and the offering would probably be better too, thus supplying ministry needs more fully. Not only did I have to confess my erroneous thinking to the Father, but I promised

> ❧
>
> *"More" and "bigger"*
> *may look "better,"*
> *but it is not always*
> *the "best!"*
>
> ❧

Him that I would never allow the **size** of the church or group dictate whether or not this ministry goes to serve them. Since that time, we have served tiny to large and everything in between. Sometimes God sends us to a specific location for just one person! "More" and "bigger" may look "better," but it is not always the "best!" The real issue is to be, not on the edges, but in the **center** of God's will.

At times, we move along in our lives and our vocations, just minding our own business, when we get an offer that appears to be really good. We feel certain that it is in the center of God's will. So we accept the invitation, and before we know it, we find ourselves facing a really tricky situation. Sometimes there is no way to see or even suspect the inherent dangers that accompany such an offer. This was the case in the experience I am about to relate.

Since my husband spent 21 years on active duty with the United States Air Force, we really have a heart for the military. Whether Army, Navy, Air Force, Marine or any other branch of our armed services, these are some of my favorite places of ministry, and God has given many opportunities to serve our military across the United States and around the world.

One of those ministries was in response to an invitation from an Air Force base chaplain in Florida. Although my husband would not be able to go with me due to his job, all the other details seemed to fall into place, and at the right time, I was on my way.

When I arrived in Florida, I contacted the liaison chaplain

by phone, and he informed me that, at the last minute, he had been given orders for temporary duty on another base in Florida, so he would not be present when I arrived at the chapel; however, he had already arranged everything, and there should be no problems. He also said that he would really like to hear about the service afterward. He noted that the base where he was temporarily assigned was right on my way home, and requested that I stop by and give him a report.

He also offered to check with the lodging office, and see whether they would reserve a room on the base so that I could rest for the night before continuing my trip. That was very thoughtful and kind. I would have to stay somewhere that night anyway, especially since I would have been driving about eight hours by then, and would need to a good night's rest for the 8-10 hour drive scheduled for the following day. So, I thanked the chaplain and agreed to stop by.

Things went well, and God blessed the Sunday ministry. Monday morning found me on the road again, praying and thanking God. However, as I drew nearer to the base where I was to meet the chaplain, I began to feel very uncomfortable. I began to wonder why I couldn't have just shared with the chaplain on the phone. Why was he so insistent that I meet him? Why did I agree? The questions kept coming, and there were no comfortable answers. The longer I thought about it all, the worse I felt (which included the development of an increasingly severe headache). I was getting worried. So, I prayed.

I told God I did not want to meet that chaplain. Maybe I shouldn't have agreed to the meeting. Had I missed God? Maybe I should just drive on by and call later. But, I had said I would meet him—should I break my word? "Yes," I thought— "there is just something not right about all this. So, God, I'm not going." But, I had no peace.

So, I continued to pray. "Father, the chaplain said he would arrange for me to have a room at base lodging," I continued, "so, OK, I will go, and if there is a room reserved for me, I will know I am supposed to be there, and I'll check in. Then I will call the chaplain and we can talk about Sunday's service on the phone. I will have kept my word, basically (that I would stop and report to the chaplain), and I can be on my way home early the next morning." With that, I turned onto the road that led to the base, and drove up to the lodging office.

At that moment, I was praying they would **not** have a room for me. So, when the clerk told me they didn't have a reservation in my name, I felt greatly relieved, and thanked her and turned to leave. "But," she said, "we also have rooms on the other side of the base—let me call and see if your reservation is there." In spite of my objections she called, and though there was no reservation in my name, they did have a room available and the clerk booked it for me. I tried to protest, but to no avail. There seemed to be no way out, but I still planned to call the chaplain and visit over the phone—no way did I want to see him in person.

On arrival at the other lodging office, they handed me a key to my assigned room, but before I went to the room I decided to call the chaplain from the lodging office. I planned to explain that I was really tired (which was the truth) and was expecting a long drive the next day (also the truth), so if it was all right with him, we could just discuss the Sunday service on the phone. Then I could go to my room, relax and forget about the whole thing.

When I called the chaplain's office, they said he was out in the field, so I told them that was fine, and that I would just leave him a message. But they insisted that they could get him on the field phone. "No, please don't—I know he is on duty, and I don't want to bother him there," I responded. But it made no difference—the one at the other end of the line insisted he should try, and the next thing I knew, I was talking with the chaplain.

It seemed that no matter how hard I tried, I could not get out of meeting with this man! I thanked the chaplain, and just as I had planned, explained that I was really tired—that it had been a long drive, and since I would need to get an early start in the morning, could we just visit by phone. But he was a bit pressed for time right then, and thought it would be much better if I would go to dinner with him. He reasoned that I would have to eat somewhere anyway, and I could give him the report there. (Actually, I could have done without dinner and been just fine.) He absolutely would not take "no" for an answer. I finally agreed, but said that I would need to get right back so I could get enough rest for the next day's drive.

As I went to my room, I continued to pray. "God, You know I have tried to get out of this, and You know how I feel about it—I'm worried and scared. For whatever reason, You must want me here, but You will have to protect me, and You will have to put your words in my mouth." I asked God to guide me, and the best I knew how, put all my trust in Him. At the same time, a silent little voice kept telling me, "There's no problem because chaplains are honorable, and besides, you are just an ordinary woman, so this man couldn't possibly have any impure motives regarding you—don't flatter yourself!"

When the chaplain came to pick me up, I was waiting outside. I was trusting God, but I still didn't trust the chaplain. Soon we were on our way to a seaside restaurant, and it was a bit of a drive. It only took a few minutes to report on that past Sunday's ministry back at his home base.

The chaplain went on to say, "The moment I saw your picture, I knew there was something different about you," and he reached over to take my hand. Instantly I withdrew my hand, and said, "You know what that something different is? It's Jesus!" And I began to tell him about how Jesus had made such a dramatic difference in my life.

I continued with my testimony, including the fact that I was a Christian for 30 years before I knew anything about the Holy Spirit. I shared how God had brought me to the place of desperation (the same experience that is related in chapter 8 of this book). I explained that Jesus had been resident in my life for a long time before He was President of my life. I shared with him how God had shown me that I needed to spend time alone with Him every day, and give Him everything—total control—all the time—every day.

As we arrived at the restaurant, I continued my story. The chaplain got his turn too. He told me that he was unhappy in his marriage. I told him that God could fix that. He told me about his goals and dreams. At one point in our conversation, I commented "In your job, you must counsel a lot of young airmen." "Oh yes," he said, "regularly." Then I responded, "May I ask you a personal question?" (I could scarcely believe the boldness God was giving me.) "Sure," he said. Then I asked, "Do you spend time alone with God every day?" He lowered his head, and said, "No, I don't." "Then," I continued, "How do you have anything to give to those young men?" He had nothing to say.

At one point in our conversation, the chaplain asked about

the room reservation, and I mentioned that when I checked with the lodging office they did not have a reservation for me. He said that he had indeed made a reservation for me, but he had made the reservation in **his** name, not mine—no wonder there was confusion.

After dinner, the chaplain suggested we take a walk on the beach, but I declined, and before long we were back on the base, and he on his way to the passenger side to open the car door for me. I still wasn't comfortable, and wouldn't be until I was safe in my room, alone with God. I whispered, "God You have brought be safe this far—I am trusting You to **keep** me safe." At that moment, the door opened, and I wasn't sure what to expect. After I got out of the car, the chaplain very kindly and humbly spoke, "I want to thank you for tonight—I heard things from you that I would never have listened to from anyone else. Thank you." Now

> *There are times that we feel completely "taken in" by deception*

I knew the real reason that God wanted me there.

I went, unaccompanied, to my room thanking God, not only for his protection, but for his direction—for letting me be His instrument. I know that chaplain heard God's message that night. Whether he did anything about it, I do not know—I have never heard from him since that time.

There are times that we feel completely "taken in" by deception, but when we give those circumstances and ourselves completely to God, He will accomplish **His** purposes through it all.

Disruptive Forces

There are all kinds of forces that can disrupt our lives, including physical problems, financial difficulties, powers of nature, family crises, even simple changes. Sometimes it seems they conspire, all at the same time, to surround us, and all together, they seem insurmountable.

Looking back, some of the things that seemed to surround and threaten us seem almost comical now. I remember returning home from a wonderful ministry tour, only to face a stopped-up kitchen sink, leaking shower, overflowing washing machine, as well as a "dead" fax machine (which had been knocked out by a storm). In addition to all of that, the ministry had received by mail a very generous contribution of $808.80, only to find out that it was a computer-generated mistake—a $783.80 payment had been erroneously combined with the intended $25.00 contribution. Even though the check was made out to this ministry, $783.80 of it didn't belong to us, and of course, we refunded the money to the people (they had intended those funds to be a mortgage payment).

At times it seems that everything is working against us in a plot to bring us down, and we feel like my friend, Thelma, who (after a particularly trying time) made the following remark: "This is too much to happen to me in one day–I think I'm just going to have to cry!" We can cry if we must, but the best thing to do when everything seems to be falling apart is just to keep on trusting Jesus: *"But the salvation of the righteous is of the Lord; He is their strength in time of trouble. And the Lord shall help them, and deliver them; He shall deliver them from the wicked, and save them, because they trust in Him."* (Psalm 37:39-40)

During a West Coast ministry tour some years back, there

were many disruptions. It had been a long, treacherous drive through the mountains of California to reach the radar site where I was scheduled for ministry. I had not realized it would take so long to get there, and felt completely exhausted by the time I arrived. There was not much time to rest before the evening concert, so after checking into my room, I just sort of fell across the bed with my feet still on the floor.

Suddenly, my ankles started itching like crazy, and before long I was itching all over. I sat up and looked down at the floor—the carpet was literally hopping with fleas! By now not only were fleas all over me, but they were on everything I had brought into the room. As quickly as possible I removed all my things from the room, went back to the lodging office and told them about the fleas. I was given another room in a different building, so after putting all my clothes into a dryer (hoping to kill the "resident" fleas), I moved into the new room. But by now, there was no time for rest before the evening concert.

My flea-bites were incredibly itchy and unbelievably numerous, though most of them were not obvious to anyone else. In spite of the extreme discomfort however, God enabled me to sing. Knowing God could have prevented it, I wondered why he permitted that most disagreeable "flea experience"–it was hard to find anything good about it. Well, there was one thing for sure–as tired as I was, the itching kept me awake to sing, and God did make His presence and power known in spite of my weakness and discomfort. *"And He said unto me, My grace is sufficient for thee; for my strength is made perfect in weakness. Most gladly therefore will I rather glory in my infirmities, that the power of Christ may rest upon me."* (2 Corinthians 12:9)

Another scheduled ministry on that same West Coast tour was at the Oregon Women's Correctional Institution in Salem.

God's Word tells us, *"If our gospel be hid, it is hid to them that are lost; in whom the god of this world hath blinded the minds of them which believe not, lest the light of the glorious gospel of Christ, who is the image of God, should shine unto them." (2 Corinthians 4:3-4).* These words remind us that our adversary, the devil, is strong, and still quite active in his attempts to keep people from knowing Jesus Christ as Savior. So we must continue to pray that God will open the eyes of the lost.

Moments before beginning ministry at that particular correctional institution, I prayed that God would remove every evil power and influence, everything that would disrupt or distract or interfere in any way, so that the women would be able to hear God's message. To my surprise, during my very first song, about half of the women got up and walked out. Even as they were leaving my heart was silently crying out, "Oh, God, no—don't let them leave—they need to hear the gospel!" But, they were gone, and I couldn't bring them back. Talk about disruption!

My heart was breaking for those women, but I continued sharing the gospel in song and word. At the close of the service when I gave an invitation for any who wanted to receive Jesus Christ as Savior and Lord, every single woman who had remained in that auditorium said "yes," and prayed, asking for forgiveness and receiving Jesus into their hearts. What I thought was a serious disruption, I now believe was God's way of answering my prayer that He would remove every evil influence. He simply let those that He already knew would not accept Him that day walk out, so that the rest of the women who were left would be undisturbed and could hear and respond to His call.

Destructive Forces

There are both literal and figurative storms, both of which can be devastating. There will be storms in every life and ministry, and they can make or break us. But, we can learn to "Wing It—Through Every Storm" (see Chapter 16).

There will be many forces in this life that would threaten to "do us in," and they are so often unexpected. There have been numerous times in this ministry that the very act of travel (particularly the problems associated with the ministry vehicle— the van) could have ended everything. But, God has always been faithful to "work everything together for good."

I can honestly say that I am a careful and defensive driver— not one to take many risks, and I always pray that God will protect and direct all of my travel. Still sometimes, there have been accidents, and it seems for all the world, at these times someone is "out to get me." Like the time I was driving home from ministry, traveling through Houston: I was in the westbound, leftmost lane of incredibly heavy three and four-lane traffic, when suddenly a car in the lane to my right sped around another vehicle, catching its bumper and spinning that car in such a way that it wound up in **my** lane, stopped—and facing me! I had no place to go! I braked hard, but the head-on collision was inevitable—the other car couldn't move, and I could not stop in time! Both our vehicles were severely damaged, but, thank God, there were no personal injuries. Though there was some soreness, God protected both the other driver and me from serious harm.

Another time, on my way to ministry in Louisiana, there had been several unavoidable delays, so I would be arriving at my destination later than expected. It was already the dusk of the evening, but my confidence was high—my arrival would not be too late if all went well. But all did not go well. Suddenly, for no apparent reason, all the lights on the van went out, and nothing I tried would restore them. What is more, I was driving on a two-lane road with no shoulder area at all—talk about possible destruction!

There was a little town just ahead, so I thought surely there would be help available. There was absolutely nothing. Whatever there might have been was already closed for the night. And…uh-oh—up ahead I spotted a highway patrol car—just waiting! That's all I needed—a ticket for having no lights. So, I prayed.

The best option seemed to be to "take the bull by the horns," so I drove over and parked alongside the patrol car, got out and asked if he could help me. I told him about the lights going out, and asked if he knew of any place open where I could get the van checked. He suggested the problem could be fuses, but there was absolutely nothing open in that little town; however, there was another town about 25 miles away, and there should be something open there. "But," I said, "It's getting dark—do you think I can make it without lights?" He answered confidently, "If you go right now, I think you'll make it."

Praying all the way, I did make it to the next town, though it was really dark by the time I got there. Thank God, there was a business open that had fuses, and in a short time, the bad fuse was located and replaced, and I was on my way again.

Not many miles down the road, I was delayed again, this time by a major highway accident that apparently had happened 30-40 minutes before I got there. Suddenly it dawned on me that if the lights had not gone out on the van, if I had not been delayed, I could have been involved in that very same accident. Could it be that God turned off the lights in order to save my life? I think so!

Another time I was on an extended ministry tour that included Indiana, Ohio, Pennsylvania, Kentucky and Arkansas. Obviously, there was a lot of driving involved. Things had gone well, but on the way from Ohio to Pennsylvania trouble came again, and the van could go no farther. The last 113 miles to Chambersburg, Pennsylvania had to be via tow truck, the second tow in two days! However, I did get to share the gospel with the tow truck drivers since I had to ride with them—they were pretty much captive audiences. While I don't know whether they ever received Jesus Christ, I do know they know how, and pray for their salvation.

From early in the morning till late at night, my only hope is You

Our troubles had already included a battery replacement, three alternators, and a "phantom" coolant leak that several mechanics had tried (without success) to find. And, oh yes, the speedometer had stopped working, making it impossible to tell how fast or how far I was going. Then there was also the "helpful" passerby, who didn't know anything and proved to be nothing but an irritant.

By this time, it was Saturday night, but Sunday was coming, with concert presentations scheduled morning and evening. Determined to "give thanks for all things," and again committing everything to Jesus, I began to sing a little chorus to Him: *My Only Hope is You.* I don't know who wrote that song, but the words were so appropriate: "From early in the morning till late at night, my only hope is You."

As I waited for that second tow-truck, I sang, prayed, and thanked God, and my faith was again strengthened. I could trust Him to direct my path, and get me to Chambersburg at the right time. Though I heard no audible voice, I knew God was telling me to press on, don't quit, do everything I knew to do, and leave it all in His hands. And, God gave me peace: *"The wisdom that is from above is first pure, then peaceable..."* *(James 3:17)*

The tow-truck finally got there. The van was loaded on the platform, and we headed for Chambersburg, arriving safely just after midnight. Guest speakers, singers, evangelists, etc., usually say they are glad to be wherever they are. Well, I **really** could say that, with renewed meaning, in Chambersburg, Gettysburg, and every other place of ministry on that tour and back home again!

In spite of what could have been "destruction," God not only took care of me and supplied all my needs, but He did some pretty awesome things. For example, in Gettysburg, a Christian lady had taken notice of our scheduled ministry and wanted to attend, but she already had a dinner engagement. She told her date, Charles, of her desire to go to the concert, and asked him whether they might go to dinner early and, following dinner, could attend the concert together. His answer was "yes," but the best "yes" of all was when, at the close of the concert, he prayed to receive Jesus Christ as his Savior—Praise the Lord! Charles must have been one of the main reasons that God really did want this ministry to get to Chambersburg.

After another particularly long ministry tour, having experienced no major problems with the van during travel, I arrived safely home, drove into our driveway, and instantly the transmission died! God kept it going until I got **all** the way home, and then let the van break down in my driveway! There have been many times of travel while driving that van that could have ended in destruction, including flat tires, blowouts, road hazards, and accidents. The van has been broadsided, struck from behind—in fact, struck from every direction. We have gone through heavy rain, severe lightning, snow and ice, hail storms, and even dust storms. Though at times, we seemed **surrounded** by destructive forces, God has brought us safely through. *"The Lord is my Shepherd" (Psalm 23).*

Discouragement—Discouragement, disappointment and despair are all closely related, and sometimes all three surround us all at the same time.

Discouragement just sort of envelopes us at times, and it is not always easy to shake. It comes to us through different faces and many channels, but one of the most difficult to handle is that which comes through well-meaning friends, relatives and co-workers.

Hearing of the travel involved in this ministry and knowing that my husband could not always go with me due to his job, a pastor-friend of ours once told me, "If you were my wife, I'd nail your shoes to the floor!" Talk about a discouraging remark! When I told my husband what this pastor had said, he just smiled and lovingly and kindly answered, "Honey, don't worry about that—he's **not** your husband, **I am**!" My husband has always been in full support of this ministry—you may remember reading in an earlier chapter how God gave the idea of this ministry first to him.

Some time back when traveling in ministry, I stopped to visit a cousin for an hour or so. She made it clear that she disapproved of my being in a ministry that took me so far and wide. She very sharply commented, "Well, I don't know how you do it—I could **never** leave my family and travel as much as you do!" I responded, "Well, if God told you to, you could." "No," she answered, "Not even then!"

Encounters like this weigh heavily on our minds, and truly invite discouragement, but in those times, we just have to take it all to God, lay it at His feet, leave it there, and trust Him. Not if, but **when** we are discouraged about any aspect of the ministry to which He has called us, we just need to remember to recall and rely on His Word: *"Humble yourselves in the sight of the Lord, and He will lift you up."* (James 4:10)

When I first began in this ministry, a pastor suggested to me that I would probably never make it, since the music industry was a very difficult one in which to succeed. And, of course, our adversary the devil, whether through whispers to our minds or through the voices of other people, often ridicules us, and tells us to give up—we can't possibly make it. He has used this same method many times before. I'm reminded of Nehemiah when he was trying to rebuild the walls of Jerusalem—boy, did he get the scorn and the taunting!

God had given Nehemiah not only the desire, but also great favor with the king, so that Nehemiah was given permission and provision by the king in order to get the work done. But enemy opposition was strong, and a number of plots were tried in order to stop the building of the wall.

Among the many ways Sanballat, Tobiah, and Geshem tried to stop the work, mockery and ridicule were especially and continually employed. Sanballat spoke to the army of Samaria: *"What do these feeble Jews? Will they fortify themselves? Will they sacrifice? Will they make an end in a day? Will they revive the stones out of the heaps of the rubbish which are burned?"* (Nehemiah 4:2) To add to the insults, Tobiah said, *"Even that which they build, if a fox go up, he shall even break down their stone wall."* (Nehemiah 4:3)

How in the world can one combat such tactics, when a few are trying to turn all of the public against you? The answer, of course, is by responding as Nehemiah did. He did not answer his enemies—he went directly to God:

"Hear, O our God; for we are despised; and turn their reproach upon their own head, and give them for a prey in the land of captivity:

And cover not their iniquity, and let not their sin be blotted out from before Thee; for they have provoked Thee to anger before the builders.

So built we the wall; and all the wall was joined together unto the half thereof; for the people had a mind to work." (Nehemiah 4:4-6)

Even though they were praying and trusting God to enable them to complete the wall, Nehemiah and all the people worked with one hand and held a weapon in the other because of the continual threats of the enemy, like this one: *"...They shall not know, neither see, till we come in the midst among them, and slay them, and cause the work to cease. And it came to pass, that when the Jews which dwelt by them came, they said unto us ten times, from all places whence ye shall return unto us they will be upon you."* (Nehemiah 4:11-12) But, through it all, from the beginning to the end of the building project, because Nehemiah had a mandate from God, he encouraged the people, *"Our God shall fight for us."* (Nehemiah 4:20)

The most impressive thing about Nehemiah was his courage and steadfastness, and his refusal to interrupt or stop the work. The enemy wanted him to come down from the wall and "negotiate." Five times they sent messages to Nehemiah to "come down" and meet with them. In the fifth message, they accused him of rebellion and insurgency, claiming that he was plotting to become the king of the Jews. But Nehemiah would not leave the work to "parley" with the enemy. He knew all the accusations were lies concocted to stop the work, and he returned such a message to the enemy and refused to come down, quit, or compromise.

It will be over when God says so, and only then. I had a broken hip, but I wasn't dead, and at this writing, I'm not dead yet!

When a believer knows he or she is in the center of God's will and is faced with mockery, ridicule, and every other form of accusation and attack, instead of accepting discouragement and entertaining defeat and despair, we must remember to do just as Nehemiah did so many years ago—take it to our great and mighty God, lay it all before Him, obey Him, and trust Him with all of our hearts.

Several years ago when my hip was broken, requiring major surgery for a partial hip replacement, there were plenty of discouraging times. During the early days of recovery, one of our pastor-friends quipped, "Well, I guess this is the end of your ministry" (almost as if he was glad). I don't think he had talked to God about that, but I had, so I responded, "Not necessarily—it will be over when God says so, and only then." I had a broken hip, but I wasn't dead, and at this writing, I'm not dead yet! I promised God from the very start of this ministry that I would sing and speak until He said it was time to stop, and so far, He hasn't given that order.

Disappointment—Another element common in this "caterpillar" world.

In relationships, events, and other things, disappointment involves expectations—either what we expect to happen doesn't, or what we don't expect to happen does. We sometimes think there will be approval and cooperation, and sure enough, it turns out just the opposite.

One of the most unforgettable disappointments in this ministry was when we were scheduling an event to celebrate the premier of one of our recordings. This recording had been arranged, orchestrated and conducted by an extremely gifted and well-known musician, who would be coming to our city for this event. Not only would those attending the celebration be blessed by the amazing talents of this godly man, but there might also be opportunities for him to be a blessing in other places of our city. However, the person who I thought would be most delighted and interested in this possibility hardly gave the noted musician the time of day.

He further explained to me that he did not think our premier celebration would be successful, so he could not promote our ministry, because, he said, "I only want to be associated with things that are successful...you understand, don't you?" I did understand, and I was crushed! Unless God had lifted me up, that major disappointment and discouragement would likely have culminated in dropping me into the depths of despair, and who knows where it would have led me from there.

Despair—when hope is hard to come by.

Without exception, every person in the world wants love and acceptance, but when we are discouraged and disappointed, we feel only rejection and despair. The longer we stay in such a state, the worse we feel. Now we are folding our wings, because we have begun to think we can't fly anymore. If we are not very careful, we will find ourselves in the midst of a big "pity party" because we have stopped looking at Jesus and focused our eyes on ourselves. We can't look at ourselves and Him at the same time. The longer we look at "us," the less likely we are to regain this thing called "hope"! When hope is postponed, the result is despair:

"Hope deferred maketh the heart sick." Proverbs 12:13

Obviously, the opposite of despair is hope—the two cannot coexist. Clearly the best answer regarding despair is to hope in God:

"Why art thou cast down, O my soul? And why art thou disquieted within me? **Hope** *thou in God: For I shall yet praise Him for the help of His countenance." (Psalm 42:5)*

"Be of good courage, and He shall strengthen your heart, all ye that **hope** *in the Lord." (Psalm 31:24)*

"For Thou art my **hope**, *O Lord God; Thou art my trust from my youth." (Psalm 71:5)*

"But I will **hope** *continually, and will yet praise Thee more and more." (Psalm 71:14)*

I have never seen God fail, because He cannot fail! He will always give direction, comfort and encouragement. It has been my experience that sometimes He speaks those things to my heart even while I am praying. Sometimes He speaks through His Word as I read the Scriptures. And sometimes He speaks through a letter, a phone call or through a friend—even through a grandchild.

This may seem like a rather simple illustration, but some time ago when our grandson, Matthew, was seven, he seemed to have trouble remembering things, like his lunch! One morning the phone rang, and when I answered there was at first a little hesitation, and then the small voice asked, "Is this Grandma?"

I recognized his voice, and said, "Yes." Matthew continued, "I forgot my lunch—could you bring it to me?" I had a million important things to do, but how could I disappoint this little one I loved so much? I said I would get it to him by lunchtime.

When I arrived at school, everyone had already gone to the lunchroom—they had just walked in and were seated. When I walked into the lunchroom, the children seated around Matthew had opened their lunches and were ready to eat. Matthew was ready to eat too, but there was nothing on the table before him.

He was not upset—he was just sitting and patiently waiting—he had **hope**! He knew I would be there, because he had talked to me and asked me to bring his lunch, and I had promised that I would. As I handed Matthew his lunch—he smiled and said, "Thank you, Grandma." I said, "You're welcome," and I hugged him and left. God used that precious grandchild and his forgotten lunch to remind me that when trouble comes, I need not despair. Instead, I need only to get in touch with Him and ask for His help, and then wait for Him with hope in my heart!

Another opposite of despair is delight. When the way is hard and the day is dark, just when we think we can't go on, or wonder if we are really in His will, God sends encouragement and affirmation, and redirection if necessary. In effect, God puts His arms of love around us, and speaks words of assurance to our hearts, and we are at once reminded:

"Thou wilt show me the path of life; in Thy presence is fullness of joy; at Thy right hand there are pleasures for evermore." (Psalm 16:11)

He **is**, after all, the Comforter! We just need to call on Him— He is listening!

"Call unto Me, and I will answer thee, and show thee great and mighty things, which thou knowest not." (Jeremiah 33:3)

"Now the God of hope fill you with all joy and peace in believing, that ye may abound in hope, through the power of the Holy Ghost." (Romans 15:13)

Dr. Vance Havner used to say that the trouble with life is that it is just so daily! We cannot know what lies ahead, good or bad, but we can be sure we will have our share of tough times. Sometimes in this ministry, when the burden of work becomes heavy and finances are low and I begin to feel weak and weary, discouragement begins to knock on the door of my mind. But at that very same time, if I am listening, I can hear God calling *"Come unto Me" (Matthew 11:28)*

So, what to do when surrounded by deceptive, disruptive and destructive forces? When surrounded by discouragement, disappointment and despair? RUN—DON'T WALK—**run** to the Father in prayer! And, for added encouragement, **run** to His Word, the Bible.

When I run to my Father, Almighty God, He not only holds

me closely right then, but He often sends fresh encouragement through someone else. The following note was one of those blessings. These are the words of one who responded to God's message through this ministry. Then he was used of God to speak His message of affirmation to my heart:

> I know God was speaking to me personally as I had reached a decision point of my life—I was discouraged and ready to leave God's work—I was disgusted by my own thoughts etc. and by the behaviour of people. Anyway God ministered to me in a very special way through your ministry, and I know you were sent by Him to do so. Your book 'Where To Go When It Hurts' was written for me.

On another occasion, I received a phone call from a young lady who was traveling through our city. She told me that she had been present at the Whiteman Air Force Base chapel when I was there four years prior to that telephone conversation. During that morning worship service I had presented the gospel of Jesus Christ through song, Scripture and testimony. The young lady just wanted to let me know that she had been saved as a result of that witness that morning at Whiteman AFB, and that she was now growing as a believer. Talk about encouragement!

God has affirmed this ministry and encouraged my heart many times through the words of people that He has touched and spoken to through this ministry. Many other experiences could be shared, but I just want to **brag on God**! *"In God we boast all the day long, and praise Thy name for ever." (Psalm 44:8)* Lest we begin to think that we are in any wise responsible for the success of the gospel, we must always remember: *"But we have this treasure in earthen vessels, **that the excellency of the power may be of God, and not of us.**" (2 Corinthians 4:7)*

For LOTS of success when surrounded:

L – Listen—just keep listening to God

*"My sheep **hear** my voice, and I know them, and they follow me." (John 10:27)*

O – Obey—just keep on going as God directs

*"Hath the Lord as great delight in burnt offerings and sacrifices, as in **obeying** the voice of the Lord? Behold, to **obey** is better than sacrifice, and to hearken than the fat of rams." (1 Samuel 15:22)*

"Know ye not, that to whom ye yield yourselves servants to obey, his servants ye are to whom ye obey; whether of sin unto death, or of obedience unto righteousness?" (Romans 6:16)

T – Trust—just keep on trusting God.

"Trust in Him at all times; ye people, pour out your heart before Him: God is a refuge for us." (Psalm 62:8)

"In Thee, O Lord, do I put my trust; let me never be put to confusion." (Psalm 71:1)

S – Sovereignty of God.

To again quote my friend, Thelma, "I've been through a lot of hard things in my life, but what I've learned about the sovereignty of God has been the most precious thing in my life."

"Be still, and know that I am God: I will be exalted among the heathen, I will be exalted in the earth." (Psalm 46:10)

*"For great is the Lord, and greatly to be praised; He also is to be feared above all gods. For all the gods of the people are idols: but **the Lord made the heavens**." (1 Chronicles 16:25-26)*

*"Let the heavens be glad, and let the earth rejoice; and let men say among the nations, **The Lord reigneth**." (1*

Chronicles 16:31)

*"Thine, O Lord, is the greatness, and the power, and the glory, and the victory, and the majesty; for all that is in the heaven, and in the earth is Thine; Thine is the kingdom, O Lord, and **Thou art exalted as head above all.**"* (1 Chronicles 29:11)

*"And the heavens shall declare His righteousness: for **God is Judge Himself.**"* (Psalm 50:6)

*"**The Lord reigneth**...Thy throne is established of old: Thou art from everlasting."* (Psalm 93:1-2)

"Blessed be the name of God for ever and ever; for wisdom and might are His; And He changeth the times and the seasons; He removeth kings, and setteth up kings; He giveth wisdom unto the wise, and knowledge to them that know understanding; He revealeth the deep and secret things; He knoweth what is in the darkness, and the light dwelleth with Him." (Daniel 2:20-22)

King Nebuchadnezzar was so filled with himself that he took all the credit for his great success. Because he would not acknowledge that it was God who made him great, he was warned by the prophet Daniel that he, the king, would become like a beast, literally, and live as such for a long period of time—*"till thou know that the **Most High ruleth in the kingdom of men**, and giveth it to whomsoever He will"* (Daniel 4:25)

It happened just as Daniel prophesied, the king lived and looked like an animal until at the end of those days:

*"I Nebuchadnezzar lifted up mine eyes unto heaven, and mine understanding returned unto me, and I blessed the Most High, and I praised and honored Him that liveth for ever, whose dominion is an everlasting dominion, and His kingdom is from generation to generation: And all the inhabitants of the earth are reputed as nothing: And **He doeth according to His will** in the army of*

heaven, and among the inhabitants of the earth; and none can stay His hand, or say unto Him, What doest Thou?" (Daniel 4:34-35)

King Nebuchadnezzar had to learn the hard way that it is really God who is in control. Sometimes we have to learn the hard way too, because we won't listen any other way. Still, even in the midst of our "lessons," we are comforted by the Word of God:

"But Thou, O Lord, art a God full of compassion, and gracious, longsuffering, and plenteous in mercy and truth." (Psalm 86:15)

God **is** absolutely sovereign—in total control and nothing can touch us that does not first pass through His hands. **Everything** that comes into our lives comes either by His direction or His permission. Our response before, during, and after a crisis should be like that of Daniel's three friends when threatened by the fiery furnace:

"If it be so, our God whom we serve is able to deliver us from the burning fiery furnace, and He will deliver us out of thine hand, O king. But if not, be it known unto thee, O king, that we will not serve thy gods, nor worship the golden image which thou has set up." (Daniel 3:17-18)

Those young Hebrew men were delivered—in fact, when you read the complete story, though the men who threw them in the fire perished from the great heat, the Hebrew children walked in the fire unharmed (and Jesus walked with them), and when they were released, they did not even smell like smoke!

We must also remember that God's purposes are not to harm us, but to strengthen, teach, and conform us to the image of His Son (Romans 8:29). He will be with us in all our troubles: *"For He hath said, I will never leave thee or forsake thee." (Hebrews*

13:5) And nothing can ever separate us from Him: *"For I am persuaded that neither death, nor life, nor angels, nor principalities, nor powers, nor things present, nor things to come, Nor height, nor depth, nor any other creature, shall be able to separate us from the love of God, which is in Christ Jesus our Lord."* *(Romans 8:38-39)*

Making Me Like Him

Jesus knew the times that I would turn

And walk in my own way,

And yet, He's never left me,

Not one moment, not one day!

He knew the pain I'd suffer,

Knew the losses I would bear,

Knew my deepest disappointments

And the depths of my despair.

Yet, He loved me and He chose me,

And saved me from my sins,

And He's walking with me, working with me,

Making me like Him!

Jesus knows my every motive,

Sees within the heart of me;

He knows my honest thinking
And my intentions to deceive.

Yet He loves me and has chosen me,
And saved me from my sins.
He's still walking with me, working with me,
My Father's making me like Him.

If you have received Jesus Christ as your Savior, but you're feeling surrounded just now, remember:

Who your Father is—The Awesome, Almighty, Holy, and Sovereign God. And yet, He lets you call Him Father!

What God is doing in your life—conforming you to the image of His Son, Jesus Christ. (Romans 8:29)

Where you are—in the His hand! (John 10:28-30)

Wherever you go, God is with you! "*Have I not commanded thee? Be strong and of a good courage; be not afraid, neither be thou dismayed; for the Lord thy God is with thee whithersoever thou goest.*" (*Joshua 1:9*)

Chapter 15
How To Wing It—
When Overwhelmed

Webster's dictionary says that the word "overwhelm" means to overcome completely, or to make helpless. I guess that's pretty accurate, because that is the way some things affect us when they loom so large and strong that we don't know how to cope. Some of the most common things that overwhelm us are: darkness, weakness, uncertainty, fear, pain and sorrow. Any one of these have the **potential** to "ground" us, but the good news is that we can "fly" in spite of them. *"I can do all things through Christ which strengtheneth me." (Philippians 4:13)*

Overwhelmed by darkness

Can't see where you are going? There are different kinds of darkness. There is the **literal blackness** of night when the moon and stars are hidden from view, and no other kind of light is available. There is the same kind of darkness in a room with no windows and no source of electrical or battery-powered light.

Darkness is a prime arena for panic, because most of us fear what we cannot see. My friend, Doreen, says we lose our identity in the dark. We can't even see ourselves! Our imaginations run wild, and we can soon become completely overwhelmed by the absence of light. The obvious solution is, of course, to move from the darkness to an area where there is light, or find a source of light to relieve the darkness we are in. But, if neither of these actions are immediately possible, what can we do?

I have read that most butterflies do not fly at night. I don't know what the little creatures do in the dark, but I do know what we can do when you and I are in the dark—we can go to God's Word, the Bible: *"If I say, Surely the darkness shall cover me; even the night shall be light about me. Yea, the darkness hideth not from Thee; but the night shineth as the day; the darkness and the light are both alike to Thee."* (Psalm 139:11-12)

Does this mean that God will instantly replace the darkness with light? It **is** possible (nothing is too hard for Him), but I rather think God is telling us there is no need to fear. Instead, we can trust Him completely because neither day nor night, dark nor light, will ever limit His power—they are both the same to Him. He can dispel the darkness literally, or figuratively—either way He will lead us through to His light. *"God is light, and in Him is no darkness at all."* (1 John 1:5)

There is darkness of mind and soul when our understanding is unclear or wrong—we are **un**enlightened. This **acquired darkness** can be overwhelming unless we turn to God and His Word for light:

"Thy Word is a lamp unto my feet, and a light unto my path." (Psalm 119:105)

"The entrance of Thy words giveth light; it giveth understanding to the simple." (Psalm 119:130)

"The righteousness of Thy testimonies is everlasting; give me understanding, and I shall live." (Psalm 119:144)

Chosen darkness occurs when we close our eyes and refuse to see. I am reminded of a time that I was watching one of our young grandsons wash his face. I observed with interest that his eyes were closed the whole time. "Matthew," I asked, "if your eyes are closed, how can you find your face to wash it?" His response was classic, "It's OK, Grandma, I know right where it is!"

Matthew chose that temporary darkness, and it was just no big deal. Personally, I choose otherwise—I much prefer keeping my eyes open when I wash my face so I will get it all clean—and I don't like soap in my eyes!

It is patently obvious that if our physical eyes are closed, we cannot see where we are going. It is also true that if our eyes are closed spiritually, it will be just as difficult to see. Even the strongest can fall down if the choice is to walk in darkness instead of light. There **is** a solution—turn on the light! We do not have to stumble around in the dark. We can, but we don't have to. It **is** our choice, and it is a daily choice to let the light of Jesus illumine our lives.

Jesus has already told us what to do when we are overwhelmed by any form of darkness—He said:

*"I am the light of the world; he that **followeth me** shall not walk in darkness, but shall have the light of life." (John 8:12)*

"For ye were sometimes darkness, but now are ye light in the Lord; walk as children of light." (Ephesians 5:8)

When things are not all the way dark, but dim

Probably everyone has heard the old saying, "Seeing is believing." Dr. Vance Havner used to say it is quite the other way around, "Believing is seeing!" Many times in this ministry, the way has seemed unclear. The only solution was (and is) to pray. We may not see instantly, but as we keep on trusting the Lord, in His way and in His time, His light will make our way clear.

If you are feeling overwhelmed by darkness just now, **believe, trust:**

Trust the **One** who created light and divided the light from the darkness. (Genesis 1:14-18)

Trust the **One** who can and will give you light, the **One** who **is** the Light:

Too weak to fly? Trust and obey the **One** *who gave you the wings, Almighty God Himself!*

"For Thou art my lamp, O Lord; and the Lord will lighten my darkness." (2 Samuel 22:29)

"The Lord is my light and my salvation; whom shall I fear? The Lord is the strength of my life; of whom shall I be afraid?" (Psalm 27:1)

Trust the **One** who will one day end darkness forever:

"And the city had no need of the sun, neither of the moon, to shine in it; for the glory of God did lighten it, and the Lamb is the light thereof." (Revelation 21:22)

"And there shall be no night there; and they need no candle, neither light of the sun; for the Lord God giveth them light; and they shall reign for ever and ever." (Revelation 22:5)

Overwhelmed by weakness

Too weak to fly? Trust and obey the **One** who gave you the wings, Almighty God Himself!

"He giveth power to the faint; and to them that have no might, He increaseth strength." (Isaiah 40:29)

"For it is God which worketh in you both to will and to do of His good pleasure." (Philippians 2:13)

We cannot depend upon our own strength or feelings. Our strength will fail, and our feelings will fool us—they even change sometimes with the weather. We must look to God, ask Him to replace our weakness with His strength, and by faith, whether we see or feel anything different, trust Him. We can go in the power of His might: *"I will go in the strength of the Lord God."* (Psalm 71:16)

One of the most striking examples of hearing and heeding and then seeing God do the impossible is found in the third chapter of Joshua—I love this story! As Joshua and the children of Israel approached the river Jordan, God gave Joshua directions and warnings before crossing over. The people were commanded:

"When ye see the ark of the covenant of the Lord your God, and the priests the Levites bearing it, then ye shall remove from your place and go after it. Yet there shall be a space between you and it, about two thousand cubits by measure: come not near unto it, that ye may know the way by which ye must go: for ye have not passed this way heretofore. And Joshua said unto the people, Sanctify youselves: for tomorrow the Lord will do wonders among you." (Joshua 3:3-5)

God told Joshua, *"And thou shalt command the priests that bear the ark of the covenant, saying, When ye are come to the brink of the water of Jordan, ye shall stand still in Jordan."* (Joshua 3:8)

Joshua had not read the end of chapter three, so he **did not know** what God was going to do, but I suspect that he may have reflected back to the time that God parted the Red Sea for the children of Israel when they fled from Egypt. Joshua must have recalled Moses' words: *"And Moses said unto the people, Fear ye not, stand still, and see the salvation of the Lord, which He will show you today; for the Egyptians whom ye have seen today, ye shall see them no more for ever. The Lord shall fight for you, and ye shall hold your peace." Exodus 14:13-14.* And Joshua surely remembered that when God parted that sea, the children of Israel walked all the way through on dry land!

According to Exodus 12:37, there were about 600,000 men, and some say that with the addition of women and children to that number, there must have been close to 2,000,000 people who walked across! As the Egyptians pursued, attempting to follow the children of Israel through the Red Sea, God closed the path and allowed those walls of raging waters to rush in upon the Egyptians, and they all drowned!

By faith, Joshua gave instructions to the children of Israel. He told them to come and hear the word of the Lord. He assured them that they would know that the living God was among them and would without fail drive out their enemies (Joshua 3:10).

"Behold, the ark of the covenant of the Lord of all the earth passeth over before you into Jordan...And it shall come to pass, as soon as the soles of the feet of the priests that bare the ark of the Lord, the Lord of all the earth, shall rest in the waters of Jordan, that the waters of Jordan shall be cut off from the waters that come down from above; and they shall stand upon a heap." (Joshua 3:11,13)

By faith, Joshua, along with all the children of Israel and the priests that carried the ark of the covenant, obeyed God, and look what happened:

"And as they that bare the ark were come unto Jordan, and the feet of the priests that bare the ark were dipped in the brim of the water, (for Jordan overfloweth all its banks all the time of harvest,) that the waters which came down from above stood and rose up upon a heap very far from the city Adam, that is beside Zaretan: and those that came down toward the sea of the plain, even the Salt Sea, failed, and were cut off: and the people passed over right against Jericho. And the priests that bare the ark of the covenant of Lord stood firm on dry ground in the midst of Jordan, and all the Israelites passed over on dry ground, until all the people were passed clean over Jordan." (Joshua 3:15-17)

Did you happen to notice that the waters parted, not before, but **when** the priests stepped into the water? It would have been a lot easier if they could have **seen** the path through the water before they started across, but there was no visual evidence of any kind of path. To make things even more challenging, the Jordan river was at flood-stage! But, when Joshua, the priests, and all the children of Israel acted in obedience to God's directions, moved ahead, and stepped **into** the floodwaters, their weakness became strength and their faith became **actual sight**!

What God has promised,

He will **always** do!

He will **always** make a way

For me and for you!

Whether the rivers of trouble in your life or mine are at flood-stage, or but a trickle, or anything in between, our God will see us through. Our own personal weakness and inability has no bearing on **God's ability** to bring us over or through our Jordan. Nor does our own personal strength and ability make any difference at all. It is our focus on God, our faith in Him, and our obedience to Him that prepares us to experience His wondrous deliverance.

Most preachers, missionaries, evangelists, and music evangelists like me can attest that there have been times of such great physical weakness and illness that it seemed it would be impossible to stand and deliver the message God has given. But just as the **Lord of all the earth** went before Joshua and the children of Israel, He goes before us and with us, and will without fail accomplish all He desires through us as we yield to Him and trust Him fully. Somehow, when we take that first "step into the waters," God ushers forth His supernatural strength and energy to "walk all the way through the sea on dry land!"

Due to poor health and associated problems with aging, the well-known evangelist, Dr. Billy Graham, has for several years continued to struggle with great physical weakness. He now has to have help just to reach the pulpit, but when he does get there and opens his mouth to speak, God's message comes through with great clarity and power—God's power!

"...My grace is sufficient for thee; for My strength is made perfect in weakness..." (2 Corinthians 12:9)

Overwhelmed by uncertainty and frustration—

If you've never gotten confused, mixed-up, or lost your way, you are rare indeed! Chances are, there will be times of aggravation and frustration in your life because of the way things are working or not working. Sometimes these are small and petty, like the stapler I was trying to use recently—only every fourth staple came out right! That was, indeed, a little thing, but it certainly was irritating and frustrating! Instead of the dependable stapler that I had been using for years, I was trying to use a new "freebie" that I had "won" as a prize. The only thing to do was to return to the "tried and true" stapler, and it worked right every time!

Sometimes we **think we can substitute** something different for a tool we know is good and right for the job. It would be ridiculous to try to substitute a table knife for a saw in order to cut through a 2x4 plank! I suppose that eventually you could cut through with the table knife, but what a job it would be! Not only would the aggravation be at an all time high, but the result would be far from satisfactory!

Frustrations often come when we attempt to use a substitute for genuine replacement parts. Case in point—the home phone system I mentioned before. With time and use the battery packs inside our portable telephones became weak, and eventually just didn't work any more. We tried some generic types—after all, the package indicated that they were replacement battery packs for the brand-name phones we had. The only thing is—they just didn't work!

By trial and error, we discovered that the **only** battery pack that really works correctly is the **one** made by the company who made the phones! Now that I think of it, in the original instructions for those portable instruments there was a little notation that said something about using only genuine replacement parts of their particular brand name. Sometimes we get frustrated in our Christian walk (and "flight") because we have resorted to a **substitute** solution rather than the precise, quality instructions and principles of God's Word. When we study His original instructions, we find that the only solutions that really work are the ones given by our Maker!

Sometimes we overwhelmingly lose our way **when we take "short-cuts."** Many times the shortcut becomes the long way or the wrong way! In chapter nine of this book, I related our experience of driving from Rome to Naples during a ministry tour in Italy some years ago. A lot of the problems we experienced on our journey were a direct result of our taking a "short-cut," combined with the lack of a map.

Many times the shortcut becomes the long way or the wrong way!

God has given us a perfect map in His Word. He not only knows the way, He **is** the way! So, when tempted to choose an alternate route, if we will first go directly to the Master and check His Map, we will know the right way, and save a lot of grief! I do realize that sometimes, through no fault of our own, things happen, and we are not sure where to proceed from where we are. Still, the best action is not reaction, but to go the Master Consultant—our Heavenly Father—and give Him our uncertainties. He will get us going in the right direction on the right path.

"Trust in the Lord with all thine heart, and lean not unto thine own understanding. In all thy ways acknowledge Him, and He shall direct thy paths." (Proverbs 3:5-6)

There were many frustrations, both great and small, during the time my husband was on active duty in the United States Air Force, particularly during some of our overseas assignments. At the time we received orders to go to Brazil, our youngest child was 7 weeks old, and our other three were 6, 8, and 10 years of age.

That first journey to Brazil was fraught with overwhelming complications—even the flight to get us there! Our plane was late taking off from Charleston, South Carolina, due to engine problems—that was a real comfort! When we finally did take off we narrowly missed a mid-air collision with another plane that was coming in for a landing! Our stop in Dutch Guinea almost proved to be an overnighter, since our plane couldn't seem to get off the ground (once again due to engine trouble)! At last, on the fourth try, we made it airborne and then the rest of the way to Rio de Janeiro. After a couple of days there, we finally boarded the plane that would take us to our desired destination, Salvador, Bahia, Brazil.

Salvador was considered a remote assignment, and we understood why when we arrived. Very few spoke English, and it was like going back 50 years in time!

We lived in a hotel in Salvador for a few weeks before finding an apartment. While in the hotel we were challenged not only with managing a family in small quarters, washing clothes in the bathtub, and getting the children in school, but we were also trying to learn the Portuguese language.

Within a short time after moving into an apartment, our household goods arrived. When trying to install the kitchen range, we found that a special adapter was needed, and since Don had to be at work, it was up to me to go to downtown Salvador and procure the part. What a frustrating experience, especially since my Portuguese language skills were somewhat— no, a lot—lacking! Suffice it to say that God worked everything out and enabled us to get the right part and get it installed— and the stove worked!

But that was only the beginning. It was almost Christmas, and we couldn't afford a Christmas tree. They were very expensive in Salvador—way out of our reach. Our budget was already stretched beyond the limit. But, the children would be so disappointed if we had no tree! It looked like a rather bleak Christmas, but, God gave me an idea. The mattresses for our beds had been packed in large, strong cardboard cartons, and we still had a couple of those cartons. We could make a cardboard Christmas tree!

After flattening the cartons into single panels, I laid two of them on the floor and drew an outline of a Christmas tree on each one. Then I cut the two "trees" out (scissors wouldn't do it—I had to use a butcher knife). Then the children colored the "trees" with crayons. I sort of glued the two parts together to make our Christmas tree look more full. Our homemade decorations were not perfect but very interesting. The "garlands" we draped around the tree were paper chains and popcorn ropes. Of course, that took a while since we kept eating the popcorn!

It wasn't the most beautiful Christmas tree I had ever seen, and it was definitely different (and somewhat crude, I admit), but it didn't look half bad! The children didn't seem to mind that the tree wasn't real—in fact, they loved it! And, the entire cost of the tree and decorations had been most insignificant. All it really cost was some time and effort. The frustration about not being able to buy a Christmas tree at first seemed overwhelming, but actually it turned out to be no problem at all.

Now our family has grown up and our children have children of their own. Whenever memories of the past are stirred, do you know which Christmas the children remember the most?

If you guessed the "Cardboard Christmas," you are right! Long ago, my mother taught me that it isn't how much money you do or don't have, but it is what you do with what you have that matters most.

Do what you can,

(You can't do everything, but you can do some things),

With what you have,

(You can't do anything with what you don't have),

Where you are,

(You can't do anything where you are not),

And do it now!

(Don't wait for things to get "better").

There were lots of other frustrations during our three years in Brazil, one of which was the purchase and delivery of groceries. Some of the things could be purchased locally, but some of our favorite American foodstuffs could not be found in the Salvador markets. However, we could place an order with the commissary located in Rio de Janeiro, and once a month, the groceries would be delivered by plane. How exciting it was when our orders came in—it was almost like Christmas!

One of our favorite items was Log Cabin syrup for pancakes. I will never forget one particular time an order came in, after waiting for six weeks—bad weather had kept the plane from coming on schedule. I had ordered a huge bottle of our favorite syrup, and as I was unpacking the groceries, I dropped the bottle, and it broke into pieces! The syrup was not only ruined, but was flowing everywhere. How could I have been so careless? I was so frustrated that I just sat in the middle of the floor and cried!

But that wasn't the only syrup in the world! In fact, our missionary friend gave us some maple flavoring and showed me how to make my own syrup. Log Cabin or other types may still be very good, but now we prefer my "homemade" syrup.

Probably one of the most dramatic times of uncertainty and frustration was when my husband received a message from the embassy office in Rio de Janeiro offering him the opportunity to transfer to Sao Paulo. We were scheduled to be in Salvador for two years, and had already been there nine months. Moving to Sao Paulo would automatically extend our stay in Brazil. Instead of staying two years, we would be staying three. We were content to stay in Salvador. So my husband answered the offer with a "no, thanks." Almost immediately he received another message, "You will report to Sao Paulo on..." We didn't have a choice after all. The decision was final—there was nothing we could do about it.

Both Don and I were disappointed, discouraged and frustrated. But, we couldn't let the children know—we would have to pretend we loved the idea of leaving Salvador, driving a thousand miles through the interior of Brazil, and staying in Brazil a year longer than we had planned. Packing up and leaving our now familiar surroundings and driving to Sao Paulo proved to be even more challenging and frustrating that we had expected.

We were told that we should not attempt to drive at night, because not only was there a danger of bandit attacks, but sometimes whole sections of the road might be missing, and there would be no warning signs or lights to prevent us from driving into oblivion! We wisely took that advice. During daytime driving we did see areas where the road had fallen in or had been washed away. Along the way we played silly word games with the children as if we were having the time of our lives. We were laughing on the outside, but inside our hearts were deeply troubled, though the children never suspected it.

We arrived safely in Sao Paulo, and there are dozens of other interesting, frustrating, and fun experiences we could share about our time there, but this much has to be told. The first Sunday we were in Sao Paulo we visited a little English-speaking chapel, and what a blessed experience that was! The pastor preached a wonderful message, and the Word of God just seemed to pour over us in wonderful, refreshing showers of blessing.

In Salvador we had tried Sunday worship services together with the Portuguese-speaking believers, but we knew so little of the language that we could only understand a few basic words. Even though we could feel the presence of the Lord in those services, our struggles to understand left us with punishing headaches. Don and I reasoned that if we were having that much trouble, and we had actually had some basic language training, our children must be having even more difficulty. So we decided to try the English-speaking church until we could get a better grip on the Portuguese language. Although there were some very good messages preached in that little nondenominational church, not everything was as it should have been for a New Testament church. We hoped matters would change, and resolved to do what we could to help, but our efforts seemed to be fruitless.

Back to our first Sunday in Sao Paulo, however—after the message that morning, we knew we had experienced a great spiritual feast! In comparison to what we had been accustomed to, it was like sitting down to prime-rib steak after almost a year of hot dogs! During the remainder of the two years in Sao Paulo, God grew us in Him through messages delivered by Pastor Shurtz and through the fellowship of believers at the

Metropolitan Chapel.   Also, during the time we were there God gave Don the privilege of being ordained as a deacon.

There seemed to be a sort of pattern that occurred a lot during our time in Brazil: first overwhelming uncertainty and frustration because of unwanted changes, then acceptance (though sometimes reluctantly) of those changes, and ultimately, victory, in spite of, or maybe because of, those changes. But all of the changes were in God's plan for us—He used them for our good and for His glory.

Wherever you are right now, and whatever uncertainties and/ or frustrations you face, simply give everything to the Father, now. Don't wait for better weather, better finances, better conditions, or better anything. Just do what God says—do it now—obey and trust Him to accomplish all He chooses to do through it all. And you know what you'll get? Contentment!

> *Contentment is not getting what you want, but wanting what you've got*
> *- David Ring*

Evangelist David Ring once said, "Contentment is not getting what you want, but wanting what you've got." That does not mean we should not have goals, but it does mean that we should yield ourselves and our goals to God, then pursue them as He leads. He may not choose to fulfill them all, or any of them, but when we know we are in the center of His will, trusting Him completely, we can be fully content, knowing the outcome will be right. The Apostle Paul said:

"Not that I speak in respect of want; for I have learned, in whatsoever state I am, therewith to be content." (Philippians 4:11)

That is quite a statement, considering all the persecution

Paul suffered! One thing for sure, contentment in our great God is a wonderful defense against uncertainty and frustration.

Overwhelmed by Fear

Fear is probably **the** most immobilizing and overwhelming factor in our lives.

Fear wears lots of faces. What are you most afraid of? Failure? Rejection? Financial disaster? Illness? Death? Probably most of us experience all these fears, and many others, during our lifetime, even if only briefly. We mentioned in another chapter that fear is one of the favorite tools of our adversary the devil in his attempts to destroy us. No wonder he uses it so much—it works so well! Small fears grow into giant anxieties, and the "what-if's" play havoc with our thoughts and emotions.

Fear is probably the most immobilizing and overwhelming factor in our lives

If only we could remember that faith cancels out fear. When we face our fears and choose to believe God and His promises, regardless of how scared we feel, those fears will actually fade away! (Isaiah 41:13)

There are all kinds of fears (phobias), but our Heavenly Father is greater than **all** of them! Some years ago, our friend, Melody, was suffering from a devastating fear—agoraphobia. Technically, that is "fear of the marketplace," but actually, it is a fear of being out among people any place away from one's secure home, apartment, etc. I understand that this kind of fear is not psychological, but is, in fact, caused by a chemical imbalance in the brain. Nevertheless, Melody became so insecure and fearful that she was almost a recluse, bombarded by frequent panic attacks which left her lightheaded, shaky, and sick to her stomach. She even became suicidal.

There was one day that I was convinced Melody was going to try to end her life, so I went to her house to talk with her, but she wouldn't let me in. How I wanted to help her, but she refused. In no uncertain terms she told me to go away. There was nothing I could do except pray, and I did. She got past that awful day, but those dreaded fears continued to harass her. I received a letter from her that said, in so many words, that she didn't want me to write or call anymore, but that I should just give up and forget about her. But, God would not let me do that. I answered Melody's letter and told her that I was her friend whether she liked it or not, and that I wasn't giving up— I would continue to pray for her.

While in prayer for Melody one day, God spoke to my heart very specifically about her. He impressed me to ask her to be the prayer chairman of this ministry. I wasn't sure I had heard Him correctly. After all, she was rather unstable. God did not explain His plan to me, but simply continued to urge me to ask her to be the prayer chairman.

So, I called Melody and told her how God had spoken to my heart, and asked her if she would consider being our prayer chairman. People often called or wrote to us and asked for prayer, and we did pray, but we felt it would be wonderful if there were someone in this ministry who could devote full-time prayer to those requests. I told Melody we would provide her with a notebook and paper and whatever other supplies she needed in order that the requests could be recorded and dated, along with dates of answered prayer and associated comments. As the requests came in, we would pray and then forward the requests to Melody. She promised to think and pray about it.

The next time we talked, Melody said that since she was pretty much home-bound and didn't have anything else to do anyway, she might as well take the job. She did assume that responsibility and began praying for people on a daily basis. Not only was that a blessing in many lives, but one of the most awesome things happened as she continued in that ministry. As Melody prayed for others, God began to heal **her!** Did He ever!

There has been much evidence of that miraculous cure. One of the most dramatic proofs of healing began in the summer of 1996 when the 1997 South Central Texas Billy Graham Crusade was in planning. Melody had always had a great respect for Billy Graham, and had even been a counselor at one of his crusades when she was 16, before the agoraphobia problem began. Her greatest desire that summer was that by the time the crusade was set to begin in the spring of 1997, she would be able to physically go to the huge Alamodome in San Antonio and attend the crusade.

Melody began to pray that God would make that crusade possible for her, and we prayed too. She was asking for three things: that she could go in person and worship together with the crowd at the crusade in the Alamodome; that she would get to see Dr. Billy Graham and hear him preach; and that through it all she would have **no** anxiety. All this for a girl who could scarcely get two miles away from her safe-haven (her mobile-home)!

God answered all three requests! That April of 1997, Melody drove herself to the Alamodome, and sat, without fear, among those 60,000 or 70,000 people (I don't remember exactly how many were there). She did get to worship there and see Dr. Billy Graham and hear him preach—and **all without anxiety**! What an **AWESOME GOD** we serve!

Since that time, Melody has been able to go to church, and even sing solos, and now teaches a Sunday School class. Now, that is healing! Looking back, we can all rejoice to see where God has brought her from, and shudder to think where she could have been if God had not rescued her just in time. Does this mean she never ever has any more problems? Of course not! There are still times when the old fears come knocking at her door, and when they do, she has to remember where her strength and salvation comes from:

"What time I am afraid, I will trust in Thee...When I cry unto Thee, then shall mine enemies turn back; this I know; for God is for me." *Psalm 56:3,9*

"Ye that fear the Lord, trust in the Lord; He is their help and their shield." *(Psalm 115:11)*

"The Lord is my strength and song, and is become my salvation." *(Psalm 118:14)*

But, couldn't God prevent fear from ever knocking again? Indeed He could, but sometimes He allows those fears and problems to come knocking, because He intends to make us stronger as He enables us to overcome them.

Some of the deepest fears we face are financial ones. We forget that we really don't own anything—everything we have is borrowed, even the air we breathe. God can remove anything and everything at any moment. He can also allow the devil to remove everything—case in point, Job! Though God did not reverse those losses, He did multiply His blessings to Job afterward, giving him twice as much as he had before! (Job 42:10) God **is** in control, even in times of humiliation and devastation. When you find yourself in great anxiety and turmoil, fearing your financial future, trust the **ONE** Who owns it all!

There are many different kinds of fears that can attack at any given moment, but here is a good "rule of thumb" for all of them:

"As for me, I will call upon God; and the Lord shall save me. Evening, and morning, and at noon, will I pray, and cry aloud; and He shall hear my voice." (Psalm 55:16-17)

Overwhelmed by Pain or Sorrow

Fly to the ONE who has suffered the most! If anyone can understand our pain and sorrow, it has to be Jesus! No one has ever endured as much extreme anguish and agony as He. Yet Jesus willingly took it all on Himself so that He could bring us to God:

"For Christ also hath once suffered for sins, the just for the unjust, that He might bring us to God, being put to death in the flesh, but quickened by the Spirit." (1 Peter 3:18)

There have been, and will no doubt always be, times of pain and suffering in every life, some of which we bring upon ourselves, but a lot of which is just part of life in this "caterpillar" world. At times we wonder if we will ever rise above it!

Now that I think about it, in the six years prior to completion of this book I have undergone seven surgeries, numerous medical tests, and three months of physical therapy. When combined with the work of the music ministry and family responsibilities too, it is no wonder I've had a lot of trouble finishing this book! Looking back, it is nothing less than a miracle of God that has kept this ministry, our family, and me going. Perhaps He is still answering the prayers that I mentioned earlier—that He would make me real, and never let me sing or say anything I did not know in my heart was positively true. I didn't put a time limit on that, and those are still my desires.

As mentioned before, even the Apostle Paul had a "thorn in the flesh," and this was his response:

"And lest I should be exalted above measure through the abundance of the revelations, there was given to me a thorn in the flesh, the messenger of Satan to buffet me, lest I should be exalted above measure.

For this thing I besought the Lord thrice, that it might depart from me.

And He said unto me, My grace is sufficient for thee; for my strength is made perfect in weakness. Most gladly therefore will I rather glory in my infirmities, that the power of Christ may rest upon me.

———❋———

...I have made, and I will bear; even I will carry, and will deliver you.

Isaiah 46:4

———❋———

Therefore I take pleasure in infirmities, in reproaches, in necessities, in persecutions, in distresses for Christ's sake; for when I am weak, then am I strong." (2 Corinthians 12:7-10)

Probably most Christians have some sort of "thorn" that we would really like to be rid of. Whatever it is, if we have honestly and earnestly committed it to God and He does not take the "thorn" from us, we can still know that He will sustain us and enable us to work through (and in spite of) that problem, whatever it is. One thing for sure, we know without a doubt that we can totally trust our Heavenly Father, for He has said:

"...I have made, and I will bear; even I will carry, and will deliver you." (Isaiah 46:4)

———

God is at work in the life of every believer to conform us to the image of His dear Son, the Lord Jesus Christ. He has put His Spirit within us, so that we can know Him better and make Him known to others. If we are "real," then we will be so transparent that others will really **see** Jesus in us. But, God has to allow us go through trials, pain, sorrow—whatever it takes to bring us to the place that His glory will always shine through.

"For God, who commanded the light to shine out of darkness, hath shined in our hearts, to give the light of the knowledge of the glory of God in the face of Jesus Christ. But we have this treasure in earthen vessels, that the excellency of the power may be of God, and not of us." *(2 Corinthians 4:6-7)*

Overwhelmed by Power Failure

When you've really "blown" it—when you stop flying and start crawling—trust the One Who **is** the Power!

Have you ever really "blown" it? What a silly question! Of course you have, and so have I—big time! And it has been so devastating to me that I felt surely the word "Failure! Failure! Failure!" must have been stamped all over my forehead! I knew better! How could I have done that? How could I have let it happen?

Some failures are more drastic than others, and some are so overwhelming that, before I know it, I am back to crawling, thinking I will probably never "fly" again. But when I humbly come to the Father, confess my sin, and turn to Him with all my heart, He cleanses me, puts me back on my feet, restores my soul, and gets me "flying" once more. Even if I don't feel all the way better at that moment, still I know, on the authority of God's Word, I am forgiven.

"If we confess our sins, He is faithful and just to forgive us our

sins, and to cleanse us from all unrighteousness." (1 John 1:9)

Forgiven

Do you know what it means to be forgiven?
What it means to taste His mercy and His grace?
How it feels to have His loving arms around you?
Do you know the comfort of His secret place?

Oh, I know what it means to be forgiven,
What it means to taste His mercy and His grace,
How it feels to have His loving arms around me,
And I know the comfort of His secret place.

"...But Thou art a God ready to pardon, gracious and merciful, slow to anger, and of great kindness..." (Nehemiah 9:17)

"He that dwelleth in the secret place of the Most High shall abide under the shadow of the Almighty.

I will say of the Lord, He is my refuge and my fortress: my God: in Him will I trust." (Psalm 91:1-2)

It is wonderful to have strength and endurance, both physically and spiritually, but when my strength is small, I can't seem to go the distance, and there is "power failure," once again I realize that even at my strongest, there are things I cannot overcome and things I can never accomplish without help.

I remember one time when a trailer hitch needed to be removed from our station wagon. I got tired of waiting for my husband or someone else to remove it, so I decided to do it myself. Surely it couldn't be that hard to do!

The more I worked at it, the more difficult the task became. The hitch was halfway disengaged from the station wagon and there were some bolts that absolutely refused to be loosened. I tried everything, but I simply did not have the physical strength to remove those bolts. Consequently, with the job only half done, and with part of the trailer hitch on the ground, the station wagon was totally unusable—it wasn't going anywhere! I had been unwilling to wait, and had taken matters into my own hands, which proved to be woefully inadequate! It was terribly embarrassing—I could not finish what I had started. I had to admit my power failure and ask for help.

That incident returned to my memory when I was visiting with a friend in another state. As she came to the assistance of one of her young children, she said to that little one, "It's OK to ask for help. Betty has to ask for help too sometimes." Even if the problem is our own fault, due to our own foolishness or our own disobedience, we can bring it to Jesus, lay it at His feet, and ask for help. I am reminded of an illustration by Chuck Swindoll, who said that sometimes we get our lives all knotted and rolled up like a ball of string, hopelessly tangled, and the harder we try to undo the knots, the more tangled it becomes. When that happens, the only solution is to take the whole ball of string to Jesus, and ask Him to fix it—ask Him for help. Remember Isaiah 41:13—God will hold you and help you!

I can't tell you how many times I have had to hand it all over to Jesus. Without fail, however, when I do give the "whole ball of string" to Him and ask Him for His help, His strength and His direction, He either gives me His power, direction, strength, and ability to take care of the problem, or works it out in a remarkable way that I could not have even imagined!

We all experience power failure at times. Success in our

spiritual growth is a lot like learning to walk—we will stumble and fall at times. We may be down, but we don't have to be "out"—we have to get up and keep on trying. In our Christian "flight," we may sometimes crash, but we don't have to burn. When we crash it doesn't mean we can never fly again, though we may need to go back and review some of our "flight" lessons.

Basically, what I'm trying to say about being overwhelmed by power failures is that when our strength is small, and if we start to crawl, this is what we need to do: R&R&R&R— Remember, Realize, and Return, and oh yes, Rejoice!

Remember: First of all, remember when it's **over** our head, it's still **under His feet—God** is in control.

"That the God of our Lord Jesus Christ, the Father of glory, may give unto you the spirit of wisdom and revelation in the knowledge of Him,

The eyes of your understanding being enlightened; that ye may know what is the hope of His calling, and what the riches of the glory of His inheritance in the saints,

And what is the exceeding greatness of His power to us-ward who believe, according to the working of His mighty power,

Which He wrought in Christ, when He raised Him from the dead, and set Him at His own right hand in the heavenly places,

Far above all principality, and power, and might, and dominion, and every name that is named, not only in this world, but also in that which is to come:

And hath put all things under His feet, *and gave Him to be the head over all things to the church,*

Which is His body, the fullness of Him that filleth all in all. (Ephesians 1:17-23)

Realize that we cannot do everything (or anything) God wants us to do in the power of our flesh. He can and will accomplish all His desire through us by the power of His Spirit. W. A. Criswell said, "Man's weakness is no hindrance to God, nor is man's strength an aid to God. He works out His purposes by His Holy Spirit."

"Not by might, nor by power, but by my Spirit, saith the Lord of hosts." (Zechariah 4:6)

Return to Him. We have to stop trying to do God's will our way, confess our sin, and let Him have control. The Bible is filled with scriptures that affirm the fact that **He** is our strength! We must return to Him in persistent, prevailing prayer. Persistent prayer, in spite of life's problems, does not always find relief from pain and does not always gain the response we want, but it can and will produce the power to endure, and it can and will produce in me a true reverence for God.

God Is Still God

I may not understand the pain and sorrow,
I may not know the path, the why or how,
But I will trust my God for each tomorrow,
He holds it **all**—the future, past, and now!
Yes, He is here, He's always been, and He is now!
God is still God! He's always been, and He is **now!**

"Return unto me, and I will return unto you, saith the Lord of hosts. (Malachi 3:7)

"...For the Lord your God is gracious and merciful, and will

> *In the joy of the Lord there is the power for the "overwhelmed" to "overcome!*

not turn away His face from you if ye return to Him." (2 Chronicles 30:9)

Rejoice! Webster's dictionary defines rejoice as: To fill with joy; to be filled with joy. It is impossible to be overwhelmed with trouble and filled with joy at the same time! In the joy of the Lord there is the power for the "overwhelmed" to "overcome!"

"...the joy of the Lord is your strength." (Nehemiah 8:10)

*"Glory ye in His holy name: let the heart of them **rejoice** that seek the Lord." (1 Chronicles 16:10)*

*"But let all those that put their trust in Thee **rejoice**: let them ever shout for **joy**, because Thou defendest them: let them also that love Thy name be **joyful** in Thee.*

For Thou, LORD, wilt bless the righteous: with favor wilt Thou compass him as with a shield." (Psalm 5:11-12)

To list all the wonderful **rejoice** and **joy** scriptures would take an entire chapter, so I won't attempt to add them all now. But, if you're feeling overwhelmed or oppressed by anything, one of the very best remedies would be to get your Bible and a good concordance and make a scripture study of those beautiful words—**rejoice** and **joy**.

*"**Rejoice** in the Lord always; and again I say, **Rejoice**." (Philippians 4:4)*

Chapter 16
How To Wing It—
Through Every Storm

W e don't usually ask for storms, and for the most part, nobody wants them. Violent thunderstorms, tornadoes, and hurricanes cause tremendous damage and devastation as well great loss of lives. We haven't learned how to stop the storms, but in recent years new high-tech early warning systems have been designed, developed, and implemented, in order to assist us in preparation for the furies of nature that are on the way. However, even these efforts sometimes fail, and the warning is too late, or there is no warning at all—thousands are taken by surprise, and a disaster of epic proportions occurs, such as the gigantic 2004 Tsunami.

There are other kinds of "storms" that invade our lives. Some of these are of our own making, and others are quite uninvited— they just come. Sometimes there are warnings, and sometimes those warnings go unheeded. Storms often take us completely by surprise, but God can and does use those storms, both the literal and figurative kind, to bring us back to Him and teach us needed principles. There are all kinds of storms—death, difficulty, physical, financial, change, impossibilities and disasters—none of which we can manage, maneuver through or conquer. But no storm ever takes God by surprise. He always has a plan—He is always in control. When we fix our eyes on Him, we will see that He can and will bring good out of every tempest in our lives.

No storm ever takes God by surprise

Literal Storms of Nature

There have been many storms during the course of this ministry, not only during travel, but also while at home with family and working in my office. Sometimes work on this book was delayed simply because of high risk to the computer during lightning and thunderstorms. There was one particular week that for three days in a row the power was off and on over and over again because of severe storms. God knew I needed to finish the work, so why did He allow the interruptions?

For one thing, we needed the rain that came with the storms. But, for another, I think, perhaps it has been to teach me to work **between** storms. I wanted ideal conditions—perfect weather, perfect everything with no interruptions or distractions. Under those conditions, I thought, I would surely be able to write well and finish the book quickly. Perhaps it is possible for some authors to have everything just right—and just write! But, I can't help but think of Paul the Apostle. He wrote under the most difficult conditions imaginable—in prison, and chained to a guard at that! Perhaps God is just re-teaching me the principle of:

> Do what you can,
> With what you have,

Where you are, and

Do it now.

When it is impossible to do it now, then we must be diligent to "do it at the first, and every, opportunity."

I never wanted **any** storms—my preference was for both this ministry and my personal life to be the "happily ever after" kind. But, God, in His wisdom, chose otherwise. If not for the rough and blustery times, how could I ever encourage others? How could I assure anyone of God's faithfulness to "fly" through the storms if I did not know what it was like to be there myself and had not experienced, first hand, those "Everlasting Arms" underneath me?

"Blessed be God, even the Father of our Lord Jesus Christ, the Father of mercies, and the God of all comfort;

Who comforteth us in all our tribulation, that we may be able to comfort them which are in any trouble, by the comfort wherewith we ourselves are comforted of God." (1 Corinthians 1:3-4)

I once heard a preacher say that when God allows or sends tribulation, we just need to "tribulate!" There have been many opportunities to do just that when physical, spiritual, financial, and literal storms have bombarded us, both personally and in this ministry.

Storms are usually quite inconvenient as well as most uncomfortable. You probably remember these words from the old song, *You'll Never Walk Alone*:

Walk on through the wind,

Walk on through the rain,

And you'll never walk alone.

I used to think those words were very noble, and they are, but now I know that even though I'll never walk alone, it can also be tough!

During a western U.S. tour, while driving from El Paso, Texas, to Las Cruces, New Mexico, the evening was growing dark, and a massive windstorm was suddenly upon me. It did not seem wise to try to make it to Las Cruces, so I stopped at a roadside park to *"rest in the Lord and wait patiently for Him"* (Psalm *37:7)* to calm the winds. I committed everything to my Heavenly Father, and closed my eyes. The wind was so strong that it literally rocked the van—in fact, it just sort of rocked me to sleep.

As I slumbered, God gave me a dream. I had been praying about whether I was supposed to go to Brazil for ministry in an evangelistic crusade, but up to that point had not been able to discern whether this was God's will. I have always said that if I **knew** God wanted me to go somewhere in ministry, then regardless of whether I could **see** the way or not, I would be willing to take the "leap of faith" and commit to that journey, wherever that might take me.

In the dream—I saw myself flying high in a plane and then landing in Brazil, and I heard these words: *"…and I will cause thee to ride upon the high places of the earth … for the mouth of the Lord hath spoken it."* (Isaiah 58:14) I know this is part of a larger text in Isaiah, but these were the words God used to speak confirmation to my heart. I knew that God wanted me to go to Salvador, Bahia, Brazil. I would not only be riding high spiritually, but I would be riding pretty high in the planes that would take me there and back.

Upon that confirmation, I began to plan and prepare for the ministry in Brazil. Although I do sing and speak in the language of Brazil (Portuguese), I don't have the ability to translate songs from English to Portuguese. This was another matter of fervent prayer, as it was my desire to be able to communicate the love of Jesus to the people in their own language. Although we had lived in both Salvador and Sao Paulo during an Air Force assignment to Brazil, it had been sixteen years since we left there, and my Portuguese language skills were somewhat rusty.

God not only provided translations and restored the language to me as I had requested, but He gave me more than I had before

As I prayed about the ministry to Brazil, I asked God to refresh the Portuguese language to my mind and my lips, and provide the needed translations for the songs. God not only provided translations and restored the language to me as I had requested, but He gave me more than I had before!

We were in a major thunderstorm as our plane approached Salvador, but God was at work in the midst of the storm. As we continued to circle the city, a member of our team called me to the back of the plane where he was seated next to a Brazilian man. They were having trouble communicating because of the language barrier. I sat down to talk with the Brazilian man, and through the written testimony of my teammate, and as the Lord interpreted through me, that precious Brazilian man came to know Jesus as his Savior. We had a wonderful time of rejoicing with this new brother in Christ. It was so exciting, I even forgot we were up in the air—we were "in the clouds" in more ways than one.

I didn't find out until a week later that during the entire time we witnessed to the Brazilian man, our plane had been circling the city, waiting for the opportunity to land. Some of the passengers were beginning to worry a little, but God had everything under control the whole time. When the witness was finished, and I returned to my seat, we immediately began the descent to the city of Salvador. We couldn't land until that man was saved! The moment he accepted Jesus Christ as his Savior, we were cleared to land! We were right on schedule— God's schedule, that is!

The storm of death

God used other storms during the 1982 ministry to Salvador, Bahia, Brazil. One of those was the **storm of death**—the death of an infant. I was asked to sing at the funeral of a tiny two-month old child who had died of malnutrition. He was the only son of one of the members of a local church in Salvador. The funeral was held in the home of the mother, and the missionary was trying to help her get all the necessary paperwork done. It would soon be sundown, and at that time the practice of embalming was not observed in Brazil, and the law required that burial occur within 24 hours of death. Cemeteries kept several graves open and ready at all times, and casket stores were open around the clock so caskets of any size could be purchased at any time.

While the missionary and the mother of the child were away, a few of our group remained in the room with the casket. As friends of the family came by to pay their respects prior to the funeral service, there were two girls in particular who came and just sat for a time. While they were there I shared with them how to know Jesus, and asked them if they would like to pray and receive Him as their personal Savior. One girl said she wanted to go home and pray privately, and the other said she wanted to think about it some more.

When the missionary and the mother returned, the memorial service began. The missionary brought a brief and beautiful gospel message. Then we prepared to go to the cemetery. The tiny body was in a small white cardboard casket. Since the family was very poor they could not afford a hearse. Some little children carried the casket to the missionary's car.

The graveyard was the ugliest thing I had ever seen—not at all like our well-kept cemeteries in the U.S. Only the wealthy can afford permanent gravesites in Brazil. All the rest are buried in public graveyards, which are dug up every three years and reused.

The graveside ceremony was very simple. The mother turned away as the little casket was covered with dirt and then mounded over. Then the children each took a flower and sort of planted it by sticking the stem in the top of the mound.

As sad as it sounds, however, there were some lovely things about that funeral. The mother was a precious Christian, and she had the assurance she would one day see her son again. And, remember the two girls who came by to pay their respects, and had listened as I witnessed to them about the Lord Jesus? Two days after the funeral, **both** girls came to an evangelistic meeting we held in their neighborhood, and **both** girls came to make their public professions of faith in the Lord Jesus Christ! God truly brought good from the **"storm"** of the death of that infant. Perhaps those girls would never have known they could have eternal **life** had it not been for that one small **death**!

There were many opportunities, including personal visits and evangelistic meetings, to share the gospel. Almost 2000 people came to know Jesus during that mission to Salvador. God truly blessed the ministry there, and I was really looking forward to the next two-week mission in Rio de Janiero. Little did I know when I said farewell to my Salvador team members that the **storm of death** would soon touch my life and ministry.

After only one service with the evangelistic team in Rio de Janeiro, the phone call came informing me of my father's death. This brought a **storm of indecision.** It did not look possible to get back for the funeral, so should I stay and finish the work in Brazil, or should I go back as soon as passage was available even though I would still miss the funeral? As you know, from reading Chapter 12 of this book, God led me through that tempest as well.

Storms of Difficulty—When the way is rough and dirty!

There are many kinds of difficulties, but some of the hardest to deal with are the physical demands we face at times. The 1982 ministry to Brazil was just such an occasion, particularly when visiting people in their homes, many of which were nothing more than cardboard shacks. In Brazil, there were many favellas—little villages with dwellings made of cardboard, combined with branches, pieces of tin or anything that could be used to put up some kind of wall and overhead protection even if it would not last. Sometimes heavy rains washed entire villages away. Most of the little "houses" in these favellas had dirt

It was physically difficult walking there—the ground was rough, and the way was dirty and repulsive. But God was there too!

floors, and there was no running water. There were also no sewer systems—human waste simply ran in what can be loosely termed the "streets." Disease, of course, was common. It was physically difficult walking there—the ground was rough, and the way was dirty and repulsive.

But God was there too. In one of the families we visited there was a grandmother who could barely walk. We did not know what kind of storms this family might be experiencing, but we did know they needed Jesus. After sharing my testimony, and explaining how they could know Jesus Christ, three members of that family prayed right then and there, and received Him as Savior and Lord.

The grandmother was one of those who accepted Christ that afternoon. I loved her instantly. She could not read or write, but she could definitely understand, and when she heard about Jesus, she responded immediately. She and all her family came to the evangelistic meeting at the local church that evening, and that grandmother made public her profession of faith in Jesus Christ. After the service, she came to me and hugged me tightly, and wept, "Oh, what would I have done if you had not come! Thank you, thank you, for coming to tell me about Jesus." If she had been the only one saved, it would have been worth it all!

There are many other places in the world where the way is very difficult, physically demanding, and often unpleasant in both sight and smell. But wherever and whenever God sends us, and however troublesome the scene, He will always give us the strength and endurance and everything else we need to make it through every kind of storm we have to experience.

"Beloved, think it not strange concerning the fiery trial which is to try you, as though some strange thing happened unto you;

313

But rejoice, inasmuch as ye are partakers of Christ's sufferings; that, when His glory shall be revealed, ye may be glad also with exceeding joy." (1 Peter 4:12-13)

Physical Storms

Just about everyone has experienced the trials of **physical storms.** If you haven't yet, trust me, you will if you live long enough. Our bodies are aging—some faster than others, but all are aging—wearing out. Still, it isn't easy going through the process. Sometimes it seems there is just one medical problem right after another, or maybe on top of another, not only for me, but also for my husband, Don, who has colon cancer. We are very thankful that if he has to have cancer, it is the best kind—it is very slow and he has no pain. We realize it could change at any time, but so far, so good. While all these things take their toll in time, expense, and loss of strength and energy, and have caused delays in ministry, we realize that "falling apart" physically is actually scriptural. Every human body is perishing, but the good thing is that we are growing spiritually day by day. The Apostle Paul said:

"But though our outward man perish, yet the inward man is renewed day by day. For our light affliction, which is but for a moment, worketh for us a far more exceeding and eternal weight of glory; While we look not at the things which are seen, but at the things which are not seen; for the things which are seen are temporal; but the things which are not seen are eternal." (2 Corinthians 4:16-18)

How could Paul, with all the physical things he suffered, call it "light" affliction? The answer is in renewal of the inner man day by day. As we grow spiritually, we can look beyond what we can see with our physical eyes. Paul's goal was to fight a good fight and to run a good race on this earth. His eyes were on Jesus, and his ultimate view was an eternity with the Him. That is how we can make it through not just the physical storms, but through every storm—by *"looking to Jesus, the author and finisher of our faith." (Hebrews 12:2)*

Financial Storms

I'm convinced that everyone will, at one time or another, or perhaps many times, have to go through financial storms, whether personally, in ministry or in business. Over and over again, in prior chapters of this book, personal illustrations have been given of urgent needs surrendered to God, and His miraculous financial provisions. There will likely be financial challenges in the future, but God never breaks His word, so we can bank on His promises!

Stormy times are great opportunities for us to practice trusting our Heavenly Father when we cannot see the resources at hand to take care of pressing financial needs. This is not spoken lightly, for I know from experience that it is not always easy to trust when I can't see. In times like these, one of the scriptures that helps me the most is found in the sixth chapter of Matthew. Jesus is saying that we cannot have two masters—we cannot serve God and money at the same time. He tells us not to be anxious, and directs our attention to the birds of the air and the lilies of the field, reminding us that He takes care of those needs and that He will most certainly take care of our needs as well. But here is the priority God has given—we must not miss it:

"But seek ye first the kingdom of God and His righteousness; and all these things shall be added unto you." (Matthew 6:33)

What things will be added? What things will be given unto us? Everything we need!

Storms of Change

Progress usually involves change, whether we like it or not. I am one of those who came "kicking and screaming" into the computer age. It wasn't so bad going from a manual to an electric typewriter, but it didn't stop there. Things kept changing—"word processors" came along, and personal computer systems, laptop computers, and more. Now it has become not just advisable but absolutely necessary to fit into the computer scenario.

Progress usually involves change, whether we like it or not

Since there are continual advances, revisions and upgrades in the computer field, I am still learning to adjust to changes! I **am** grateful for the many things that can be accomplished using this incredible tool, but the process of learning has been and still is most challenging! There have been times when I have done something on the computer and the thing I was working on disappeared never to be seen again! There are times when I forgot to "save" my work, so I lost everything I was working on and had to start all over again. Maybe you've never done that, but I can guarantee—it is truly frustrating, aggravating, irritating, and more!

All of life is like that. Just about the time we get comfortable in one situation, things suddenly change. I laughingly say that about the time our children were grown and we had an "empty nest," some of them came back home—with reinforcements (children of their own)! I deeply love our children. They are all precious blessings from God, and I thank Him for our big, fun, wonderful and sometimes loud and crazy family. But, it is still true that with children there will be continual changes. It is best not to get too comfortable in one stage of life, because change is probably just around the corner.

We do expect changes from time to time, but some of them are extreme surprises that require dramatic adjustments, such as serious illnesses, accidents, and job and career crises, to name a few. The list goes on, but to weather all these storms, instead of resisting or resenting changes, we must, as with everything else, yield these to the God Who holds our present, past and future in His hands. He has never lost any of His power, and His mercy endures forever!

The One Who Never Changes

Life is full of changes,
Nothing ever stays the same!
I'm so glad there's one who never changes—
Jesus is His name!

How Long?

Oh, God, that's how long Your mercy lasts—forever!
That's how long Your faithfulness will be!
That's how long Your love and grace goes on enduring,
Forevermore—for all eternity!

Lord, You promised You would not forsake or leave me,
So there's no need to fear what I can't see;

There's not the slightest need for me to worry,

For You are with me now and for eternity.

Storms of Impossibilities

"Is anything too hard for the Lord?" (Genesis 18:14)

In the 15th chapter of Genesis, God promised that Abraham and Sarah would have a son. In the 17th chapter of Genesis, God reconfirmed that promise and even named the son that would be born: *"Sarah thy wife shall bear thee a son indeed; and thou shalt call his name Isaac..." (Genesis 17:19)* Abraham was 100 and Sarah was 90 years old at that time. In chapter 18, we read that Abraham and Sarah were old and "well stricken" in age when God confirmed His promise again, and in Chapter 21 we read about the birth of Isaac, just as God had promised. In our own reasoning, we would say that having a child at the ages of Abraham and Sarah would be totally impossible. But, nothing is too hard for God!

"For with God nothing shall be impossible." (Luke 1:37)

Probably everyone recognizes these words spoken by the angel Gabriel to the virgin Mary, informing her that she would bear a son, the Son of God. Now if having children when the man and wife are between 90-100 years sounds difficult, then for a virgin to bear a child would have to be impossible. But, not with God! These are His words:

"Behold, I Am the Lord the God of all flesh, is there anything too hard for me? (Jeremiah 33:27)

We can only repeat with Jeremiah, *"Ah, Lord God! Behold, Thou hast made the heaven and the earth by Thy great power and stretched out arm, and there is nothing too hard for Thee." (Jeremiah 32:17)*

We have had lots of what looked like "impossibles" in this ministry, but they became "do-ables" when we knew it was God's will to pursue them. God has always made a way, and given countless, often unique, opportunities to tell the good news of His love and life through the Lord Jesus Christ.

When the invitation came for me to participate in the Billy Graham Amsterdam 2000 Global Evangelism Conference, it looked like a financial impossibility. Though I tried to forget about it, God continued to bring it before me until I gave it back to Him in prayer. Though it appeared to be an impossibility, God made the way, not only for me, but for Don as well. We both had the privilege of being a part of this marvelous conference. God makes a way when there is no way!

Though we cannot truly know this side of Heaven all the ways God uses this ministry to touch and change the hearts of men and women, I am convinced that sometimes He originates an entire tour in order to answer the heart-cry of one person who is desperately needing Him. God will always do whatever it takes to answer the searching heart.

"And ye shall seek me, and find me, when ye shall search for me with all your heart. And I will be found of you, saith the Lord..." Jeremiah 29:13-14. In his book, *My Utmost for His Highest*, Oswald Chambers declares that God will tax the last grain of sand and the remotest star to bless us if we will obey Him.

In late December of 2004, when my participation in the 2005 ministry to China looked like an impossibility, God made a way—it was a confirmed, "done deal" within three days! Within six months His plan culminated in the actual experience. It was a mission effort filled with blessings (and difficulties, too). The witness of the Lord Jesus Christ was shared many times and in many ways. I believe, however, that one of the basic

> *I am learning that with God, there is no such thing as impossible!*

reasons God made it **all possible** was the heart cry of one Chinese girl, the one I mentioned in chapter ten of this book. Remember her words when she received Jesus Christ? "I was just waiting for the chance!"

Well-known pastor/teacher, Chuck Swindoll, has said that life is full of wonderful opportunities cleverly disguised as impossibilities. Over the years, both in this ministry and personally, there have been many such "opportunities—lots of "impossibles"—but I am learning that with God, there is no such thing as impossible!

Impossible?

When you cannot understand, worship Jesus,
Bless His name when you cannot see His hand.
For the God who created all Heaven and Earth
Will be with you, and show you His plan.

Though everything about you may be crumbling,
Jehovah God is faithful day by day;
He will never leave nor yet forsake His children,
If you are truly His, He'll make a way.

If the challenge you face looks impossible,
Run to Jesus—lay your burden at His feet.

With God there's no such thing as impossible,
And every single need, He'll more than meet.

Throughout this ministry and our personal walk with the Lord, we have had the privilege of facing and enduring many different kinds of storms. It has been shown through the pages of this book how God has brought us through those storms, and the things He has taught us through these storms as we continue to learn to trust in and rely completely upon HIM.

God is in the process of conforming each and every one of His children into the image of His dear Son, the Lord Jesus Christ, and it takes time—all of our days on this earth! We must continue to learn and grow as long as we draw breath on this earth. We **will** one day be perfect at last, **when** we see Jesus—at the end of this earthly journey—not before or until then. In the meantime, there will always be room for improvement in each of us.

Storms of Disaster

None of us can forget the disaster that gripped our nation during the event of September 11, 2001, when enemy attacks brought the destruction of the New York twin towers, and with it the death of 3000 of our people. We know there could be other 9/11 times in the future, perhaps just around the corner. There will be wars, terrorism, and death. Remember, we live in a fallen world in which evil abounds. Yes, God is greater, and we've read the back of the Book, and we will win! In His time and in His way, He will make all things right.

In the meantime, we must not lose heart, but continue to fix our gaze on the Lord Jesus Christ, staying victoriously on course as we take our "flight" in this caterpillar world. We need not fear, but we do need to pray for each other as Paul did for the Christians in Ephesus (Ephesians 3:16-21). That is our prayer for all who read this book—that your roots would reach the

Not only can God calm the storm, but He is able to calm you and me in the midst of the storm!

depths of God's love, that you would be filled with His fullness, and that you would grow strong in the power of His might.

Thus, **when, not if, but when** the storms of life come, you won't fall apart. To quote Jeff Harris, "Some want to stay just on the other side of broken, never moving any farther on." Maybe that's where you've been or are now, but you don't have to stay there. Remember: *"Be of good courage, and He shall strengthen your heart, all ye that hope in the Lord." (Psalm 31:24)*

No matter what kind of storm you face, no matter how fierce and violent the conditions, no matter how desperate, weary and alone you may feel, nothing can separate you from the God who loves you, and in whose grip you are safely held. You can trust Him—the **One** who can calm the storm:

"Then they cry unto the Lord in their trouble, and He bringeth them out of their distresses. ***He maketh the storm a calm,*** *so that the waves thereof are still." (Psalm 107:28-29)*

"And He (Jesus) arose, and rebuked the wind, and said unto the sea, Peace, be still. And the wind ceased, and there was a great calm." (Mark 4:39)

Peace is not the absence of storms—it is the presence of God **in** the storm. He gives peace not only **after,** but **in** and **through**

every storm. Not only can God calm the storm, but He is able to calm **you and me** in the midst of the storm! Trust Him, and remember:

God's providence put me here,

God protects me here,

God knows I am here,

God's Word comes to me here,

God's power sustains me here,

God is with me here (and wherever else I go),

God will never leave me!

God will be faithful **through every storm**.

Through Every Storm [10]

Sometimes I feel like the great rains of trouble
Just keep on coming, wave after wave,
And it looks like the floods will overwhelm me—
Oh, a shelter my weary soul craves.

My heart cries out, Does my life really matter?
Are all my longings and prayers really heard?
Then God, my Father, whispers so softly,
"Lo, I am with you to the end of the world."

Dark Storms without may still be raging,
And torrential rains may be still coming down—
Within my heart there is peace and assurance,
Only in Jesus can this rest be found.

No circumstance can ever alter
The Word of my God, my Savior, my King,
Though strong and fierce the storm all about me,
My God will give a song I can sing.

Through every storm, there is provision,
Through every dark and lonely hour.
For every storm, there is a purpose,
For every storm, there is God's power!
Through every storm, there is God's purpose,
Through every storm, there is God's power!

"O Lord, Thou art my God; I will exalt Thee, I will praise Thy name; for Thou hast done wonderful things; Thy counsels of old are faithfulness and truth.

He will swallow up death in victory; and the Lord God will wipe away tears from off all faces; and the rebuke of His people shall He take away from off all the earth; for the Lord hath spoken it.

And it shall be said in that day, Lo, this is our God; we have waited for Him, and He will save us; this is the Lord; we have waited for Him, we will be glad and rejoice in His salvation." (Isaiah 25:1, 8-9)

Whether it be a howling gale or soft summer breeze, we must simply choose to fly with the winds God sends or allows, and trust and obey Him completely. That's how to endure and get through **every** kind of storm!

Chapter 17
How To Wing It—
No Matter What!

How to "wing it?" As we have said before, the butterfly does it God's way by instinct. If we would successfully "wing it," we too must do it God's way, but it will not happen for us by "doing what comes naturally." It can only be by doing what comes **super**naturally! We have come full circle back to: *"Christ in you, the hope of glory." (Colossians 1:27)* And, He didn't make His home in us to be a temporary occupant: *"For He hath said, I will* **never** *leave thee, nor forsake thee." (Hebrews 13:5)*

So, **no matter what** comes our way, we can make it through, not just somehow, but victoriously!

Remember, there will always be forces that could halt our "flight" and tempt us to go back to "crawling." Our human nature will always be exposed to temptation, and on the surface, it often appears to be innocent and right. But, once we surrender to the temptation, the true nature of that enticement begins to be revealed, and we find the end result to be far different from what we expected. It is then we realize we have not only been deceived, but we have deceived ourselves—"we've been had!"

How in the world did it happen?

"Let no man say when he is tempted, I am tempted of God; for God cannot be tempted with evil, neither tempteth He any man: But **every man is tempted, when he is drawn away of his own lust, and enticed.** *Then when lust hath conceived, it bringeth forth sin; and sin, when it is finished, bringeth forth death." (James 1:13-15)*

No matter what comes, no matter what the temptations may be (and there **will** be temptations), God has already made the way for us to fly through, around, and above them all:

"There hath no temptation taken you but such as is common to man; but God is faithful, who will not suffer you to be tempted above that ye are able; but will with the temptation also make a way to escape, that ye may be able to bear it." (1 Corinthians 10:13)

Do we have any personal responsibility to take action, or can we just sit in the midst of it all, do nothing, and wait for God to miraculously "pluck us out" of the temptation? God can and sometimes does do just that, but He has also given clear directions on what we are expected to do. Some very specific instructions are found in 1 Timothy 6:11-14. In a "nutshell," we are told to: **Flee, Follow, and Fight.**

To get the whole picture, read the entire sixth chapter of First Timothy. In that chapter we are warned about false teachers and their "sick" instruction (lacking sound doctrine) leading to all kinds of evils, not the least of which is the love of money. Note that money is not evil in itself—it is the **love** of money that leads to all kinds of evil:

"But they that will be rich fall into temptation and a snare, and into many foolish and hurtful lusts, which drown men in destruction

and perdition." For the love of money is the root of all evil; which while some coveted after, they have erred from the faith, and pierced themselves through with many sorrows. (1 Timothy 6:10)

"But thou, O man of God, **flee** *these things; and* **follow** *after righteousness, godliness, faith, love, patience, meekness.* **Fight** *the good fight of faith..." (1 Timothy 6:11-12)*

Temptation comes to every one of us, regardless of our station in life, but it does not come to everyone in exactly the same way. It comes at the point of each one's greatest vulnerability. Alcohol has not been much of a temptation to me—I think the stuff stinks, so it must surely taste horrible. But aside from the disgusting smell and flavor, I have also seen the devastation wrought in the life of an alcoholic, so I don't want to open the door even a tiny crack to that monster. Alcohol may not be a problem to me or you, but in the life of every one of us, there are little (or big) pockets of different varieties of weakness—areas where we are individually most vulnerable.

If you know anything about Greek mythology, then you have heard about the "sirens"—the sea nymphs that were said to dwell in certain coastal areas of the Mediterranean Sea. It has been told that when ships passed through those particular areas, the sirens would sing such alluring songs that the sailors would be irresistibly drawn by the music and they would jump overboard and be drowned.

The story is told of a hero named Odysseus who knew his ship would pass by an area where songs of the sirens were known to have lured many a man to his destruction. So Odysseus took drastic measures—he ordered that he be tied to the mast, and that the ears of every crewman be sealed with wax so they would not hear the seductive songs of the sirens. Thus Odysseus and his crew sailed safely past that coastal area and they did not yield to the music of the sirens.

Though the Odysseus account is mythology, the fact is that today there are "sirens" of all kinds calling out to us—to nonbelievers and Christians alike, with the intention of snaring us and drawing us to destruction. The only way not to be trapped by such "enchanting music" music is to get away quickly—**flee!**

Flee—Run like crazy!

"Flee also youthful lusts…" (2 Timothy 2:22) Lust is wanting to satisfy my desires, my own way, i.e., "I must have it, and I must have it now!"

"Abstain from all appearance of evil." (1 Thessalonians 5:22) If it looks wrong, it probably is—don't even go there!

Satan will always try to satisfy our own legitimate needs and desires in an illegitimate way. In the wilderness, Jesus Christ endured and conquered the most severe temptations ever known to mankind. Each time Jesus was tempted, He used "Word-warfare"—He answered the devil by quoting the Word of God: *"It is written…"*

Satan will always try to get us to satisfy our own legitimate needs and desires in an illegitimate way

God could have intervened. At any time during the earth-life of His Son, Jesus Christ, He could have sent 10,000 angels and more to help Him. But God did not interrupt or eliminate those temptations. I believe He allowed them all so that Jesus Christ could experience all the allurements of the flesh and overcome them all without sinning. Being sinless, Jesus was the **only** one qualified to be our

Redeemer and our Great High Priest. With that perfect redemption, He has given us the freedom to come before Him in absolute confidence:

"Seeing then that we have a great high priest, that is passed into the heavens, Jesus the Son of God, let us hold fast our profession.

For we have not a high priest which cannot be touched with the feeling of our infirmities; but was in all points tempted like as we are, yet without sin.

Let us therefore come boldly unto the throne of grace, that we may obtain mercy, and find grace to help in time of need." (Hebrews 4:14-16)

Incidentally, there is a special promise for all who endure temptation, not giving in, but trusting God and remaining strong in the power of His might:

"Blessed is the man that endureth temptation; for when He is tried, he shall receive the crown of life, which the Lord hath promised to them that love Him." (James 1:12)

Follow! If we would follow righteousness, we must follow God's Word.

Righteousness—what does that mean? How is it achieved? Webster's dictionary defines the word "righteous" as "ethical, chaste, honorable, good, virtuous, good, noble." Well, those are the qualities the Word of God teaches us about! Simply stated, if we would follow righteousness, we need to read and heed God's Word, the Bible, for that is where we find the directions—the maps! I love the quote from Warren Wiersbe in the January 25, 1989 Back to the Bible Radio Broadcast:

"When the child of God

Looks into the Word of God,

He or she is transformed by the Spirit of God,

Into the image of God,

To the glory of God!"

The Scriptures are replete with the encouragement and prayers of other faithful followers. In one of the wonderful "Our Daily Bread" devotional booklets, Dennis DeHaan has written:

"No greater help and care is given

To others in their need

Than when we bear them up in prayer,

And for them intercede."

The psalmist cried out in prayer for righteousness, and so do we:

"Set a watch, O Lord, before my mouth; keep the door of my lips. Incline not my heart to any evil thing, to practice wicked works with men that work iniquity; and let me not eat of their dainties." (Psalm 141:3-4)

"Hear my prayer, O Lord, give ear to my supplications; in Thy faithfulness answer me, and in Thy righteousness." (Psalm 143:1)

The entire 143rd Psalm is a cry for help and deliverance—does God hear? Well, just look at Psalm 145. You will be blessed in reading all 21 verses, but here is just a portion:

"The Lord is righteous in all His ways, and holy in all His works. The Lord is nigh unto all them that call upon Him, to all that call upon Him in truth. He will fulfill the desire of them that fear Him; He also will hear their cry, and will save them. The Lord preserveth all them that love Him; but all the wicked shall He

destroy. My mouth shall speak the praise of the Lord; and let all flesh bless His holy name for ever and ever." (Psalm 145:17-21)

Fight! Fight the good fight of faith.

Some people seem to be born "spoiling for a fight." But that kind of hostility is not the kind of fight we are here promoting. We are talking about standing firm against the destructive powers of evil. Since Satan cannot have the souls of Christians, he will try to ruin their lives and reputations, giving God a "black eye," so to speak.

Once we have been born into God's family, nothing and no one can ever reverse that birth!

Once we have been born into God's family, nothing and no one can ever reverse that birth! No person or power can ever take away the new life God has given us! Of course, even we who are believers will all die physically unless we are alive at the time Jesus Christ returns and calls us to meet Him in the air:

"For the Lord Himself shall descend from heaven with a shout, with the voice of the archangel, and with the trump of God; and the dead in Christ shall rise first; Then we which are alive and remain shall be caught up together with them in the clouds, to meet the Lord in the air; and so shall we ever be with the Lord." (1 Thessalonians 4:16-17)

In the meantime, Jesus has told us to "occupy" until He comes. As long as we are on this earth there will always be a "fight"—whether spiritually, physically, mentally or emotionally, because our adversary, the devil, is still alive and well:

"Be sober, be vigilant; because your adversary, the devil, as a roaring lion, walketh about, seeking whom he may devour; whom

resist steadfast in the faith..." (1 Peter 5:8-9)

It is very clear that this formidable adversary will continue to attempt to kill and destroy until the time of the end when Jesus will consign him to everlasting torment.

Fighting is never easy. Most people don't want to fight, but the alternative is to submit to the demands of the opponent. So what does God say about Christian warfare?

"Finally, my brethren, be strong in the Lord, and in the power of His might.

Put on the whole armor of God, that ye may be able to stand against the wiles of the devil.

For we wrestle not against flesh and blood, but against principalities, against powers, against the rulers of the darkness of this world, against spiritual wickedness in high places.

Wherefore take unto you the whole armor of God, that ye may be able to withstand in the evil day, and having done all, to stand.

Stand therefore, having your loins girt about with truth, and having on the breastplate of righteousness;

And your feet shod with the preparation of the gospel of peace;

Above all, taking the shield of faith, wherewith ye shall be able to quench all the fiery darts of the wicked.

And take the helmet of salvation, and the sword of the Spirit, which is the Word of God;

Praying always with all prayer and supplication in the Spirit, and watching thereunto with all perseverance and supplication for all saints." (Ephesians 6:10-18)

Many have given their lives in battle, physically fighting to secure our freedoms, and you may or may not be one of those called to fight in such conflicts or wars. But, make no mistake, there are times when a country **must** go to war to protect its people, and it is the right thing to do. If you doubt that, read the Old Testament, starting with the book of Genesis. The Bible tells us that there will be wars and rumors of wars until the end of this age. There will be major battles, both literal wars and conflicts of the soul, until Jesus Christ returns to this earth as King of Kings and Lord of Lords. Then, and only then, will there be everlasting peace.

In the meantime, don't quit! You may fall at times, but that is no reason to give up. In a very real sense, the first time I "lost my footing" was when I was five years old, and was stricken with an illness so serious that the doctors said there was no hope—they sent me home to die!

But there was one Who did give me hope—His name is Jesus! I did not yet know Him as my Savior, but He came to me and let me know everything would be all right. I was in bed for a long, long time—so long that I forgot how to walk. I remember spending my sixth birthday in bed. By the time I was well enough to walk again, I was afraid to try. It's a scary thing when you can't remember how to walk. I will always be thankful that the Lord gave me a patient, godly mother who loved and encouraged me, and insisted that I try. It was a real struggle to learn to walk again, but she wouldn't let me quit!

Every believer is admonished to "**Fight** the good **fight** of faith." The Apostle Paul gives us great encouragement in his testimony:

"I have fought a good fight, I have finished my course, I have kept the faith; Henceforth there is laid up for me a crown of righteousness, which the Lord, the righteous Judge, shall give me at that day; and not to me only, but unto all them also that love His appearing." (2 Timothy 4:7-8)

If we would win—"wing" a successful "flight," and find victory in the battles of life, not only must we flee, follow and fight, but we must also learn to **"Faith it!**

"For yet a little while, and He that shall come will come, and will not tarry. Now the just shall live by faith; but if any man draw back, My soul shall have no pleasure in him." (Hebrews 10:37-38)

"But the just shall live by his faith." (Habakkuk 2:4)

"The just shall live by faith." (Romans 1:17)

"But that no man is justified by the law in the sight of God, it is evident; for, The just shall live by faith." (Galatians 3:11)

> *Faith must be tested, because it can be turned into a personal possession only through conflict.*
>
> *-Oswald Chambers*

Faith must be tested to be perfected. In Oswald Chambers' devotional book, *My Utmost for His Highest,* he writes:

Faith is not intelligent understanding, faith is deliberate commitment to a Person where I see no way.

Chambers goes on to say that our faith will be tested:

"Faith must be tested, because it can be turned into a personal possession only through conflict. Believe steadfastly on Him and all you come up against will develop your faith. Faith is unutterable trust in God, trust which never dreams that He will not stand by us."

If you are needing a "faith-lift," remember others who have gone before, have fought the battles, and have stood the tests.

Be encouraged by the testimony of those who are real heroes—
"heroes of the faith." Read about Joseph, Joshua, Esther, David,
Stephen, Paul, and many others whose stories of faith are written
in the pages of history as well as recorded faithfully in God's
Word, the Bible.

*"But without faith it is impossible to please Him; for he that
cometh to God must believe that He is, and that He is a rewarder of
them that diligently seek Him." (Hebrews 11:6)*

There follows in the eleventh chapter of Hebrews a long list
of actual heroes of the faith. These men and women were human
and made mistakes like you and me. Their struggles were real,
their battles intense, and their hardships severe. What is more,
they did **not** have the advantage of reading the "back of the
book." They had to walk, fight, and endure by faith, and they
didn't give up—they kept on trusting the Lord.

There have been many other heroes of the faith not recorded
in the Bible—some have gone before us, and some are still here.
Some who have personally inspired me are well-known, such
as: Nate Saint and his son, Steve; Dr. Adrian Rogers; Dr. Roy
Fish; Dr. Billy Graham, and his daughter, Ann Graham Lotz.
Some of my heroes of the faith are relatively unknown to the
world: Ed Rock, Leonard Conner, Cheryl Watson, Thelma
Hemenway, and Helen Cade have all lived exemplary lives of
faith and service, and have left lasting impressions of trust, hope,
and enouragement.

Probably everyone has heard of Jim Elliot, a great hero of the
faith and an inspiration to many people. In this one quote he
summed up the "follow" and "fight" of 1 Timothy 6:12: "He is
no fool who gives up what he cannot keep for what he cannot
lose." Elliot and his fellow missionaries had such a burden for

the Auca Indians that they gave up everything including their lives, in the attempt to share the gospel of Jesus with that hostile tribe.

Nate Saint was one of the missionaries who was murdered along with Jim Elliot. But the end of their lives was not the finish. It was only the beginning. In later years Nate's son, Steve, went back to the Auca tribe (now called the Waodani), and God gave him great success in sharing the love of Jesus with them! Many of the Waodani have come to know Jesus as their personal Savior.

At the Amsterdam 2000 Billy Graham Evangelism Conference in Holland, Steve Saint not only gave his personal testimony—he brought with him a Waodoni who gave his own personal testimony of salvation through Jesus Christ. That man was the very one who had murdered Steve's father! What a joy and blessing to personally meet both Steve Saint and his friend, and now, brother! Now you've heard the rest of the story!

Probably only a few reading this will recognize Thelma Hemenway's name, but she was a faithful prayer warrior, a lady of great humility, and a kind and loving encourager and helper. Thelma was a true friend. This is the poem God gave me for her:

Friend

Every good and perfect gift
Comes down from God above;
Great and small, He sends them all
As tokens of His love!

I know He loves me very much!

He's proven that is true,

Because He's given me the joy

Of being friends with you!

Of the multitude of good things

That from His hand descends,

One of the very best God gives

Is a kind and loving friend.

And that's just what you are to me,

A very special blend

Of God's sweet love and mercy;

You're His "good gift" to me, my friend.

There are young and old heroes. Cheryl Watson was very young when cancer took her life—only 40 years old. But she loved Jesus intensely and was faithful to share the gospel until the day she died.

Ed Rock was a great hero of the faith. He was still writing poetry at the age of 90 and still singing duets with me at 92. He was truly a "rock," serving the Lord faithfully all the way to his death at the age of 93.

Leonard Conner has not only been a constant inspiration by his life and witness, but has also been a great encouragement and help through his active participation in this ministry for many years.

Helen Cade was another of my heroes. She was a great Bible

teacher, prayer warrior, and friend—and what an encourager! She was a "walking revival" everywhere she went. There must be hundreds (at least) in heaven because of her faithfulness to tell people about Jesus. You have probably heard the saying that "when God takes a friend, He leaves a fragrance." Helen Cade was, indeed a beautiful example of God's fragrance!

There are many others—real heroes of the faith, some who are still here, and others who have already passed from this life into the presence of our Great Savior, the Lord Jesus Christ. These and others who are still alive at this writing (some named in this book, and others unnamed) have truly impacted my life and ministry, and still encourage me when I need a "faith-lift."

Of course, none of our heroes of the faith, except the Lord Jesus Christ, are to be worshipped or placed on pedestals above us. They were people just like us, who didn't always get it right, but what they did do was, by faith, "fly" right (fight the good fight).

Faith

Sure, I can smile when I don't know what lies before me,
But can I smile when I know, and it's bad news?
Can I walk with total confidence in Jesus,
Even though He leads in paths I would not choose?

When the way that God is leading looks uncertain
And likely to be long and filled with pain,
I will look with eyes of faith unto my Father,
Knowing He will bring me safely through again.

He will never waste a single sorrow,

Neither circumstance nor loss, nor tears nor pain;

He will work all things together for His Glory

And for the good, and for my gain.

If in my future lies a fiery trial,

I can smile, though bitter tears may come;

My hope and joy is in my Heavenly Father,

And in my Saviour, Jesus Christ, The Son.

No, God will never waste a single sorrow,

Neither circumstance nor loss, nor tears nor pain.

He will work all things together for His Glory,

And for the good, and for our gain.

As we continue to fight the good fight of faith, we must remember, at the same time, to rest in the Lord and wait upon Him:

*"Rest in the Lord, and **wait** patiently for Him." (Psalm 37:7)*

" My soul, wait thou only upon God; for my expectation is from Him." (Psalm 62:5)

"The Lord is good to them that wait for Him, to the soul that seeketh Him." (Lamentations 3:25)

"Wait on the Lord; be of good courage, and He shall strengthen thine heart; Wait, I say, on the Lord." (Psalm 27:14)

WAIT, WAIT, WAIT, WAIT, WAIT! Why do we need so

many reminders to rest in the Lord and wait on Him? Perhaps it is because it is so hard for us to do! It has been difficult to have this book in a "holding" pattern for such a long time. But, I know God is "holding" me, and He invented time—He already knows about every single disruption before it ever gets to me.

Of course, it would be really foolish to lay paper all over the office, lean back in the recliner, and expect God to drop ink in all the right places, and "presto," the finished book would appear. As we have said before, to wait doesn't mean total inactivity (though it can include that at times). We have to learn to **actively** abandon ourselves to God, listen for His voice, be obedient to His choice, and wait, walk, and work as He leads. Even then sometimes we still seem to be "on hold." In times like these, when nothing or not enough is happening, no matter how desperate we feel, our focus must be wholly on Him:

"Neither know we what to do, but our eyes are upon Thee." (2 Chronicles 20:12)

Waiting on the Lord is the state of totally trusting Him, with absolute confidence in Him—the One who holds us in His Hands.

"My sheep hear My voice, and I know them, and they follow Me; And I give unto them eternal life; and they shall never perish, neither shall any man pluck them out of My hand. My Father, which gave them Me, is greater than all, and no man is able to pluck them out of My Father's Hand. I and My Father are one." *(John 10:27-30)*

In My Father's Hands [11]

Whatever change may come my way,
And when I cannot understand,
There is One I fully trust—
He holds me in His hands.

There may be great confusion,
There may be fear and pain,
But Jesus lives within my heart,
And God, my Father, reigns!

Whenever troubles come my way,
And things just don't go as I plan,
I need not worry, fear, or doubt,
I'm in my Father's hands.

In my Father's hands, in my Father's hands,
Nothing can snatch me from my Father's hands.
His grip is strong and sure, and I'm eternally secure,
For God, my Father, has placed me in His hands,
I'm in my Father's hands.

My Heavenly Father holds me,
With loving hands He molds me,
In faithfulness He keeps me
Secure within His hands—I'm in my Father's hands.

Chapter 18
Free To Fly—Free To Soar— Free Indeed

Fashioned for Flight

Just as the little butterfly was fashioned to fly, you and I were designed to rise above our circumstances—to "fly" in spite of our "caterpillar" world. We have been set free to live in the light of the love of our great God and Father. *"Ye shall know the truth, and the truth shall make you free." (John 8:32)* What— Who is the truth? It is none other than Jesus Christ Himself! Jesus said: *"I am the way, the **truth**, and the life: no man cometh unto the Father but by Me." (John 14:6)*

Once we have been born into God's family, even though there will still be allurements of the flesh, we are no longer subject to the flesh—we have been set free. All of our lives, our adversary, the devil, would keep us in the dark, in confusion, in bondage to the old way of life, but **Jesus has set us free**! According to the Word of God, *"If the Son, therefore shall make you free, ye shall be free indeed." (John 8:32)*

If, however, we do not know the Word of God, the Bible, we may not realize we are free from the power of the enemy. If we do not **know** God's precepts, then we are most likely not practicing them, and we can easily be duped into believing the enemy's lies, half-truths, and assaults, such as:

Assault #1: You are no good, and never will be—there is no hope for you.

The Truth: It is true that "*in my flesh dwells no good thing*"*(Romans 7:18)*, but God loved me so much that He sent His Son to die for me, so that I could live forever with Him. He has transformed me into a new creation in Christ Jesus, and made me a new creation in Him (2 Corinthians 5:17). Furthermore, God has wrapped me in His righteousness. We read in 2 Corinthians 5:21 that God made his Son, Jesus (the One who knew no sin), to be sin for us that we might be made the righteousness of God in Him! As the old song says, "My **hope** is built on nothing less than Jesus' blood and righteousness!"

His Righteousness Covers Me

His awesome love has made it so,
And by His Word I truly know
That God the Son has set me free—
His righteousness now covers me!

Assault #2: You are a Christian, and you have sinned. You have really done it this time! You have sinned too greatly—there is no more forgiveness for you!

The Truth: "*There is therefore now no condemnation to them which are in Christ Jesus.*" *(Romans 8:1)* When Jesus died on the cross, He paid the penalty for **all** our sins, not only for those we committed before we were saved, but also for those we have committed after we were born into His family, and every sin we will ever commit. Does this mean I can live any old way or submit to any old kind of desire? God forbid! We should never go back to "crawling" when God has set us free to "fly."

Yes, Jesus paid for all our sins. This does not, however, give us license to sin. It does give us liberty to live in obedience to the Lord Jesus Christ. If, as a believer, one can sin easily without feeling any guilt, it is questionable whether this person has ever been born into God's family, because God the Holy Spirit indwells every believer, and the Holy Spirit always convicts us of sin. Perhaps we can "get away with it" for a time, but the true child of God will not continue to practice sin as a lifestyle.

When we became new creatures in Christ (were born into God's family), we were not taken out of this caterpillar world, but given the power to overcome as we travel through it. When we sin, our new birth is not reversed. We cannot get unborn spiritually any more than we can physically. God does the birthing, and God does the keeping of our souls. However, when we sin, fellowship with God is broken, and cannot be restored until we return to Him, confess and forsake our sins, and yield our lives back to Him. God knew this would happen, and He made the provision for us to come back to fellowship with Him:

"If we confess our sins, He is faithful and just to forgive us our sins, and to cleanse us from all unrighteousness." (1 John 1:9)

In the meantime, until we return, confess and receive God's cleansing, we become servants of sin, and the devil is an awful taskmaster.

"Know ye not, that to whom ye yield yourselves servant to obey, his servants ye are to whom ye obey; whether of sin unto death, or of obedience unto righteousness?" (Romans 6:16)

The fact is that Jesus Christ has paid for every sin of every person who has ever been born

The fact is that Jesus Christ has paid for **every** sin of **every** person who has ever been born, from the beginning of time to the end of the age, but that payment is not automatically credited to every person's account. Every one of us owed a tremendous debt of sin which we could never pay! Jesus fully paid that enormous debt of sin which He did not owe, but that payment is applied **only** to those who receive Jesus Christ as Savior and Lord. Every one who does receive Jesus Christ is given new life and freedom from the bondage of sin. We are now no longer servants to sin and the devil. We have been set free to serve the living God!

Assault #3: Even if you have been forgiven, the butterfly with the broken wing will **never** fly as high again. Forget it, you are not worthy to serve God. He will **never** use **you** in His service again.

The Truth: The truth is that though our "wings" may be broken through sin, they can be mended when we confess and forsake our sins and return and yield to God. The half-truth of Assault #3 is the "never" part. Healing may take time, and whether we "fly as high" again is God's decision. It is possible that we can so grieve the Holy Spirit that, as mentioned earlier, we can be "sidelined" or "shelved" in terms of the kind of service we once enjoyed.

But even if that happens, the "never" part of usefulness to God is a half-truth. Even though we may never reach the full potential that could have been, God can and will still use us if we will fully yield to Him.

"For the Lord your God is gracious and merciful, and will not turn away His face from you, if ye will return to Him." (2 Chronicles 30:9)

In the pages of world history, Winston Churchill stands out as a courageous statesman. The speech he is perhaps most famous for was composed of only a few words: "Never give up, never, never, never give up!" History also reveals men and women who have exhibited outstanding humility, such as Oliver Cromwell who, when his portrait was being painted, instructed the artist to paint him "warts and all!" In the Bible we see the pictures of great heroes of the faith. They too are painted "warts and all," with their true humanity on display, revealing not only their great courage but also their weaknesses and failures. They too had to confess their sins and return to God.

David was a man after God's own heart, but there were times when he sinned, and those failures were devastating. When David numbered the people of Israel and Judah, he did this against God's will, as pointed out by Joab, captain of the army. This action was evidently a sin of pride—David wanted to see how strong "his" people were. Joab's response was, in a nutshell, that God was in control, so why would David want to number the people? But, the king's word prevailed, and this is what happened:

"And David's heart smote him after that he had numbered the people. And David said unto the Lord, I have sinned greatly in that I have done; and now, I beseech Thee, O Lord, take away the iniquity of Thy servant, for I have done very foolishly.

For when David was up in the morning, the word of the Lord came unto the prophet Gad, David's seer, saying,

Go and say unto David, Thus saith the Lord, I offer thee three things; choose thee one of them, that I may do it unto thee.

So Gad came to David, and told him, and said unto him, Shall seven years of famine come unto thee in thy land? Or wilt thou flee three months before thine enemies, while they pursue thee? Or that there be three days' pestilence in thy land? Now advise, and see what answer I shall return to Him that sent me.

And David said unto Gad, I am in a great strait; let us fall now into the hand of the Lord; for His mercies are great; and let me not fall into the hand of a man.

So the Lord sent a pestilence upon Israel from the morning even to the time appointed; and there died of the people from Dan even to Beersheba seventy thousand men." (2 Samuel 24:10-15)

Think of it—70,000 men died as a result of David's sin. As we read the rest of the story in 2 Samuel 24:16-25, we see that God stayed the hand of the destroying angel, and David again confessed his sin and prayed to God on behalf of all those affected by his sin of pride. At the end of this awful experience, David built an altar where he gave offerings to the Lord, worshipped and yielded to Him: *"So the Lord was entreated for the land, and the plague was stayed from Israel." (2 Samuel 24:25)* Of all the sins of mankind, pride is probably the most odious to God, so we must always obey Him in humility and contrition.

"For thus saith the high and lofty One that inhabiteth eternity, whose name is Holy; I dwell in the high and holy place with him also that is of a contrite and humble spirit; to revive the spirit of the humble, and to revive the heart of the contrite ones." (Isaiah 57:15)

The point is, even though we have been forgiven, sin **does** have consequences, and they are never pleasant ones. Our sins not only have an effect in our own lives, but also in the lives of others. The seeds (good or bad) that we sow and nourish will bear fruit! Whatever we plant is exactly what we can expect to harvest. If we choose to sow poorly, we will reap in kind. I heard one pastor say that when sin's harvest comes, we often pray for a "crop failure," but Dr. Charles Stanley has affirmed that not only will we reap **what** we sow, but we will reap **more** than we sow, and **later** than we sow.

None of us will ever be able to depend upon or glory in our flesh. The truth is that our flesh will never be worthy, but God has forgiven and accepted us and covered us with the righteousness of His Son, the Lord Jesus Christ, so that now when He looks at us, He sees us in Jesus. He does not throw us away as useless because we have failed.

Of this I am sure, that when Jesus saves, He saves completely—we will **never stop** being God's children. He will **never stop** loving us, and we will forever be secure in Him. It all comes down once again to freedom of choice. God does not make us accept Jesus Christ, and even when we do receive Him and are born into His family, He does not make us obey Him. He does give us the

Freedom comes not through religion, but through a relationship— knowing Jesus Christ personally

power not to sin, but He also gives us the freedom to choose, even if we make the wrong choice.

Freedom comes not through religion, but through a relationship—knowing Jesus Christ personally, not just knowing about Him, but receiving Him as Savior and Lord. Jesus Christ is the Author and Founder of our freedom. And when we truly know HIM, we are not only fashioned for "flight," but we are favored for "flight."

Free Indeed [12]

Freedom's never free, it always costs somebody something,
And the freedom I enjoy was bought for me,
Not with wealth and riches or the armies of my country,
But with the precious blood of Christ at Calvary.

Jesus is the Way, He is the Truth, He is the Life,
And as He promised in His Word, He'll make you free.
You will know the Truth when you receive Him as your Savior,
And He, the Truth, will make you free indeed!

Free indeed, free indeed!
If the Son shall make you free, you shall be free indeed!
Free indeed, free indeed!
If the Son shall make you free, you shall be free indeed!

We have genuine and lasting freedom when we have Jesus Christ. Hallelujah, what a Savior!

"If the Son therefore shall make you free, ye shall be free indeed!" (*John 8:32*)

Favored for flight

*"For the **Father Himself loveth you**, because ye have loved me, and have believed that I came out from God. I came forth from the Father, and am come into the world; again, I leave the world, and go to the Father." (John 16:27-28)*

*"Yet a little while, and the world seeth me no more; but ye see me; **because I live ye shall live also**." (John 14:19)*

Fueled for Flight—God has given us freedom, favor, and even the fuel for successful "flight" in this caterpillar world. Though I wish I had known much earlier in my life, it has only been during the years of this ministry that I have begun to realize pure power—the fuel that God has already provided to each one of us personally:

The Word of God before me.

The Holy Spirit of God within me.

The Armor of God about me.

The Word of God before me—To list all the scriptures that tell the benefits of God's Word to my life, my "flight"—your life, your "flight"—would take another whole chapter, or maybe another whole book! The Scriptures were written not just for us to read and to feed upon, but also for us to heed. *"And I will walk at liberty; for I seek Thy precepts." (Psalm 119:45)* When we follow the precepts of God's Word, we find not only freedom of flight, but the power as well.

The Holy Spirit of God within me— Successful flight is impossible in the power of our own flesh. *"Without me, ye can do nothing." (John 15:5)* The real power is God Himself, the One who, in the person of the Holy Spirit lives within us (Colossians 1:17). It is He who is the fuel, the power, and the strength of our lives—"*I can do all things through Christ which strengtheneth me.*" *(Philippians 4:13)*

The Armor of God about me—In another chapter we talked about the armor of God—complete protection for the Christian. He has given us everything we need for total protection. It only remains for us to put it all on!

"*Put on the whole armor of God, that ye may be able to stand against the wiles of the devil.*" *(Ephesians 6:11)*

Real, Enduring Freedom from Sin

"*Wherefore He is able also to save them to the uttermost that come unto God by Him, seeing He ever liveth to make intercession for them.*" *(Hebrews 7:25)*

Jesus saves entirely—to the uttermost! He gives us complete freedom from sin: Past, Present, and Future!

The Past—the Penalty of Sin. Jesus paid it **all!** He has given us full pardon, and absolute freedom from the **penalty** of sin, which is death, hell, and eternal separation from God.

The Present—the Power of Sin. Jesus paid it **all!** He has given us freedom from the **power** of sin in this present earthly life. If we are not experiencing that freedom it is because we are not allowing Jesus Christ to have control of our lives. Instead, we are trying to do God's will our own way.

The Future—the very Presence of Sin. Jesus paid it **all!** It is done! His perfect salvation includes freedom from the very presence of sin which we will experience in the future—the moment we leave this earthly tabernacle of our flesh and go to be with our Savior in Heaven! From that day on, we will never again be exposed to the presence of sin!

Heaven [13]

Well, I went to bed and I dreamed a dream last night,
I was up in Heaven, and what a beautiful sight!
There were loved ones I had known before,
And mansions bright and so much more!

What a thrill, what a joy, what a sight!
What peace, what pure delight!
As I visited Heaven that night,
I didn't want to come home!

But the most exciting thing about that place
Was to look into my Savior's blessed face.
I beheld His hands, His feet, His side—
T'was for me that He was crucified.

Oh, His eyes were filled with wondrous love and grace,
As He led me gently through that glorious place,
Through the streets of gold by the crystal sea,
And it's all awaiting you and me

In the land where there's no night,
Where the blind receive their sight,
Where Jesus is the Light!
I didn't want to come home.

Well, I soon woke up, and brother did I feel good,

For my dream was clear, and I really understood

That my troubles on earth are very small,

And Heaven will be worth it all!

What a thrill, what a joy, what a sight,

What peace, what pure delight,

As I visited Heaven that night,

I didn't want to come home.

What a thrill, what a joy, what a sight,

What peace, what pure delight,

Oh I visited Heaven last night—

That's my new home!

Now that we are fashioned, favored, and fueled for flight, we are **Free to Soar**! Perhaps this acrostic will help us remember to practice the freedom Jesus has given us:

S—Say Goodbye!

O—Obey!

A—Abide!

R—Rejoice!

S—Say Goodbye! Not, see you later!

Say goodbye to old fears, failures, sins of the past, and even old successes! Accept God's complete forgiveness and commit everything into His Almighty Hands. (Incidentally, Webster's Dictionary says that "goodbye" is a contraction of "God be with ye").

"Brethren, I count not myself to have apprehended; but this one thing I do, forgetting those things which are behind, and reaching forth unto those things which are before, I press toward the mark for the prize of the high calling of God in Christ Jesus." (Philippians 3:13-14)

O—Obey—Listen to the voice of God and obey Him:

BE still—and listen, and do: Dr. Charles Stanley has said that being still does not mean being idle, but being still on the inside, trusting God, seeing things from God's perspective.

"Be still, and know that I am God; I will be exalted among the heathen, I will be exalted in the earth." (Psalm 46:10)

"Draw nigh unto God, and He will draw nigh to you…" (James 4:8)

"I will instruct thee and teach thee in the way which thou shalt go; I will guide thee with mine eye." (Psalm 32:8)

"But be ye doers of the word, and not hearers only..." (James 1:22)

BE filled—with His Spirit and follow His directions.

"See then that ye walk circumspectly, not as fools, but as wise…be filled with the Spirit..." (Ephesians 5:15,18)

"Wherefore gird up the loins of your mind, be sober, and hope to the end for the grace that is to be brought unto you at the revelation of Jesus Christ; As obedient children, not fashioning yourselves according to the former lusts in your ignorance." (1 Peter 1:13-14)

"For the weapons of our warfare are not carnal, but mighty through God to the pulling down of strongholds; Casting down imaginations, and every high thing that exalteth itself against the knowledge of God, and bringing into captivity every thought to the obedience of Christ." (2 Corinthians 10:4-5)

BE-lieve—Trust Him. Take Him at His Word.

"In Thee, O Lord, do I put my trust; let me never be put to confusion." (Psalm 71:1)

"Cause me to hear Thy lovingkindness in the morning; for in Thee do I trust; cause me to know the way wherein I should walk; for I lift up my soul unto Thee." (Psalm 143:8)

"Trust in the Lord with all thin heart; and lean not unto thine own understanding. In all thy ways acknowledge Him, and He shall direct thy paths. (Proverbs 3:5-6)

A—Abide — Stay in close fellowship with Him. Keep your focus upon the Jesus. Rest in the Lord, worship and praise Him, and pray. There is no better way to soar!

In thinking about abiding (staying), I am reminded of our grandson, Thomas who has always been a dynamite, 100-mile an hour kid. Pre-kindergarten was a real challenge for him and everyone else until he learned the principal of "abiding" or "staying on the green," as they called it in his class. By way of explanation, on the classroom wall there were three big circles—one red, one yellow, and one green. If a child was disobedient his name was put in the red circle; if his name was in the yellow circle that meant he was dangerously close to trouble, but if his name was in the green circle that meant he had been good and obedient. Thomas was having trouble getting in and staying in the green circle until finally his mother told him the only way he would be allowed to play his favorite video game at home was to stay "in the green" all day at school.

When Thomas realized the benefits of not only being in the "green circle," but staying (**abiding**) there, his whole school life turned around, and from then on he was "in the green" every day.

He didn't lose any of his bounce or joy, but he was much better off for his obedience, and so were we! One thing though, Thomas couldn't possibly be good enough in one day to keep him "in the green" all month—he had to do it one day at a time— sometimes 10 minutes at a time. And so do we! Be encouraged— keep abiding in Jesus. Your difficulties may not instantly vanish, but when you make up your mind to abide in Jesus, and let His words abide in you—moment by moment, step by step— God will turn your life around. You will be better off and so will everyone around you.

Your difficulties may not instantly vanish, but when you make up your mind to abide in Jesus, and let His words abide in you —God will turn your life around

One of the great passages on abiding in Christ is John 15:1-10. How very rich this entire chapter is! Jesus said:

"I am the vine, ye are the branches; he that abideth in me, and I in him, the same bringeth forth much fruit; for without me, ye can do nothing." (John 15:5)

As we abide in Jesus, and let His words abide in us, we cannot help but **worship and praise Him**:

"O worship the Lord in the beauty of holiness; fear before Him, all the earth." (Psalm 96:9)

"O come, let us worship and bow down; let us kneel before the Lord our maker." (Psalm 95:6)

Song of Worship [14]

Oh Lord, Your throne is the heaven,
And you walk on the wings of the wind.
You formed the sun, the moon, the stars, the earth,
And all that is therein.

You send the rain and snow
And fire and hail as well,
And when You speak, they hear You,
And obey Your "Peace, be still!"

Oh, Lord, You're altogether holy
And righteous in all of Your ways,
To You alone belongs all power,
All glory, all majesty, and praise.

You are absolute in righteousness,
And You are perfect purity,
Yet Your mighty hand of boundless grace and love
Extends to even me.

Oh Father, You are high and lifted up,
Exalted far above all,
Yet, You're filled with loving, tender mercies,
And You hear me when I call.

And what have I that You did not give?

What merit can I claim?

Nothing of self, my sinful soul cries out,

But all in Jesus' name!

How I love the name of Jesus,

Son of God, Incarnate Word!

Oh, my God, I bow before you,

King of Kings and Lord of Lords!

How I love the name of Jesus,

Son of God, Incarnate Word!

I will praise Your Name forever,

King of Kings and Lord of Lords!

King of Kings and Lord of Lords!

Forever! King of Kings and Lord of Lords!

"Praise ye the Lord. Sing unto the Lord a new song, and His praise in the congregation of the saints." (Psalm 149:1)

Praising God doesn't depend on how we feel or where we are in life. We praise Him for who He is and for His great mercy, love and grace.

"Thy mercy, oh Lord, is in the heavens; and Thy faithfulness reacheth to the clouds.

Thy righteousness is like the great mountains; Thy judgments are a great deep; O Lord, Thou preservest man and beast.

How excellent is Thy lovingkindness, O God! Therefore the children of men put their trust under the shadow of Thy wings.

They shall be abundantly satisfied with the fatness of Thy house; and Thou shalt make them drink of the river of Thy pleasures.

For with Thee is the fountain of life; in Thy light shall we see light." (Psalm 36:5-9)

"This I recall to my mind, therefore have I hope. It is of the Lord's mercies that we are not consumed, because His compassions fail not. They are new every morning; great is Thy faithfulness." (Lamentations 3:21-23)

His Mercies Never Stop

Whether in the midst of a valley,

Or whether on a glorious mountaintop,

Or whether in the quiet of the morning,

His new mercies—they just never stop!

Prayer—there is no way to abide in Christ without prayer. *"Pray without ceasing."* (2 Thessalonians 5:17) This does not mean that we are literally on our knees in prayer 24/7. What it does mean is that we abide in such close communion with God that at any moment we can speak with Him knowing He is listening. We can bring any person, problem or trouble to Him instantly. And, we can **hear** His voice! *"My sheep hear my voice, and I know them, and they follow me."*

We can bring any person, problem or trouble to Him instantly.

(John 10:27) We **can** abide in Him every moment. But once again, though God truly wants intimate fellowship with each one of us, He will not make us abide. We must decide—daily!

R—Rejoice—and give thanks. Frustration, discouragement, complaining and fear (and other wrong attitudes) always affect our "flight" in negative ways, but when we rejoice in the Lord, with praise and thanksgiving all those, negatives "fly" away!

"But let all those that put their trust in Thee rejoice; let them ever shout for joy, because Thou defendest them; let them also that love Thy name be joyful in Thee. For Thou Lord wilt bless the righteous; with favor wilt Thou compass him as with a shield." *(Psalm 5:11-12)*

"Giving thanks always for all things unto God and the Father in the name of our Lord Jesus Christ." *(Ephesians 5:20)*

"Thanks be to God, which gives us the victory through our Lord Jesus Christ. Therefore, my beloved brethren, be ye steadfast, unmovable, always abounding in the work of the Lord, forasmuch as you know that your labor is not in vain in the Lord." *(1 Corinthians 15:57-58)*

"Rejoice evermore. Pray without ceasing. In everything give thanks; for this is the will of God in Christ Jesus concerning you." *(1 Thessalonians 5:16-18)*

If you are not sure you know how to start rejoicing and praising God with thanksgiving, practice by reading the Psalms. You could begin with Psalm 135 about the greatness of God, and Psalm 136 praising God for His past and present blessings and affirming His great mercy. In that one Psalm the affirmation "for His mercy endureth forever" is stated 26 times!

One of the best ways to rejoice is to sing to the Lord. If you can't sing, at least you can make a joyful noise!

*"O come, let **sing unto the** Lord; let us make a **joyful noise** to the Rock of our salvation. Let us come before His presence with thanksgiving, and make a **joyful noise** unto Him with psalms."* (Psalm 95:1-2)

*"Make a **joyful noise** unto the Lord, all ye lands. Serve the Lord with gladness; come before His presence with **singing**. Know ye that the Lord He is God; it is He that hath made us, and not we ourselves; we are His people, and the sheep of His pasture. Enter into His gates with thanksgiving, and into His courts with praise; be thankful unto Him, and bless His name. For the Lord is good; His mercy is everlasting; and His truth endureth to all generations."* (Psalm 100)

If you can't think of any other reason to rejoice, think about Jesus, who is our highest joy!

Jesus, My Highest Joy[15]

You put a song in my heart, You put a smile on my face,
You fill my mouth with laughter.
You took away all my sin, You made me clean again,
You gave me life ever after!

You give me peace that passes understanding,
And riches that money cannot buy,
And love that's deeper than the ocean,
And hope that's higher than the sky!

You are the solid rock of my salvation,
You turn my dark and lonely nights to day.
You are my strength and song in times of trouble,
And You always hear me when I pray.

What a blessing just to talk with You!
How I love to hear Your voice!
When You speak, my fears all fade away.
Thank you Jesus, You are my highest joy!

One day our time on earth will end. It may be by physical death or perhaps you and I will be alive when Jesus returns to receive His bride (that's the church—all who have received Him as Savior and been born into His family). One of our greatest rejoicings is the assurance of His Glorious Appearing!

The Glorious Appearing

What thrilling words of hope!
What a song to sing!
The prophecy has been fulfilled—
Born is Christ our King!

He who was in the beginning,
Is now, and ever shall be—
Jesus Christ came in the flesh
For all the world to see!

Eternal Life has now been offered.
To whosoever will believe;
This life is in the Son of God—
Have you this life received?

Some hearts were closed to Jesus
When He on earth was born,
But for all who have received Him,
He will return one glorious morn!

For all that God has promised
He will always surely do,
And He has given you His word—
He will come back for you.

Fear not, just keep on looking up,
Rejoice, the day is nearing—
Jesus Christ will soon return.
What a Glorious Appearing!

(References: Galatians 4:4; Isaiah 9:6; John 1:1, 14; Luke 2:11; 1 John 4:14; 1 John 5:11-12; Romans 10:9-12; John 1:12; 1 Thessalonians 5:23-24; John 14:1-3; Revelation 22:12-13; Titus 2:13)

Jesus encouraged His disciples and us when He said:

"Let not your heart be troubled; ye believe in God, believe also in me. In my Father's house are many mansions; if it were not so, I

would have told you. I go to prepare a place for you. And if I go and prepare a place for you, I will come again, and receive you unto myself, that where I am, there ye may be also." (John 14:1-3)

The day will come when our work on earth will be ended, and we will take that final "flight" when all who have become new creations in Christ will "fly away" to be forever with Him in Heaven. Until then, we can rejoice in the "here and now," knowing that we will certainly rejoice in the "there and then!"

During this entire book we have talked about the little butterfly, and compared our own earthly "flight" (sometimes, "crawl") with that of the little winged creature. Perhaps it is now time to progress a little higher—to the "wings of eagles!"

"Hast thou not known? Hast thou not heard, that the everlasting God, the Lord, the Creator of the ends of the earth, fainteth not, neither is weary? There is no searching of His understanding. He giveth power to the faint; and to them that have no might He increaseth strength. Even the youths shall faint and be weary, and the young men shall utterly fall; But they that wait upon the Lord shall renew their strength; they shall mount up with wings as eagles; they shall run, and not be weary; and they shall walk, and not faint." (Isaiah 40:28-31)

"The Eternal God is thy refuge, and underneath are the everlasting arms." (Deuteronomy 33:27)

Remember, being transformed into a new creature (salvation) occurs the moment we receive Jesus Christ as our Savior, but learning to "fly right" takes a lifetime! The Master Designer, however, knows each of us so intimately that He can and will direct every second of our flight—if we will let Him. Whether you are just beginning the "butterfly life," or have been in the air for quite some time, my prayer is that your heart and mind will be continually open to hear the Spirit of God speak to you. May you from this time forward have the "flight of your life!"

"And now, what wait I for? My hope is in Thee." (Psalm 39:7)

It's time to fly! You have everything you need in Jesus! You are free—**Free Indeed!**

Index of Poetry and Songs
by Betty Moni

Some of the poems in this book are also songs which have been written and recorded by Betty Moni. These songs are available on CD and cassette rcordings as listed below:

	Song	Recording
1	The Pity Party Song	*Don't Touch The Glory*
2	Butterfly Life in a Caterpillar World	*Jesus, My Highest Joy*
3	Lamb of God	*The How and Why of Christmas*
4	Hold Him in my Heart	*Jesus My Highest Joy*
5	The Book of the Lamb	*Free Indeed*
6	Kept	*Kept*
7	Jehovah My All	*Free Indeed*
8	Little One	*Little One*
9	The Higher Purpose	*More Than Conqueror*
10	Through Every Storm	*Jesus, My Highest Joy*
11	In My Father's Hands	*Jesus, My Highest Joy*
12	Free Indeed	*Free Indeed*
13	Heaven	*Free Indeed*
14	Song of Worship	*Don't Touch The Glory*
15	Jesus, My Highest Joy	*Jesus, My Highest Joy*

Resources Available through
Betty Moni Ministries/Sacred Music, Inc.

Recordings (CD and Cassette)

Joy Comes In The Morning

Thank You, Lord

New Creation

More Than Conqueror

Kept

It Is Well

The How And Why Of Christmas

Don't Touch The Glory

Free Indeed

Little One Jesus,

My Highest Joy

Publications (Books)

Where To Go When It Hurts

Butterfly Life In A Caterpillar World

Ministries

Concert Presentations
Inspirational Speaking and Singing for:
    Conferences, Retreats, Revivals, Chapel & Worship Services and other

*For more information about Betty Moni Ministries/Sacred Music, Inc.,
or to order recordings/publications, additional copies of this book, or to
inquire about ministry schedule, please contact:*

Betty Moni Ministries
Sacred Music, Inc., P.O.Box - 701115
San Antonio, TX 78270